INCOMING

SEX, DRUGS, AND COPENHAGEN

EDITED BY

JENNIFER CORLEY,
JUSTIN HUDNALL,
TENLEY LOZANO,
FRANCISCO MARTÍNEZCUELLO

SO SAY WE ALL

Cover design by Adam Vieyra
Interior design by Olivia M. Croom

ISBN: 978-0-9979499-3-3

So Say We All (SSWA) is a San Diego-based 501c3 non-profit organization whose mission is to help people tell their stories, and tell them better, through providing education, publishing, and performance opportunities.

www.sosayweallonline.com

ACKNOWLEDGEMENTS

So Say We All, its *Veteran's Writers Division* from which many of the stories in this collection originated, and the *Incoming* print and public radio series are proudly supported by the California Arts Council's Veterans in the Arts (VIA) initiative, the City of San Diego's Commission for Arts and Culture, Cal Humanities, the Creative Forces: National Endowment for the Arts Military Healing Arts Network, the KPBS Explorer Program, and the individual supporting members of So Say We All.

We especially want to recognize a gift made by Kelly Patterson in the name of her uncle, Gary Armstrong, whose dedication to his memory is contained within—it is a deeply appreciated and poignant moment of kindness to all of us at So Say We All, and an example of how veterans never cease to give.

If you would like to support the education, performance, and publishing programs of So Say We All—and we'd love it if you would—please visit our website at www.sosayweallonline.com and click on "donate."

Thank you to all of the veterans, military family members, and foreign national interpreters who have bravely shared their stories. And thank you, the reader, for hearing us.

—*So Say We All*

CONTENTS

DEDICATION TO GARY ARMSTRONG

My uncle, Gary Armstrong, would have been so very pleased to know that the gift made on his behalf to support the So Say We All Veteran Writers Division—and the publication of this collection—will give other veterans an opportunity to speak their truth. His involvement in a writing group was a godsend. His writing gave him a vehicle to express joy, to honor the loves of his life (especially my aunt, Anita and their cat/son Freedom), to show fondness, appreciation and gratitude to his friends, and to share things that made him laugh or made him curious. It also provided him a place to air frustrations, vent righteous anger and work through difficulties. He called himself, "The Bard of the Bus Stop", because you could find him living, learning and experiencing much that he wrote of from that very vantage point. His writing is unconventional, like the man himself.

Gary loved music. In my youth, he would DJ audio tapes and send them to me. He turned me on to new artists and those before my time, he entertained me (his DJ name was, "Uncle Billy Bob Blues Boy Bear"....), and shared his broad and eclectic musical legacy. His musical range was blown wide open while he was in the military. The men he served with were as varied as the music they brought to him; blues, old gospel, classic rock, early rock, rock-a-billy, bluegrass and country, zydeco, native American and international music…I *could* go on. His ears had a thirst for new sound and true sound. He especially loved songs that told the story of human longing and suffering, those deep strings that join us all. He could never fail to stop and listen to a woman singing her heart out.

Emmylou Harris to Ella Fitzgerald, Billie Holiday to Bob Marley, Clifton Chenier to Sunny Ade, and Bonnie Raitt to Van Morrison, his ears craved the music. There may be people who are bigger music-heads than Gary, but not many. Music was the thread that could make sense of it all. One of my great pleasures was being able to return the favor as I discovered artists he didn't already know. With such a lyric soul, when he began to write, it was natural for him to hear melody behind his own words. (Some of his poetry *was* put to music!—Thank you mama Christy!) When he read his work aloud, he did it as the spoken word poets do, with music and percussion in the delivery.

In his lifetime, he never had much money and he suffered many losses. An over-fondness for alcohol limited his options and landed him on the street more than once and for long stretches at a time. Through it all, he retained a deep humanity, a sense of fairness, of hope, and a love of life. He knew he was a man blessed. No matter his circumstances he could always find a synchronicity to prove it to you, he could always work the experiences of his life into rhyme, or near rhyme and that sense of wonder was never far from his consciousness.

Though he did not write these words, he spoke them often and lived by them, I think he'd approve of me sharing.

"Love life, be gentle and take care of one another." —(unknown) and always remember to, "Keep the faith, baby!"—(Adam Powell)

Blessings All!

—Kelly Patterson, August '17

FOREWORD

The most dangerous thing you can hear in a warzone is, "Hey sir, watch this!"

That musing by our friend and contributor Benjamin Busch pretty much encapsulates why we wanted to curate an entire anthology of true stories about boredom and escapism as experienced by US military personnel. The experience of "hurry up and wait" is ubiquitous throughout all branches of service, makes no distinction between officer or enlisted class, rank, MOS, or era.

There's a joke where a captain tells the 1st lieutenant they move out at 0600, and the 1st lieutenant then tells the 2nd lieutenant that the captain said be ready by 0530, who then goes and tells the men about their 0500 formation, when the gunny yells for every swinging dick to be out by 0430, the sergeants kick it up to 0400, and the corporals push the rest out by 0330 just to cover their ass—and then they all wait and wait and wait until 0900 when the captain returns to say he just got word they move out at 1100.

And with that kind of waiting comes longing—to be anywhere but where one is, to find distraction from the dismal and interminable boredom no matter how short-sighted or riddled with consequences—and whenever a service member has dared to pursue that longing, however it turned out for them, a story earned its wings.

We title this collection of those stories, "Sex, Drugs and Copenhagen," after the three big categories we saw escapism falling into, with Copenhagen (the chewing tobacco so popular when staying awake on post, not the city in Denmark) representing The Suck, the unavoidable and inescapable periods of living waking purgatory where things just get weird.

It's strange to think that our previous volume in this series—which dealt with the process of coming home from deployment and transitioning back to civilian life—might actually be easier to relate to for a civilian than these stories of escapism sought under duress, because in most cases civilians at the breaking point have the option of abandoning their situation and just walking away. But for the armed forces, that's where the story begins.

—Justin Hudnall
Executive Director,
So Say We All

TRACERS
Colin D. Halloran

The thing about sex is that it's fleeting. Ethereal, even. Like the thrill of combat. Great sex and great killing, the creation and taking of life, are surprisingly similar. In the throes of the moment, time seems to slow. Senses are heightened as your neurochemistry surges. Images are sharper, you can feel—sense—every bead of sweat, yours, hers, it doesn't matter. When a drop falls, from a forehead or a breast, and lands on your arm, you can feel it shatter, feel it spread its saline shrapnel across every micrometer of your skin. It's only when it's over that you realize just how little or how much time has passed, a simultaneous moment and eternity. Reality, of course, is somewhere between the two.

And so it is with relationships. If we look at them objectively, every romantic encounter is essentially a binary: this is the person you will be with until one of you dies, or they're not. It's simple. Like war. You survive and make it home. Or you don't. But it's the neurochemistry that brings the nuance, and most romantic encounters will land somewhere between a one-night stand and happily ever after.

I don't remember the first time I told a girl I loved her. Probably middle school, when I had no idea what it meant, clumsy words made non-sequitur on an ignorant tongue. I'm guessing the first time I said it with some comprehension was to my long-term high school girlfriend, now happily married to a woman. I meant it, and she meant it when she said it back. But part of love is helping the other person grow and supporting them as they do, even when that means the relationship can't last. Maybe that's why I view it differently. If all of my tried and failed romantic encounters have taught me nothing else, it's that the Beatles were wrong: you need more than love.

I went to war at age 19, a little more than a year-and-a-half into a new relationship. I still remember the white dress she wore to the Providence airport when she picked me up for my first leave after Basic Training and Infantry School. That white dress was love in thread and cotton. I could feel it spun into her mother's oatmeal raisin cookies, the batch she made for me when I headed south to fulfill my deployment orders. I left my car at her parents' house, a sign we both believed our relationship strong enough to survive the war, even if my own survival wasn't guaranteed. Before I left, I went to Build-A-Bear, found a shaggy brown teddy bear and a camouflage uniform to dress it in—we named him Halo, my first call sign.

There was a little audio device you could put in the bear that allowed you to record a personal message. I don't know how long I sat in that dark back room of a bear shop in the mall. I don't know if the people in the blue and yellow shirts when I came out were the same as those who led me there for privacy and the elimination of background noise. I don't know how many times I leaned close to the plastic circle to whisper the words, "Goodnight, Ally, I love you." And I don't know if that bear was still on her bed as someone else slid into it, while I was half a world away.

There's little room for love in war.

Maybe it's the brain chemistry. A single brain can only handle one source of such surges: love or war. Or maybe it's that the love of war is different, rooted in the Greek *philo*, a brotherly bond, like Philadelphia: the city where a uniformed bear might still be hidden away in a closet, a recording device that's run out of battery, if not from overuse, then from time. Like love.

Ally and I tried to make it work when I got back. I may have tried harder, but only because I couldn't see that I just wasn't the same person anymore. The man she'd had a future with didn't make it back from Afghanistan. But I kept trying. Kept making those 2 A.M. drives from Connecticut to Philadelphia after closing the bar. Kept bringing wholesale-size boxes of her favorite Kashi granola bars. Even after we'd broken up.

I'd make the drive, leaving at 2 A.M. Get off the exit that used to lead me home. To our home. I'd leave the granola bars on her car, then turn around and drive the three hours back up to Connecticut. I still wasn't sleeping. Still needed a mission. Even if it was only my own desperate grasping at the ghost of something long gone.

I don't know who or what or how to pluralize what came after Ally. Too much of that time is lost to my mind's own compartmentalization. Some people might call it survival mode, like that time I got hit by a car and lost the memory of the next 36 hours. But my attempt at survival in this instance was more destruction than preservation. Working to exhaustion, late nights, girls, boys, booze, drugs, anything to stop from actually feeling…anything.

But scattered consistently throughout blurred memories and one-night stands are particular women, oases where I allowed myself to rest a time, open up—slightly—be vulnerable. Where I let myself tumble headlong—or ease cautiously—into the comfort of something built on hope, which is the last thing I felt. There was a fiction writer, a marathoner, a fellow vet, each of whom gave so much, offered me shelter in their unconditional caring.

But in between and during and amongst those three were flares, like tracer rounds between the bullets that kill: brief, but intense, illuminating; lifting me out of a darkness emanating more and more strongly from inside myself, allowing me to adjust my aim. It's not that those long-term relationships were bad. It's not like I was being neglected. But there came a point, or multiple points, in each where I found myself longing for war. The fear, the danger, the thrill.

I hadn't expected to make it home from Afghanistan, and now that I was home I rarely ended a night expecting to make it to the next morning. But in the same way that the drinking, drugs, and hazy sexual encounters were an attempt at numbing the heightened neurochemistry of combat—the negative remnants of war—the love was an attempt at getting something from war back. That camaraderie. *Philo.*

In the military, we use the phrase, "Got your six." The basic understanding of this is that it's one soldier telling another, "I've got your back. I'm watching out for you." But it's more than that. There's an implied second part; essentially, "...and I know that you've got mine." It's a symbiosis. The kind not found in a one-night stand. Not found in pulling a trigger to take a life. Love implies a partnership, a shared understanding. And understanding was what I craved more than anything after coming home. Between highs and lows, institutionalizations and books published, for better or worse, I sought refuge in that depth of connection. And when I felt that connection waning, even the slightest bit, when I felt those darker pieces of myself threatening the warmth and safety of these relationships, I ran. And I cheated. Every time. I betrayed my partners.

It was never out of spite. Never out of anger or some sense of betrayal on their part. And it was never, not once, for the empty thrill of a one-night stand. It was a subconscious crying out, seeking the sense of knowing, of belonging, of understanding. In each case there was some part of myself that I had lost without knowing it, and this other person, whoever she happened to be, showed it to me again. With the darkness inside me rising, she gave me light, no matter how brief, to adjust my fire, get back on track. And I felt whole again, if only for a time.

I don't say this to fault my exes. Or to boast. In fact, I feel great shame over those I've left behind like so many spent shell casings. The love I felt for each of them was real, but I broke it.

But what most people don't understand is that the love I felt for those others, those fleeting flare ups, was just as real. It was different, maybe, but it was real. And it served a purpose. In the decade I've been back from war, the closest I've come to getting back to it—back to the heat, the violence, the pain, and the thrill—is when I've found myself in some dark corner with some-one who understands. And we'd sit there, in a bar or a bed or on a Manhattan bench while the world raced around us, tracing each other's scars and hoping to create something just as permanent.

MONKEY BUSINESS
Joshua Callaway

Mee-sta, Mee-sta…" The soft croons of a small boy beckoned from just the other side of the wire.

I stepped out of the confines of a small sandbag bunker to engage the child and see what he wanted.

My platoon was on base security rotation, which meant we were responsible for manning the eight towers surrounding the base and the two access gates. Forward Operating Base (FOB) security was widely regarded by infantry soldiers as the worst job you could have. It was like riding the bench during the Super Bowl. We wanted to be out there fighting, doing what we were meant to do. FOB security also meant twelve-hour shifts, every single day, for a month straight. If I was on day shift, I was at the mercy of the sun, which beat down with relentless anger. By the end of every shift my exposed flesh was flushed red and my cheeks were hot to the touch. During the night shift, I looked forward to spending each teeth-chattering night spooning with my battle-buddy for warmth, and praying for daylight to come fast so my bones could thaw. Even without the elements included, FOB security was still a shitty job. I stared at the same strip of barren land for twelve uneventful hours.

Our small operating base was attacked regularly by indirect fire, which meant they fired their weapons without relying on line of sight, usually with mortars and rockets. The Taliban established mortar launch sites in the mountains and far enough back to avoid detection. Once they set up their sites, they would connect their mortar rounds to a kitchen timer, delaying the attack so they could be long gone before the rounds even launched.

So we would spend each and every day miserable and bored, hoping and praying that somebody *would* attack us. If anything, to break the monotony.

I was always assigned to the south gate. The south gate wasn't *great,* but it was the best position to have, due to the lack of an observation tower. It was a no-frills sandbag bunker, big enough for three people to sit side-by-side, but not tall enough to stand without being hunched over, with a strand of razor wire that we were responsible for moving to allow convoys access to and from the FOB. Patrols rarely used the south gate and opted to use the much wider and more maneuverable north gate. Due to the lack of traffic at the south gate, along with the fact that the position called to be manned by three personnel—one to move the wire, one to act as a radio operator to call in arrivals and departures, and one Non-Commissioned Officer to be in charge—we were able to kind of chill out at our gate. We spent our days trading stories and jokes or reading magazines, which we'd be unable to do from the towers. In the towers it was imperative to stay vigilant, and constantly scan the area for signs of attacks, regardless if we were confident it wouldn't happen.

"Mee-sta," the boy called again.

"Yeah, I'm coming man, chill out!" I adjusted the chin strap on my Kevlar helmet, "Whadda ya want, anyway?"

"Mee-sta, Mee-sta, you come, look. You like? You buy," he smiled. The kid was wearing the traditional Afghan garb: baggy blue cotton pants and a shirt cut from the same material. His untucked shirt hung down to his knees. The tips of each of his fingers, down to the second knuckles, were stained orange with henna, a type of dye made from a flowering plant of the same name. The boy's hair was an unnatural shade of red and more like burgundy. He accomplished this color by mixing mud with the same type of henna he used on his fingers. After mixing the mud-dye concoction he would smear it into his hair and leave it in for a week, sometimes more, until most of the mud had flaked away. He would rinse the remaining mud out of his hair and only then would he have this wine-red coif of hair that I saw before me. The kid was all of ten with the charm of a used car salesman.

"Well whatcha got for me?" I asked.

"Mee-sta, look." Sitting between the boy's feet was a small monkey. "Look, see? I have monkey! You like?" The monkey was a blend of tan and white, with a human-like face and hands, and a short blue nylon rope hastily tied around his neck.

"Fuck yeah, I like!" I could finally fulfill my childhood dream of having a pet monkey.

"You want monkey? He nice monkey. Make very good pet, you take home to America."

"Hell yeah, I want that monkey."

"Good, you like, then you buy," he raised his hand, offering up the leash.

"Well, hang on now. How much do you want?" My right middle and index finger rubbed my thumb, to communicate what I thought was the universal sign for money.

The boy understood most of what I said and spoke enough broken English that communication was possible.

"Mee-sta, you have poo*say* mag? You give…" with both hands he gestured, "I give you monkey."

"Wait, what do you want from me?" I was confused.

"Poo-*say* mag. You give me."

"What's a poo*say* mag?" I asked. "I don't understand what you're asking for."

"*Poosay*. Poosay mag," he said, his frustration mounting with each repetition.

"POO-*SAY!*" he formed a diamond shape with his hands down by his crotch and thrusted his hips.

"Pussy!" I laughed, "you want a pussy magazine?"

"Yes! Yes!" The boy's face lit up and he said again, "You have pussy mag? You give me."

Ah, goddammit!! I don't have any porn! And even if I did, it would be kind of fucked up to give it to a little Afghan kid! Especially here, where porn is illegal in the whole flipping country. If they find the poor kid with it they'd probably stone him to death, or at a minimum beat him half to death. Man, I don't want that, but I really want that fucking monkey!

"Hold on," I said. "Let me see what I got in my bag."

The kid's eyes drifted. I think he was excited at the thought of getting his hands on some good ol' American Porn.

I didn't have the heart to tell him just yet that I had no porn, and even if I did I wouldn't hand it over. I wouldn't want to be contributing to the delinquency of a minor, and not just because he was living in a country controlled by religious fanatics, and he would probably be killed if he was found with it, but also because I don't believe in corrupting innocent children. Besides, porn was valuable currency. No matter how badly I wanted the monkey, giving up pornography wasn't worth it.

I rummaged through my assault pack and was surprised to find a dated Maxim magazine. I knew it wasn't exactly what the boy was after, but pictures of a bikini clad Anna Kournikova surely would be enough.

"How about this?" I handed him the magazine through the stacks of razor wire. The boy quickly leafed through the pages and looked up.

"No pussy?" the sound of disappointment matched the expression on his face.

"I'm sorry, I don't have any pussy mags. That's the best I can do."

The boy stared back in silence.

"Come on," I pled. "It's still a good mag. Just look."

I held my breath while he thumbed through the pages once more, slower this time, inspecting every picture. He paused every few pages to smile and his eyes grew wide, nearly popping out of their sockets.

He lifted his eyes and closed the magazine, "OK, we have deal."

"Really?!" Finally, after twenty-three long years of wishing, I had my very own monkey! The boy passed the monkey's leash to me and scooted the monkey forward with his sandaled foot.

"Hell yeah!" I shouted. "Mustoe, Edwards, get out here. You guys gotta see this!" I called for the two soldiers sitting in the bunker. Staff Sergeant Mustoe and Private First Class Edwards scrambled out of the bunker.

"What's wrong, Cal?" Mustoe asked.

"Wrong? Nothing's wrong. Check it out. I just got me a monkey."

"What?" Excited, Edwards responded, "Too cool!"

"Holy Shit!" Mustoe said. "Cal, you can't have a fucking monkey."

"Why not, Mustoe?"

"Um, 'cause it's against the rules."

"Says who?"

"Uh, says everybody. It's in the fucking briefing we got coming over here! Remember?"

My heart broke.

"Maybe we could just keep him out here, and keep it on the down low," I suggested.

"Yeah, right," Mustoe said sarcastically. "I am sure everyone that comes out here will be able to keep their mouths shut and won't say a thing."

Staff Sergeant Mustoe was right, there was no way I could keep my monkey, but that didn't make it any easier.

"You're right," I accepted defeat.

I walked back to the wire where the boy stood leafing through his new prize. The monkey stayed put and refused to move.

"Come on buddy, you gotta go back home," I attempted to coax the primate but he wasn't having it. The monkey stood his ground. I tugged the leash quickly to get him to move but he didn't budge. This time the monkey reached up and grabbed the leash with both hands and tugged back hard. I was not prepared for the monkey's strength and almost fell to the ground as a result. I jerked back, harder, but the stubborn beast stood fast. The monkey appeared angry and screeched at me while yanking back on his cord. I tightly held my end of the blue leash wrapped around my hand so as not to lose my grip. The monkey was deceptively strong. I couldn't understand how this tiny creature was manhandling me, and *manhandling* was exactly what he was doing. Each pull on the leash unbalanced me.

"Hey, kid!" I called to the boy, "I can't keep your monkey. You've gotta take him back."

"No, you keep." I sensed fear in his voice. I didn't know if he was afraid of the monkey or that I'd make him return his new jerkoff material.

"Look, kid. You can keep the magazine, but you gotta help me with this fucking monkey!" I pled as the monkey jerked me around.

Mustoe and Edwards both watched and laughed as the monkey tossed me around like a rag doll.

"C'mon kid, I can't keep him."

"No Mee-sta, I don't want. Monkey mean," he pulled up his pant legs to reveal two thin calves littered with fresh bite marks.

"You *son-of-a-bitch!* You told me he was a nice monkey!" I was pissed that I'd been duped by a child.

"No, he bite. He mean, he bad monkey."

"I should kick your little ass."

The boy gave me a wicked smile, comforted by the safety of distance and the concertina wire separating us.

Edwards and Mustoe, entertained by the exchange, laughed harder. Mustoe had to lean against the bunker to keep from falling over.

Frustrated, I screamed, "Agghhh!"

"Cal. You. Still. Can't. Keep. The…Monkey!" Sergeant Mustoe struggled to speak between his cackles of laughter.

"Yeah, I know that. Thank you." My free hand palmed my face.

The monkey stared and hissed loudly, bearing teeth. The little bastard was trying to intimidate me *and it worked!*

I thought about Alaska, where my unit was located, and the day that I arrived. In the Anchorage airport there was a giant, full size, stuffed Kodiak brown bear. The bear stands on hind legs to reach fourteen feet and it weighed an impressive 1,600 pounds when alive. When I first laid eyes on the stuffed bear I thought to myself, *If I was in a fight with this monster, I could win! As long as I had my knife and if I could get in close, I could take him.*

Now reality was slapping me in the face as this small monkey, an animal that wouldn't even come up to that bear's knee, was outmuscling me.

I tugged the monkey once more toward the wire fence, but he screeched again and lunged forward. He was trying to bite me.

"Oh, shit!" I kicked at the attacking monkey. I completely missed and my back landed on the dirt while my hand let go of the monkey's leash. I scrambled to get back on my feet to defend myself.

The liberated monkey bounded on top of our bunker.

"Get out of here, you damn dirty ape! Go on, get!"

The monkey ignored me and remained on his perch.

No one would believe this story without proof. I asked Edwards to take a break from giggling and snap a photo of me and the monkey. After several difficult attempts, Edwards successfully took the photo. I had to move slowly, closer and closer to the bunker to get in position to get both me and the monkey in the frame. If I started to move too quickly, the monkey would stand on his back legs and scream, flashing his sharp fangs.

Once Edwards had snapped the photo, I announced my new strategy, "OK guys, I say we just ignore this stupid monkey and go back in the bunker. Maybe he'll just leave on his own."

Edwards and Mustoe both agreed to try my plan, but the moment we started to walk into the bunker, the monkey leapt from where he was sitting like one of Notre Dame's gargoyles and began screeching wildly and snapping his teeth at us. The animal had decided that the bunker now belonged to him and refused to allow us back in.

"Well, now what's your plan, genius?" Sergeant Mustoe asked.

"I don't know."

"Hey, I got an idea!" Edwards enthusiastically interrupted. Without explaining his thought, Edwards picked up the receiver of the tactical radio and called the Sergeant of the Guard.

The Sergeant of the Guard, or the SOG, was responsible for driving everyone out to their towers and ensuring a proper change of guard took place. Lunch was always MREs, but breakfast and dinner were hot meals prepared in the dining tent. Since we would miss these meals, the SOG was also responsible for bringing breakfast and dinner out to all the positions.

Edwards spoke into the radio mic, "SOG, SOG, this is the south gate, over."

A moment passed and then the radio crackled to life, "South gate, SOG...Send it."

Edwards started, "Roger, SOG, we were wondering if you had picked up chow yet?"

"Not yet, south gate. Why?"

"Roger, we were hoping that you could pick us up some bananas."

"Um...OK. Any reason why?"

Edwards looked to me for what to say next. I shrugged not really sure what to tell him at this point.

"We'll explain when you get here," Edwards told him, smart enough not to talk about the monkey over the radio.

"Roger that, see you in a bit, SOG out."

When the SOG did finally make it out to the south gate about an hour later, he found the three of us still standing outside the bunker and the monkey sitting on top, hissing if we got too close to his territory.

"What the holy hell is going on here?" The SOG asked, "Why are the three of you standing around out here?"

I knew there was no point in trying to lie to him. The truth was right in front of his face, "I traded this kid," I said pointing to the boy who was still loitering on the other side of the wire waiting to see how this all played out, "a magazine for a monkey. But now the monkey has decided that he owns the bunker, and won't let us in."

The SOG started laughing hysterically, "Jesus Christ, Cal!" He said, still laughing, "You go out looking for trouble?"

"No. It's just, I always wanted a monkey. Didn't really think it through."

"Yeah, no shit," he said, handing me the bunch of bananas he'd brought with him.

I peeled one of the bananas and broke it in half. I handed one piece to the monkey with my arm stretched out in front of me as far as I could. The moment the monkey realized what I was offering, he snatched it out of my hands aggressively. The monkey bit off large bites filling his cheeks with chunks of the fruit. I held up the other half of the banana for him to see. Before the monkey could tear the second half out of my hand I tossed it onto the other side of the wire, next to the boy. The monkey took the bait, scurrying off the bunker and through the wire after his treat.

The boy accepted his cruel pet back, picking up his leash without a word of protest.

And just like that, my dream was crushed, snuffed out like a cigarette butt. I stood in silence and watched the boy and his monkey until they were out of view. I turned back to the guys who made no attempt to stifle their laughter. While they laughed,

I sighed loudly, filled now with the knowledge I would never own a monkey. Worse, I knew I wasn't a badass who could take a bear in a fight—I had just been bested by a primate. The remainder of the deployment would pass without any more monkey business.

PASS THE HOT SAUCE

Susanne Aspley

Camp Dobol, Bosnia, 1996.

Bosnia was once gorgeous. Busy towns flourished and quaint farming villages dotted the countryside. The capital, Sarajevo, hosted the Winter Olympics back in the early '70s. But from 1992–1995, the civil war between Bosnian Serbs and Bosnian Muslims destroyed all that.

The cities were pocked with artillery rounds, landmines, and shells. Near our army outpost stood a humble, pale green mosque. Chunks of the exterior were blown away, and a path of bullet holes wound all the way up the minaret. So, here we are, part of the US-led NATO Peacekeeping mission.

It's not war. But it's certainly not peaceful. Yesterday, a family attempted to move back to their home, but were beaten with 2×4s by their neighbors. The local police never showed up, so the scouts from our camp had to go deal with the mob.

The next morning, about oh-dark-thirty, I headed into the female shower trailer to get ready for another long day.

I dropped my cigarette, surprised as a male soldier walked out of the trailer. A clean, fresh waft of warm air followed him, which threw me off guard. (Infantry guys don't always smell the best.)

Irish Spring. Definitely Irish Spring soap. His chest must've still been wet, because his gray PT shirt stuck to it. He saw me and froze; the flimsy door banged into his shoulder, his olive drab towel hung limply around his neck.

What the hell was he doing, coming out of the female latrine? He stared at me in terror for a moment, speechless. I didn't ask; he didn't tell. I only looked down. He then took off like a bat out of hell, and ran across the pallets lining the path through the rows of large army tents. Stopping at a corner, he glanced back, then made a hard left and disappeared. I was sure I'd never see him again.

Later that morning, I ate breakfast in the chow hall, an overly bright, simple plywood building on short stilts. One wall was covered with cards to Any Soldier from American grade school kids with messages like, "Thank you hero!" and "Don't die!"

When it was my turn in line, I handed my melamine tray to the sulking Serbian cook, with deep-set yellow-green eyes, hairy ears and every other tooth missing. The plexiglass over the food looked snot stained, or something stained…not sure. But I asked for over easy eggs rather than a scoop of his premade scrambled. I tried those once, but they tasted like oily urine. He probably pissed on them in back for all I knew.

"Piff da," he muttered, annoyed, cracking the eggs on the griddle. He then brutally slapped them around with his spatula. Finally, he slopped them on my plate. Bloosh.

"Thank you," I said.

"Douche ya," he answered.

As I ate the overcooked eggs, the soldier that walked out of the female latrine sat down across from me. He wasn't necessarily good looking, but good to look at. A comfortable sort of attractiveness, the kind that would increase once you get to know him. His lips were thick and his teeth kinda crooked. His eyelashes didn't curl up like most people's do, but rather feathered across his soft brown eyes, just like a cow's.

"Excuse me, are you the public affairs lady?" he asked in the most endearing drawl.

Gawd. Those infantry guys acted like they'd never seen a woman in uniform before. One time a private asked me if I was in the Army. What? I'm in full battle rattle in the middle of bumscrew Bosnia with US ARMY on my uniform.

"Excuse me?" I answered, a little miffed.

He swallowed, looked at my rank, my last name, and my unit patch, which he should have to begin with. Not that it's anything spectacular.

"Specialist Aspley. Morning," he said, snapping back to army professional mode.

"Morning, Staff Sergeant Curry," I answered, reading his uniform as well.

"Yes," he said, and quickly glanced around the chow hall to see who was watching us.

On deployments, I missed something I never knew could be missed. Always wearing olive drab and muddied boots, I missed color. I missed the warmth of red, the calmness of blue, the luxury of purple. No makeup or nail polish allowed. Hair slicked back tight in a boring bun, because I was a soldier. But there's one thing I did to feel happy underneath those fifty shades of camo. I wore hot pink panties.

"Will you please pass the hot sauce?" I said to him.

Never taking his big cow eyes off me, he reached for the greasy bottle, slid it across the table, and handed it to me. Marvin started singing Let's Get it On over the chow hall muzak. I pulled the greasy bun out of my hair and shook it loose. Then, I slowly placed the bottle of hot sauce to my lips, pulled it down my neck, and drip…drip…dripped a few drops down my shirt.

OK, that didn't really happen. I didn't really do that.

I just doused my eggs with hot sauce and started to eat.

"Uh, I'm the guy that walked out of the female latrine. Sorry, that was me. I want to own up to it, and uh, tell you, sorry," he said.

The sergeant looked like a little boy who got caught, well, in the girl's bathroom.

He continued, "I'm so sorry. You don't have to tell anyone about that. We were up all night on patrol, and just got back. I needed a shower and just went in, not paying attention. No one else was in there but me. Please don't think I'm a creep, OK?"

No, definitely not a creep. And no, no wedding ring, check. But that rank. Trouble. Too high. It was two above mine, pushing him out of my fraternization zone. Relationships are not allowed here, and certainly not between junior and senior enlisted.

I realized then and there I wanted to fuck him so bad I could hardly stand it. Why? I don't know, and neither did he. Every once in a blue moon you come across someone that you know you'll end up having a past with, but dive in anyway, without plugging your nose.

This all made me smile. He smiled back. And sure enough, by the end of the week we were screwing in the back of the chapel when the Chaplain and his assistant went to Tuzla for the day. And every day from then on when the chapel was empty.

Praise the Lord and pass the hot sauce.

AFTER THE 'NAM

John DiFusco

After the 'Nam, back in my hometown, Webster, MA, I buy my first car. A white MGB with a red racing stripe. A cool, low-to-the-ground sports car. It's December 1968 and I'm a twenty-year-old California Dreamer, rollin' down Rte. 66.

When I get to sunny SoCal, I enroll in a community college. The first college girl I meet is a chick named Debbie Garcia. Debbie Garcia likes to smoke pot and drop acid. She hangs out with artists and activists. She wears gypsy hoop earrings and silver bracelets. She's a Mexican Hippie. A Mexa-Hippie. Her favorite expression is "far out." She uses it so much that I nicknamed her "Debbie Far Out." She hears me using some GI slang, Boo Coo, Com Sai and blurts "Far out, far out! You gotta meet my brother Danny. He was there too. He's a little crazy, but he's cool. He'll be at the party. This is gonna be really far out!"

So, Debbie rolls a big fat doobie, we hop into my little MG and head for the party. I'm stoned. We walk in. "White Rabbit" is blaring through big speakers: "One pill makes you smaller and one pill makes you tall…" I immediately feel self-conscious. I'm the only guy there with short hair.

I mutter, "God I hope my fucking hair grows out fast!"

Debbie knows everybody, and everybody knows Debbie. She laughs and disappears into the party with the words, "Far out! Far fuckin' out!"

I wander into the kitchen. Beer and wine bottles randomly piled up all over the counters. I meet a tall lanky brother who calls himself Slick. He's sportin' a huge afro, wearing a dashiki and purple sunglasses. He leans down like some slinky caterpillar and offers me a joint rolled in American flag paper.

"Want a hit, good brother?"

"Sure man." I take a couple of hits and it feels like my brain is expanding. All I can say is, "Whoa. Far out!"

He looks me in the eye, "That's right, my brother. That is some Humboldt County Purple Haze."

I take another hit and ask, "Hey man, you know where the bathroom is?"

"Sure brother, you just walk down that long motherfuckin' hallway till you see the red light."

The walls of the long motherfuckin' hallway are covered with posters: Jimi Hendrix, Electric Lady Land, Dennis Hopper flipping the bird from his Easy Rider Harley, Uncle Sam pointing a long finger at me, "I WANT YOU," an orange day-glow peace sign with the words "Fuck the War" scrawled across it. I hear Cream coming from one of the rooms: "Born under a bad sign. Been down since before I began to crawl…." I take a peek in. There are some people sitting around a circular coffee table smoking weed from a long wooden peace pipe. I continue down the hallway slowly. My hands begin to shake and sweat. I can't feel my feet on the floor. Looking over my shoulder. Feeling really paranoid.

At last I see the red light of the bathroom. I go in. Take a long, slow leak and stare in the mirror. Wishing. Wishing I could come down. Wishing my fucking hair would grow! I start to leave and notice a picture of an Indian warrior on the door. At the bottom are the words, "Hear me my Chiefs. I am tired. My heart is sick and sad. And I tell you from where the sun now stands, I will fight no more forever. —Chief Joseph"

On the way back, I slide into the smoke-filled peace pipe room. My focus is drawn by a girl with long black hair sitting in front of an elaborate tapestry of a gray wolf, circled by eagle feathers. She lights some incense. The smoke around her face makes her look ancient. Like from another time.

Sitting around the table are four people. Slick is there, along with a white dude in a fatigue jacket, a frizzy-haired braless blonde chick, and a long-haired Chicano who looks up at me with Apache warrior eyes and says with a rasp, "When'd you get back, Homes?"

"Back from where?"

"Lemme tell you something Ese, you could take the kid out of The 'Nam, but you can't take The 'Nam out of the kid." He clasps my hand in the Vietnam handshake and says, "I'm Danny Garcia. I was there too, man. Come sit down. Let's get wrecked."

So, I sit down with my new friends and smoke the peace pipe. The blonde chick is chattering endlessly. Nothing but anti-war shit. Danny hands around a tequila bottle and we all take shots.

Debbie explodes into the room. "Far out! Far out! I'm so glad you guys met. Johnny's a little lost." She grabs my arm and drags me over to the girl who'd caught my eye. "Come on, I want you to meet my best friend since we were kids. Johnny D., meet Lupe Marie."

We exchange awkward hellos and she leaves the room. Time stops as I watch her walk down that long hallway. She has classic native features. Light brown skin, warm dark eyes, high cheekbones. A chiseled nose. Long shiny black hair dancing down to the small of her back, waving back and forth with every step of her perfect legs. An Aztec princess in a short black skirt.

I feel a tug on my arm. Debbie's in my ear, "You like her don't you. That's far out! Listen, there's a party at the beach and I'm gonna go. Can you drive my brother home? Pleeease, Johnny D."

"Ah, a…OK," I say, and she splits with some surfer dude named Todd.

So, me and Danny Garcia hop into my little MG. We drive east, away from the university, and I have my first experience of the barrio.

When you cross over to the East Side, it's obvious. The streets are littered with trash. The buildings are all run down, faded, pink and turquoise. All the signs are in Spanish. Every house has five or six cars parked in front of it. Chevys and Buicks scattered across front lawns. Radios blaring the oldies. Vatos leaning on them. Baggie khakis, cigarettes, red bandannas and dark shades. All checking me out. Not too many MGs on the East Side. All the way, Danny is raving on about the fucking war.

"You wanna know, man? You wanna know who made me go to that fucking war, man? John Wayne, Audie Murphy, and Vic Morrow, man! Yeah, man I used to watch that show *Combat* every day, man! I seen *Sands of Iwo Jima* seven times, man! John Wayne was my fucking hero, man! Audie Murphy was like a God to me, man. He just got into firefight after firefight and never got a scratch. Just medal after medal. I think he's the one I hate the most. He did this to me." He rips open his shirt to reveal the scars and welts of five bullet holes across his chest. "Yeah, man, I stood up in the middle of a firefight. I thought I was Audie Murphy, but I was only Danny-fucking-Garcia and they shot the fucking shit outta me! And you know what else, man? Nobody cares. Nobody wants to fucking hear about it. Nobody gives a fuck about us, man! We're not the heroes our fathers and uncles were, man! We're just survivors. Sing Loy motherfucker. Sorry about that shit, GI! Fuck it, man! Fuck it!"

He storms out of the car and melts into the barrio night, hands raised to the heavens.

As I'm watching him go, I begin to feel really angry. It's as if Danny's anger leaps into me and I'm possessed by it. I turn on the radio. Conga drums tapping out a jungle beat. Mick Jagger making jungle sounds, wailing jungle wails.

Please allow me to introduce myself
I'm a man of wealth and taste
I've been around for a long, long year
Stole many a man's soul and faith

I'm on the freeway. Punching the gas. Picking up speed. Interstate 15 North, out to the desert. I don't know where I'm going, but I'm going. Fontana, Foothill exit Rte. 66. I fly past at about 90. The car is so low to the road that I see pavement rolling underneath. Faster and faster. Jagger is wailing. Barstow 40 miles. Death Valley 200. I just keep going faster and faster. Las Vegas 280. I just keep going faster and faster. Suddenly I'm airborne. I am flying in slow motion over a fifty-foot cliff. Flying up to the stars. Flying free. Then down, down to the sand and cactus below. Miraculously the car lands right side up. I look out the windshield and see an old papasan standing in the middle of a rice paddy.

He's pointing and laughing, "Ha ha, you Dinky Dau GI. You Dinky Dau!"

I hear my mother calling, "Johnny, come home. It's suppah time."

My only injury is a cut on top of my head. The crown chakra. The point where the spirit enters. I feel a gentle touch on my shoulder and a voice whispers in my ear, "Live. Love."

I climb out of the car and look back. Totaled. My first car fucking totaled. The cops find Danny's tequila bottle and they arrest me.

As they're taking me in, one of them says to me, "Why'd you do that?"

"I don't know, man. I just got back from Vietnam. Maybe that had something to do with it." He says, "Well, that's your problem, isn't it?"

In the morning I take the fucking bus home. I have two thoughts. One is that I hope this is all one long bad dream. Two is that chick, Lupe Marie. Fuck! I should have talked to her instead of just standing there with my hands shaking. Now I don't even have a fucking car! Fuck me! This is not the way Audie Murphy came home. Damn it! I served my country.

Debbie Far Out puts us together in a few days and we talk. Her name comes from the fact that her mom prayed to the Virgin of Guadalupe every day for her dad's safe return from WWII. She promised to name her first born girl after the Virgin. Lupe Marie in Spanish is Maria Guadalupe. Her first love was killed in the 'Nam two years before we met. On our first date, we go to see the movie *Camelot*. We kiss. And then we talk. We talk a lot. We married in 1970 and yes, we are still talking.

SPACE
Ellen Wright

It's 12:04 on Thursday afternoon, and I'm sitting on the couch in my brother's girlfriend's house in San Antonio. I got here Tuesday night. He's been here almost a year and it's my first visit. It's an obnoxiously oversized place in a gated community. There's a mass-produced panorama of Paris on the puke-salmon-beige wall behind me. My brother is passed out in their bedroom, which is upstairs and bigger than my apartment. He's on his back with his mouth agape, and I know this because I went in a little while ago to sneak an Adderall out of his bottle on the dresser to try to take the edge off my hangover.

My brother moved to Texas last fall to be with Katie, who had a job and owned a home. My brother was renting a room in a friend's house in San Diego and working at a new job he hated, his first since being discharged from the Army seven years prior, after seven years in. He and Katie met while she was temporarily working remotely from his office. He passed a note to ask her out, feeling too self-conscious to talk to her in front of an office full of dudes. They did the long-distance thing for about seven months, one or the other flying out every three or four weeks.

I'm older by three years and eight months, and we had a standard sibling dynamic as kids, very love/hate. He masterfully pushed my plentiful buttons, still does. He used to knock on my bedroom door while I was shut inside and run down the hall, which unfailingly had me yelling after him. We would play together for hours, his Ninja Turtles riding in my Barbie Corvette. Over the years we exchanged countless blows, both physical and verbal, but if anyone or anything threatened the other, we were the first line of defense. As I succumbed to adolescence, I really didn't like him; I thought he was annoying and immature. But to be fair, I didn't really like anyone, least of all myself.

After 9/11 he decided to join the Army to defend his country. He was 18, still gangly and pimply and goofy. I went to his graduation from boot camp in Kentucky. It took me a long moment to pick him out from the group, everyone identically shorn and uniformed. And so, so young. He couldn't turn his head the first day of our visit—he hadn't been allowed for weeks and couldn't break the habit. His one request was a box of Trix cereal, which he ate in one sitting.

We wrote letters back and forth while he was stationed in the US, and I began to appreciate him in a way I never had before. I had taken him for granted, my pesky little brother always underfoot, poking me or teasing me or repeating a joke until someone yelled at him to stop, but now that he wasn't around, I missed him. The morning he was to fly to Iraq on his first deployment I was working at a cafe and spilled blisteringly hot coffee across the top of my hand, I was so distracted.

We continued our correspondence, my letters now addressed to a forward operating base. Once he complained about the lack of pornography available, and I made a trip to a news stand to pick some out for him. It's a delicate state of mind to be in, deciding what you want your little brother to beat off to. When shipping that package I got major side-eye from the postal employee, when he read my description of "magazines."

"You know it's a crime to mail pornography, right?" he said as I felt myself turning red, because I am a terrible liar.

"My baby brother is getting shot at in a war zone, let him have his porn!" I thought defiantly.

I eagerly awaited his visits home.

His first leave after Iraq was over the 4th of July holiday, and we spent it at our dad's house BBQing. In the midst of the fireworks I realized he wasn't outside with us, watching. I found him in the living room, staring at the comics section of the paper. Whenever we went to Disneyland we always left before the big finale. He'd say he was OK, that it wasn't a big deal; he just preferred not to be around for them, but I saw the flinches and the far off look in his eyes. I know he saw terrible things, the kind of things that change a person, the kind of things I'll never understand. I know he saw friends of his killed right beside him, in the same vehicle.

After he got out of the Army we were closer than ever. He was my best friend. Others marveled at our relationship—someone once said to me, "You know that's not typical, right?" And I did, kind of. I was proud of what we had. We didn't have to explain ourselves, and we had so much fun. We drank together, a lot. It's a small miracle I survived those years, regularly driving the nine miles home double-vision drunk.

We comforted each other through breakups: he tossed my phone aside and took me out when a boyfriend I was leaving texted me 30 times in two minutes; I listened to his girl troubles when he'd show up at my door with tall cans and chips from the 7-11 around the corner; he slept on my floor, without me asking, the night before I went to file a restraining order against an ex; I picked him up from a trolley station in City Heights, tripping on acid, when his girlfriend left him on the side of the freeway after he grabbed the steering wheel of her car and tried to swerve them into traffic. That girlfriend approached me about trying to convince him to enter an in-patient treatment center to get help, but we didn't get anywhere. That was the girlfriend before Katie, two years ago.

They broke up, and knowing firsthand the madness that can come and go with a toxic relationship I expected him to bounce back, but he didn't. That holiday season, he flaked on Thanksgiving and Christmas both. I brought the family's presents to him a few days later. Drunk and strung out on Adderall, he nastily mocked every gift in turn. I took mine back, assuming he'd throw it out. He blasted the superficial consumerism and shrugged off missing the gatherings—"I just didn't want to go," he said.

One day he told me he sometimes heard voices when he drank, that he heard the neighbors talking shit about him, that he couldn't be sure how much of it was real. He was increasingly distant with our mom; he didn't like all her questions. He stopped talking to our dad altogether. I got myself into yet another shitshow of a relationship right about the time he met Katie, and between that and their frequent visits, we saw less and less of each other.

My brother really pulled away after he announced he was moving. No one in my family has ever handled distance well. My mom recently told me about the dynamic of my dad's navy deployments when I was a child: he would get upset at her telling him she missed him, angry at her letters. When he came home to her he would be distant and cold, and they would inevitably fight until he left again, for months or a year at a stretch. He retired from the Navy when I was 12 and was around regularly for the first time.

A typical weekend for our dad included a case of beer, along with pitchers of margaritas shared with mom. He was either affectionate and funny when he drank or an ugly bully. The wrong tone or look sent him into a rage, and he would be inches from my face, his eyes bleary and red and angry. Sometimes, when he really got mad, he hit or grabbed. My brother got it worse. He never laid hands on one of us in front of the other, or in front of my mom, but I heard my dad's yells and my brother's cries from elsewhere in the house. There's a patched hole in the wall behind the door of my brother's old bedroom where the knob went through as the door was thrown open.

My parents finally split up when I was almost 17 and my brother was 13. Our mom contends she tried to keep the marriage going for so long for us, my brother and me. My brother, younger and extremely sensitive, took the divorce hard. I was in full teen angst mode, busy sneaking alcohol and cigarettes, unaware and unbothered by what was going on with him. After our dad moved out, I didn't talk to him for almost four years. My dad credits my brother for keeping him from jumping off the Coronado bridge during this time. He remarried four years later, and shortly after his new wife gave him an ultimatum: alcohol or their marriage. My dad did for his new family what he couldn't or wouldn't for ours.

Recently, while talking about his concern for my brother's drinking, he shook his head sadly and said to me, "I can tell you all about living with an alcoholic," referencing his childhood with my grandfather.

Stunned, I replied, "I know what it's like."

He looked at me, truly confused, and said, "I wasn't that bad when I lived there."

It was my mom who broke the news that my brother had left for Texas. I had been texting him earlier that day. "Want to watch my cat while I go camping?" I asked, thinking he'd be happy to get a break from his shared house, but he said no, he'd be in Texas. Taken aback by the suddenness of it, I snidely texted, "Are you planning to say goodbye?"

"Yes," he replied.

A few hours later my mom called to tell me he'd come by to pack up a few things he had at her place before heading to the airport. It was a punch to the gut. I demanded an explanation, expected an apology. I got neither. He didn't seem to see what the problem was. I ping-ponged between hurt and anger. I texted Katie, "Good luck." I wanted her to know what he'd done, this man she had the poor taste to love and was taking away. I wanted someone else to blame for what he'd done.

I apologized for that text this morning, eleven months after I wrote it. I wrote it sarcastically, out of anger and frustration, but I had no idea how sadly appropriate it would turn out to be. Katie asked me to come out here. Things had been really bad the past nine months, she told me, and she didn't know what to do anymore. He needed his big sister. I had such a mixed-up mess of emotion, hearing that. I felt guilt for not coming out sooner, without being asked, for selfishly spending the better part of a year being hurt and defensive and taking the way he left personally.

I felt somehow responsible as his older sister, but completely helpless. I felt like a hypocrite; I couldn't come out to lecture him about coping with depression while I was battling a particularly nasty bout of it, or give him shit about his drinking when I couldn't remember my last day sober. I felt resentment at being asked to do the impossible, and at the reminder of how far removed I was, both physically and psychologically. But I felt hope, too, that maybe I could do something, and at least I'd be trying. If nothing else, I'd get to spend some time with my brother.

My brother and I had planned to drive from San Antonio to Austin today. He came downstairs a while ago to get something to eat. "I feel like shit," he mumbled.

"What time did you go to sleep?" I asked. He wasn't sure. He knew he fought with Katie after we came home from the karaoke bar, but couldn't remember what about. Sometime around 3 A.M. I heard her yell, "Stop fucking drinking!" then a lot of crashing and banging that sounded like things being thrown. He's back to bed now. I fly home to San Diego in just about 24 hours. I don't know if I should have a serious sit-down talk with him.

We talked a little yesterday. He said he's depressed, he said he's seeing a psychiatrist who he thinks doesn't care, whom he just tells what he thinks he wants to hear. He takes his medication, when he remembers. A buddy of his, a husband and father, hung himself a month ago, so that's got him a little wound up. He just needs a job, he said. He just needs to exercise. Things are better than they were, he's careful not to drink so much that he punches holes in the walls. He wants to move to South Dakota with Katie, get away from big cities and all the stupid sheeple. California was worse, he said, everybody in such a goddamn hurry all the time, and he'll never move back.

I'm afraid if I tell him what I'm really thinking—that he's in serious, life-threatening peril and needs intensive professional help—he'll shut me out entirely. Katie is scared of the same thing, told me when she's been stern with him he won't talk to her for days after. She's begged him to go to therapy and he refuses. She worries about leaving him at home with alcohol and guns when she goes to work. She doesn't understand what happened and feels like it's her fault.

I think part of what scares me is I see so much of myself in him: the generations of mental health problems and substance abuse, the way we grew up, so much of the way we think and see and know the world. But there's this space between us that's never been there, and I'm so afraid it's there for good. I fumble for the line between being supportive and being abused, and he's so negative and angry and misanthropic these days that I don't like being around him. I was jealous when he came out here for Katie, but now don't envy her in the least.

I'm looking so hard for the boy who would cry half the car ride home from Chino after a weekend with my cousins, every time; for the man who would shoot the dirtiest look at someone being rude or mean to someone else more vulnerable. He's in there somewhere, under booze and pills and PTSD and depression and fucking *life*. I just hope he has some kick left in him. Because as much as I want to figure it out and dissect it and make it better, this is another war that's not mine to fight, and that I'll never completely understand.

STABLE ON MEDS
Michelle Kerouac

I didn't think when I joined the Navy at 22 as a nurse that I'd become a patient as well. Anybody would become depressed being stationed on a ward taking care of other service members' kids with cancer. I learned quickly though, being depressed in the military doesn't get you discharged. Mania, on the other hand, now that's dangerous.

I loved my job, and the kids I took care of. But being in San Diego, away from my support system back in the Midwest, a single mom, and working longer hours than I ever had before left me feeling depleted. I found myself increasingly unable to pull my mind out of destructive, self-loathing thoughts that left me feeling hollow and heavy. I could do no more than I absolutely had to, just to make it through my day.

When I met with my primary physician on my birth month for my routine annual physical, I was honest during his questioning.

"Do you feel down, depressed, or hopeless?"

"Yes."

"Do you have trouble falling asleep, staying asleep, or sleeping too much?"

"I sleep all the time."

I left with a prescription for an antidepressant and a referral to the mental health clinic.

I took a few days to decide whether or not I was going to start the meds. I wasn't sure I was ready to admit to needing them. I'd had bad times in the past and got over them, but this time was different. I was different.

At the time I worked nights, so it wasn't unusual that I slept all day, but I slept all day every day.

My 6-year-old son saw the bottle of pills on my nightstand one afternoon.

"What are they for? Are you sick?" he asked.

"These are to help Mommy feel better and not need to sleep so much."

He seemed worried. I had to get better.

And once the pills started to take effect, I did stop spending days in bed, barely being able to get up long enough to even make a meal. Instead, I became more productive than I had ever been before. I kept my house immaculate. My son would come home from his weekends at his dad's to the furniture rearranged, and then the next day I would rearrange again. I paced non-stop, going from one task to the other, unable to sit still. I alphabetized absolutely everything in the house that could be alphabetized, and if it couldn't, then I color-coded it. I didn't just sleep less, but stopped needing hardly any sleep at all.

Within days, I felt the heaviness lift off me. I couldn't remember ever feeling this good, I wondered if I had been depressed so long that I'd forgotten what it was like not to be.

I took the hardest assignments on my unit and still finished my rounds in time to help the other nurses pass meds or start IVs. I had no need to take breaks or to eat; my energy seemed to be suddenly self-rechargeable. I was too busy to notice I wasn't taking care of myself.

Just a few weeks on the meds, I had a night on the unit that was oddly empty of patients. There were several rooms without pint-sized occupants in them. I gave the two corpsmen on my team each a box of adhesive remover wipes and challenged them to see who could clean the old layers of tape off the footboards of the hospital beds, where allergy labels and code status signs typically hung. To make it even more entertaining, we raced from room to room on rolling stools. Because why wouldn't we do this at 3 in the morning? I tired out even the most motivated of my corpsmen.

I was manic as fuck.

This newfound normal didn't only make me better at my job, but it made me believe I was better at everything, including sex. I had so much sex—and not just with my fiancé, who was living on the East Coast at the time.

I would drink all night long and never feel like I'd had enough. I had to force myself to eat, if at all. I'd show up to work hours early to make the schedule for the nurses, months in advance. I made friends everywhere I went. The friends I would go out with couldn't keep up with me and my ever-changing plans and would call it a night long before I was ready to go. So, I made more friends wherever I ended up after they left. I changed my wardrobe from the status quo officer approved casual wear, to wearing the most brightly colored vintage dresses I bought in droves at thrift stores. I lost so much weight in such a quick time. I felt great. I looked sick.

When the month passed, I kept my appointment with the psychiatrist. I'd still managed to keep my responsibilities intact, despite my thoughts not just running together at a rapid changing pace, but whirling without direction, an incomprehensible chatter. What I didn't know at the time was that mania triggered by the onset of antidepressants was a classic sign of Bipolar Disorder, and lack of sleep is both a cause and a symptom of mania.

In my first and only appointment with the resident psychiatrist, I'd try to focus on one thought, but get so easily distracted by another, on and on, that all I really heard him say were the words "Bipolar," "I'm giving you a mood stabilizer that will help," and "this diagnosis makes you unfit for duty."

He wrote me two more prescriptions and told me to make a follow up at the front desk. I took the prescriptions, but never stopped at the desk to schedule. I never went back, hoping my file would be lost in his pile of work, and to my relief, he never followed up with me.

At first, having a name given to what I was experiencing provided a sense of relief. Now that I knew what was going on with me, I could get better. Right? But then I let "unfit for duty" sink in, and I could hardly breathe.

I did not want to be discharged from the Navy. I needed my job. I was a single mother with healthcare and a steady paycheck, but just as importantly, what I did gave me a sense of purpose. Being marked as unfit for duty could mean I would have a hard time finding any job as a nurse, even in the civilian world.

I filled the prescription for the mood stabilizer and went to ask my unit's social worker to find out if I was truly at risk of being discharged from the military.

I didn't give her much to go off, and she didn't probe why I was coming to her with questions. What she did do was call down to the mental health clinic. Keeping the phone on speaker, when the nurse answered the phone, the conversation was as quick as it was devastating.

"If a service member is diagnosed with bipolar disorder, is it grounds for discharge?" she asked.

"Yes! Who would want to deploy with someone like that?"

He said it so quickly and matter of fact, as if it were a mandatory sentence. Those words cut through me. I had to be better.

I started the new prescriptions, and with the mood stabilizers I slowly started to slow down. I hadn't thought at first about what I'd do when my pills ran out. They did help treat my depression, but they also created problems—I was destructive, but at least not suicidal.

The antidepressants ran out first. I spent several weeks experiencing the effects of withdrawal from Paxil. Uncontrollable feelings of electricity pulsated through my hands, out of my fingers, and through the top of my head. I went back to sleeping all the time, mostly to combat the nausea and headaches from withdrawal, but with only the mood stabilizer left that was meant to treat the mania, I very quickly began a downward spiral.

I was smarter about stopping the short supply of the mood stabilizers I had left. The withdrawal symptoms I'd read from them were much more daunting.

May cause seizures if abruptly stopped.

I rationed my last few weeks of them, and cut what I had in half, then in half again, until there were no pills left, and I was left feeling as empty as the prescription bottle.

There weren't any more nights out meeting new people. I didn't return calls or make plans with friends anymore. I showed up to work and did my job. I repaired my relationships. The enthusiasm I had just weeks before was gone. I stuck to my own assignments and tried to stay under the radar. I felt like I was the mental health equivalent of Don't Ask, Don't Tell. I couldn't go back for help.

I learned to deal with my mood swings on my own, enough to go unnoticed. I worked a lot, which helped, if only for those 12 hours at a time, and I transferred duty stations shortly after.

My next duty station was in Japan, which didn't leave me with options to seek care off base without getting noticed. I was a newlywed and shortly after, a new mother again to twins. I had to lie during my postpartum depression screening.

My husband helped me keep some sense of balance by taking responsibilities away from me like cooking, and he supported my continuing to work night shifts, bringing our newborn twins to the hospital at night for me to nurse them before they went to bed. He would keep track of the fluctuations in my moods, sometimes more aware of where I was headed than I was. The lines between the highs and lows were sometimes blurred.

I continued to suffer dark periods of depression, but then at times I would again have so much energy, and feel so good, that it made the lows seem almost worth it. It never failed though: the more manic I would get, the more depressed I'd become after. Because of me, and in spite of me, I chose not to eliminate either.

Now, all my medical record from my time in the military has in it about my mental health is one line:

24-year-old female. Bipolar. Stable on meds.

DIP

Joseph S. Pete

H e wasn't proud of it, but the specialist dipped Folgers instant coffee packets rat-fucked from MREs in a desperate attempt to stay awake during endless guard shifts and overwatches that stretched into the ashen-tipped cigarette butts of morning. They told him to "stay alert, stay alive," drumming that mantra into him from Basic to the staging grounds of Kuwait, but the terrifying prospect of death often wasn't enough to hoist his eyelids aloft under the duress of deployment's long, unending slog. Death seemed remote, abstract when you weren't far removed from high school. The ever-present threat of imminent death worked a little to keep him awake, but the well-worn saying wasn't nearly as persuasive as it should have been, especially not at zero dark thirty when he'd only had a few intermittent hours of sleep.

In the end, the grainy instant coffee just wasn't potent enough.

Real coffee would have perked him up, but it wasn't exactly readily accessible in Iraq. He sometimes mixed the instant MRE coffee with sun-warmed canteen water, but it seldom resulted in anything that resembled the genuine article and it certainly didn't keep him awake. So he started dipping the stuff, which seemed to transmit more caffeine directly into his cheeks but was gross, since it didn't pack into a wad the way real dip did, and it was a constant struggle to stop himself from swallowing coarse Folgers grains.

An ex-smoker, though reformed after basic training, the specialist eventually gave in and reverted to old habits and started stuffing Copenhagen or—more often—the cheapo off-brand equivalent into his cheeks to make it through guard duty. It was gross, undeniably gross, and it made him want to vomit but, hey, he would likely die soon anyway.

What was the alternative? He couldn't smoke. He couldn't light another cigarette, as he had for years. They told the specialist snipers would see the spark, and fatally drive an AK-47 or .50 cal round into his temple. He was too cowed to light another death stick but still needed his tobacco fix. He still filled his cheek pouch with addictive tobacco and hoped to stay stimulated enough to witness any threats early enough to avoid the big suck in the sky.

Dip was, frankly, disgusting. Saliva welled up in his cheeks like bilge water. It was nasty whether you spat it out into the hot sand, deposited the blackened, brownish nicotine-stained spit into empty water bottles everyone always feared they'd accidentally take a swig of, or held the noxious swill in the pouch of your cheek for as long as you could stand. Reluctantly, the specialist chewed it like cud, and expelled the nasty brown juice every few minutes.

He fell in with the dippers in his platoon, joined the herd. They didn't quite have the same camaraderie as a huddled gaggle of smokers, but met up to insert chewing tobacco outside the chow hall and coordinated on the occasional trips to the PX on the other side of the Forward Operating Base (FOB) so they would never be short of supply.

Swallowing a slug of the brown juice became an obsession among the group, an unattainable Mount Everest they bantered about every so often. They had seemingly infinite time back on the FOB and few diversions. And they had money. The soldiers had a lot of money saved up. They spent scarcely a cent from their paychecks while deployed—room, board and every expense were covered and they rarely had the chance to set foot in any place of business.

So, they started pooling money—$20, $50, $100—to try to convince someone, anyone, to gulp dip spit from a repurposed Gatorade bottle. It was just a way they killed time if no one had a card game going or any video games to watch.

One day, the pool somehow rose to $200. That seemed serious. That was about a third of a private's paycheck at the time. The specialist started to consider it, seriously considered, which the others took note of. His platoon mates tried to goad him.

"Come on man, come on."

"You'll be a legend."

"This is the only thing that'll make this deployment bearable."

He was thinking about how he could spend all that money, trying to talk himself into it. His battle buddies circled round.

"You gotta do it. You gotta do it. This'll be the greatest thing ever. The whole FOB will be talking about you."

"Damn it," the specialist thought. "I could die tonight. I could go on patrol, and never come back. I could use this cash, go to the hajji shop, get a leather jacket or a Turkish rug. It's good money."

He grabbed the Gatorade bottle, suddenly resolute. He could do this. He could muster the courage. He didn't know what he'd even do with a Turkish rug, but God he wanted one in that moment.

They were goading him on, chanting his name.

He lifted the dip bottle toward his lips, caught a powerful whiff of rotten tobacco and stagnant spittle. It was pungent. He was nauseated, started retching a little. He tried to suppress his disgust, force himself to do it, but the revulsion was too strong. He was strong enough to go to a war zone, return fire and withstand nightly bombardments of mortar rounds. But he wasn't courageous enough to choke down nasty brown dip spit.

Pvt. Henderson suddenly ran forward, snatched the dip bottle out of his hand and knocked back a shot.

"Ooooh," everyone screamed, shouting in disbelief. The soldiers whooped, hollered and jumped around. It was like the party scene at the end of a movie as the end credits rolled.

Pvt. Henderson wiped his mouth and declared it was nothing. He was from Chicago and had downed Malort before. That was way worse, much harder to choke down. He put up a good front of bravado for a little bit. But he soon looked like he was starting to yellow.

Even as Pvt. Henderson started to hunch over and dry-retch and demand water to rinse his mouth, the specialist felt dejected, defeated. He could face the enemy, IED blasts and the like, but he couldn't will himself to do that. He wasn't disciplined enough. He wasn't strong enough. Maybe he just wasn't headstrong enough.

After spitting on the floor a few times, Pvt. Henderson regained his vigor.

"Pay up," he yelled exuberantly. "Everyone pay up."

GRAFFITI

Brandon Lingle

May, 2012.

While cruising a main drag in southern Afghanistan one night, I saw Eazy-E eyeballing me from one of the Jersey barriers lining the sidewalk. I tried not to stare at his ball cap, shades, and twin-crossed pistols. About 20 feet later, he peered at me from another wall, and again 20 feet after that. Eazy-E was everywhere three years before *Straight Outta Compton*.

These stenciled images of the rap artist follow the style of British street artist, Banksy, and they are one example of a trend in wall art at one of the largest NATO bases in Afghanistan. About the diameter of a helmet, and usually spray-painted in black on concrete blast walls, these counterculture artifacts offer mini-mental escapes for those working on US-led Kandahar Airfield, or KAF.

At the time, more than 30,000 people from at least 25 countries lived on KAF. After my run-in with Eazy-E, I paid attention to the tags, and KAF's best graffiti gallery adorned a row of Texas barriers outside the Base Exchange. A montage of symbols clung to these fortifications with a slant toward '90s culture. Hand-sprayed words framed the bottom of the ad hoc exhibit, "When Johnny Comes Marching Home," the letters black except for three red letters: W-A-R.

Besides Eazy-E, the rappers Dr. Dre, Vanilla Ice and D.J. Docmojo Worldwide graced the walls along with movie icons like *The Big Lebowski's* Walter Sobchak wielding a .45, Jack Nicholson's character from *The Shining, Star Wars* mercenary Boba Fett, Private Pyle from *Full Metal Jacket*, Ron Burgundy and John Wayne.

Other KAF tags mixed pop culture, sarcasm, and military life: smiling, walking lunchboxes toting AK-47s, walking ticking bombs, fists grabbing barbed wire, green feet, gangs of mini-soldiers carrying giant booze bottles, Mario Brothers characters, Calvin, Iron Man, biohazard signs, ducks saying "look at this duck," men using mind power to bend spoons, panda bears sporting headphones, skunks, ladybugs, dogs, tigers, buffaloes and moose.

Stencil art seemed a perfect fit for the military, a subculture focused on uniformity and limits. Well-defined rules govern life for service members within the base perimeter. Often associated with protest movements and adrift between free-form graffiti and sanctioned signage, stencil art is a subversive form caught within borders. The very edges that seek to restrain actually form the art. These boundaries also ask to be broken. With stencils, conformity becomes liberating.

An international phenomenon, stencil graffiti decorates cities around the world, but a public affairs officer told me that Americans produce most of the stencil art at the Kandahar base.

At KAF, where the stench from the "Poo Pond"—an open-sewage facility as big as a football field—rides the air and soldiers enjoy dinners at T.G.I. Friday's, or play roller hockey on the boardwalk, boilerplate language mediates life. Signs announce the rules everywhere you go, and none say, "Have a nice day" or "Don't worry, be happy."

Many offer safety pointers: "Actions on rocket attack—lie down, put on helmet and body armor, move to shelter after 2 minutes if attack has ended, wait for the all clear, report casualties and damage." Or: "Hazardous Snakes, Do NOT Attempt to Play With, Feed, Capture, Handle or Engage ANY Wildlife, Especially: Indian Krait, Sind Krait, Saw-scaled Viper, Indian Cobra, McMahon's Viper, Halys Pit Viper, Levant Viper, Central Asian Cobra." And: "No sleeveless shirts or tank tops."

Other signs address security: "No loaded weapons beyond this point." Or standards of behavior: "Phone usage—time limit, 20 minutes—do not damage phones—do not deface booths."

These widespread letter barrages quickly numb base occupants. Most people need no reminder to avoid Central Asian Cobras. So, random images—like that of *Family Guy's* Stewie on shipping containers, "Super Freak" on the front of an MRAP, or spider monkeys riding bombs on T-walls—bring welcome relief to the absurdity of life on a forward operating base.

The officer I spoke with couldn't pinpoint when the graffiti began, or who started the tradition. He said base visitors cared more about the larger murals decorating the base. I'd heard rumors that base officials planned to whitewash the street art. The officer hadn't heard of such plans or an official position on the graffiti. At least with this small issue commanders appeared more worried about the war than base aesthetics. He said the tags would likely stay since they weren't profane.

With this, Tim O'Brien's words from *The Things They Carried* echoed within me: "If you don't care for obscenity, you don't care for the truth; if you don't care for the truth, watch how you vote. Send guys to war, they come home talking dirty."

Besides protection, graffiti provides the blast walls' only redeeming quality. On a certain level, the very existence of the wall art is obscene. Maybe the stenciled patterns should be explicit. Maybe the art should make us uncomfortable. Maybe the walls themselves are the obscenity.

*

June, 2012.

Twice in a year I traveled through the wing of Leipzig-Halle's airport reserved for US forces surging to and from America's wars—to Iraq in 2011, and from Afghanistan in 2012. The former Soviet Bloc terminal—sealed from civilians—serves as a halfway house for people sporting tactical backpacks and camouflage on their way over there and back. Not a war zone and not home, the airport features expensive telephone and Internet use and shops peddling chair massages, beer, energy drinks, schnitzel, cuckoo clocks and chocolates.

German and US flags hang draped next to each other on ashen walls. Grime from tired heads form dark ovals above the worn airport seats. A German map and poster of "famous people who lived close to Leipzig" looms above a photo of John F. Kennedy's Berlin visit and his famous words. And, a sign: "Leipzig took part in the fight for freedom in East Germany, through weekly peace prayers and protests."

During each visit, fogged by jet lag and adrenaline, I'd planned to send an e-mail home or buy a trinket for my kids, and each time I spent the layover mesmerized by soldier graffiti dominating the concourse.

Under gym-style fluorescent lights and heating ducts, my boots slid along the tiled floor as I tried to digest the words from thousands of decals and notes scrawled in Sharpie or ballpoint onto the airport walls and glass partitions. The history books don't say who started the display, or the airport authority's position on such vandalism, but the graffiti remains. The layered writings gave a conflicted feel—art gallery, billboard, and war memorial. For me, the display captured a mosaic of America.

The decals popped with personal messages, hometown pride, endorsements, and wishes. IEDS Suck. OEF X. Iraq & Afghanistan Veterans Assoc. I love Kabul. I love Guam. I like

Scotch. Cover your Cough. Clean your Hands. WTF. Tip of the Spear. Fobbitry Approved. MAINEiacs. American Samoa. Puerto Rico. Charleston, SC. I love the Dairy Palace, Canton, TX. If Route Clearance were easy it would be called your MOM! Support your local artist. Support your local veterans M/C. Support Boozefighters M/C. Shooting Star Tattoos. Honest Evil Tattoos. Mountain Dew. Shiner Bock. In-n-Out. Never Forget. I'd rather be studying, University of Maryland, College Park.

One sticker recalled a missing soldier: "PFC Bowe Bergdahl–Captured in Afghanistan 6-30-09–Please help find me" printed in a yellow circle with a photo of Bergdahl in the middle.

Other decals boasted unit character through their fearsome, comical or fanciful logos: thunderbirds, doves, seahorses, wolves, warthogs, lions, tigers, bears, cobras, elephants, alligators, sharks. Winged skulls, smiling skulls, scowling skulls, eye-patched skulls, skulls above swords, flaming skulls. Aces, clubs, spades, diamonds, shamrocks, green feet, red crosses, iron crosses, iron fists, knives. Centurions, cavemen, vampires, pinups, pirates, Jolly Rogers, Jolly Green Giants. Kilroy, Bugs Bunny, Tasmanian Devils, Kenny Powers, Darth Vader, and Curious George hefting a machine gun.

Unit names adorned the walls: Banditos, Blackhats, Blackhearts, Black Sheep, Black Widows. Bladeslingers, Desert Gators, Dustoff, Expendables, Green Mountain Boys, Guardians, Hookers. Misfit Medics, Painkillers, Palehorse, Pathfinders, Pedros, Rogue Rollergirls. Role 3. Roughriders. Secret Squirrels, Swamp Foxes, Task Force Troy, Voodoo, War Donkeys, Warlords.

And mottos: All American. Be polite and professional but have a plan to kill everyone you meet. First There. Kiss our asp. Laghman Pride. Re-enlist for the Thor Battalion. Veneer o Morir. Unleash hell. That others may live. The way of the shield.

Soldier graffiti can't be foreign to Leipzig. The city has seen much war. Nearly 100,000 men died in the Battle of Leipzig in October 1813. After World War I, Leipzig's Supreme Court hosted one of history's first war tribunals, where 12 German soldiers were tried and six received prison time. The harshest sentence, four years, went to two junior U-boat officers for torpedoing the hospital ship, H.M.H.S. Llandovery Castle, and machine gunning more than 200 survivors.

Just 72 miles from the US and British firebombing of Dresden, Leipzig also suffered heavy losses from Allied attacks throughout World War II. Bombings killed thousands and left many more homeless. A 1943 attack created a firestorm. In 1944 bombs destroyed most of the Leipzig airport where I stood. In April 1945, the US Army's Second and 69th Infantry Divisions fought house-to-house until capturing Leipzig and liberating two Buchenwald sub camps in the city. The US turned Leipzig over to the Red Army in July 1945.

The name Leipzig springs from the Slavic word Lipsk, which means "settlement where the linden trees stand." Lindens, the tree of lovers, are symbolic as places to celebrate, restore peace and seek truth. Linden flowers are ingredients for perfume or medicines. The wood is a preferred choice for crafting musical instruments and window shutters. Vikings made shields of wood from linden trees.

And lindens provide a solid canvas for notching initials. Indeed, a 1970s-era American veteran told me that while stationed in Germany, he carved initials with World War II dates in trees as a joke. I wondered if any of Leipzig's lindens bore Napoleonic soldiers' names. I thought of a family relic—a Civil War bullet from Shiloh embedded in an initialed hunk of sycamore—dusty and resting in a cabinet at my aunt's house.

A British archaeologist writing a dissertation on soldier tree carvings in England and France says the messages get more personal as the carver approaches combat. She's found grave markers bearing names she found on trees. The researcher said that despite heading to war, none of the carvers complained about their situations. Only three contained profanity. Most of the carvings, known as arborglyphs, expressed love for those at home.

In the Leipzig airport, the soldier graffiti is filled with profanity. There's not much love on these walls, but there is a little. Penned in black or red hearts one can read: Smith & Hinkle, Together 4-ever. Padilla + Parcell forever. SGT Scorzelli + SSG Scorzelli. At the end of this deployment David M. Norris is going to make Stefanie R. Niromiya his EX-wife, Gen 2:24. (the "EX-" likely came after David wrote his note.)

You'd think Leipzig's walls would hold many memorials to those lost in Iraq and Afghanistan. I found two.

One read: "R.I.P. Stansbery 101st July 30, 2010." I later checked a Pentagon news release, which explained: "Spc. Michael L. Stansbery, 21, of Mount Juliet, Tenn., died July 30 near Kandahar, Afghanistan, of injuries sustained when insurgents attacked his unit with an improvised explosive device."

The second, a pink highlighter gravestone with fluorescent green writing said:

> R.I.P.
> SPC Mills
> SSG Estavano
> SPC Johnson
> SSG Proctor
> SSG Altamirano
> 1LT Vincent

Most of these soldiers died during my 2011 tour in Iraq. I didn't know them, but I'd read incident reports and reviewed images. I knew the circumstances of their demise before I learned their names or saw their faces.

The Defense Department said this:

"Spc. Adrian G. Mills, 23, of Newnan, Ga., died Sept. 29 in Kirkuk, Iraq, of wounds suffered when his unit was attacked by insurgents using indirect fire."

"Staff Sgt. Estevan Altamirano, 30, of Edcouch, Tex., died Sept. 18 in Tikrit, Iraq, of injuries suffered in a noncombat related incident."

"Staff Sgt. Russell J. Proctor, 25, of Oroville, Calif., and Pfc. Dylan J. Johnson, 20, of Tulsa, Okla., died June 26, in Diyala Province, Iraq, of wounds suffered when enemy forces attacked their unit with an improvised explosive device."

Lieutenant Vincent died a few days after I left Iraq, the second-to-last American serviceman to die in the campaign: "First Lt. Dustin D. Vincent, 25, of Mesquite, Tex., died Nov. 3, in Kirkuk Province, Iraq, of wounds suffered when enemy forces attacked his unit with small-arms fire."

The lives of thousands of young people, in limbo, are condensed on these walls. Their words ambushed me. Mostly, these are walls of bravado. The wall-writers' friends could see them unguarded if they wrote honest. But how does one get more honest than a name and a date to prove your existence? On the way out of Baghdad in 2011, I signed the California flag painted on a T-wall near the base gate—that ink has surely succumbed to the dust and wind by now. I ignored the chance to add my name to the transient art on Leipzig's walls.

This summer I'll carve my family's initials on a smooth-trunked tree. My kids will help.

ELEPHANTS
Kurt Savage

n April of '93, Cowpens was on her way home after what we thought of in those days as an especially difficult deployment to the Middle East...because we would be at sea for Christmas. The rest of the ships in our battle group had spent most of their time off Somalia, delivering food and medicine in Operation Restore Hope while we had gone on alone to the Persian Gulf.

Somalia made CNN. I got a letter from my wife while I was in the Gulf, telling me how proud she was of the humanitarian work I was doing. Except I wasn't doing humanitarian work. I was twenty-five hundred sea miles away, enforcing sanctions against Iraq.

When we launched Tomahawk cruise missiles, that made CNN, too. By then, my wife was too busy with her new boyfriend to do much writing. That part of her last letter seemed abysmally clear. Her last letter. The one that came *after* she told me how proud she was. I knew, of course, as soon as I read *that* letter, that the ocean between us, between my wife and me, was receding. The way it does before a tsunami comes and changes everything.

When we dropped anchor off Thailand, I was hellishly exhausted. Thoughts of alcohol and sex had my shipmates vibrating like a prolonged chord in some familiar but alien music. Not me. In the last five months, I hadn't slept more than 3 hours in any single 24-hour period. Just when I needed those long hours to keep me from thinking too much about my crumbling marriage, the mission changed, and the hours abandoned me. In their absence, my imagination filled every moment with helpless torment. Once, while jerking off in the shower, I pictured myself watching my wife and her lover. The thought became a fantasy, again and again. I'd lay awake in my rack, my arousal unbidden, wave after wave of shame crashing over me.

All I wanted from Thailand was a full night of uninterrupted sleep.

Even so, Phuket's beauty overwhelmed me. The bay was clear and emerald blue, the sand almost white, and the surrounding hills rose sharply from the water, covered with vibrantly green jungle. Even the *color* seemed alive.

That afternoon, as I watched my hyper-animated shipmates go ashore, I wanted to go, too. I wanted to explore this beautiful country. I wanted a souvenir. I wanted to not have to get on a boat to get there. I wanted too much to drink. I wanted a woman, to see a woman, to talk to a woman. I wanted to be a good husband. I wanted to laugh and forget. I wanted to run away. I wanted to *hide*. I chose to stay in my rack. I hoped for sleep.

On the morning of the third day, my buddy Jerry dragged me out of bed and threatened to use force if I didn't go ashore with him. Reluctantly, I followed him down the accommodation ladder to a waiting water taxi, and we sped off toward the beach.

Three-quarters of a mile later, we stopped alongside a "longtail canoe." (We all called the longtails "bonka boats" because of the "bonka-bonka-bonka-bonka" sound made by their one-cylinder outboard motors.) Jerry hopped aboard and immediately began removing his shoes and socks, since the bonka boat would only take us to shallow water, where we'd have to wade ashore. Awkwardly, I did the same.

Jerry practically charged up onto the beach. I followed more slowly, looking back at the canoe and at Cowpens more than a mile away. I decided immediately that whatever happened on liberty today, I'd make sure I could get back to the ship on my own. I don't trust anyone to carry me back. I never have. No drinking. OK, not much drinking.

As we came ashore, a slender blonde in her mid-thirties walked up to us and said, "Well, MacArthur didn't look as good returning to the Philippines." She had clear blue eyes and a confident way about her. Exactly the type I can't keep my eyes off of. Exactly the type that never seemed to pay much attention to me. She turned out to be a photojournalist from Los Angeles, in Phuket on assignment, and anxious for some American company. She promised to show us around.

Our first stop was the bar at her hotel. Jerry figured out quicker than I did that she was mostly interested in a good old American roll in the hay. I pleaded married, as though I was invoking the Fifth Amendment.

Your honor, my client is clearly under an enormous strain as a direct result of the inferences he made from his wife's most recent letter, and he is therefore not responsible for the attraction he feels for Ms. Nikon. Also, he has no desire to expose himself to potential rejection by Ms. Nikon. At this time, we wish to invoke his right to silent self-recrimination.

Unable to bring myself to attempt cheating on my unfaithful wife, I drowned my sense of irony with another beer, and headed out to explore the city of Phuket on my own.

Souvenir shopping always made me feel less homesick, spending the whole day thinking about my wife and daughter, and it helped with the homecoming to be able to give them a gift that included a story. Where it came from. How I got it. Why I thought of them when I bought it. The shop owners would greet me with, "Hey, Joe, you come see my shop?" Almost invariably, his "shop" would turn out to be a flattened refrigerator box featuring a helter-skelter display of mediocre wood carvings or haphazardly tanned leather goods. Once, in Kenya, it was art. Nothing original, but excellent copies. I was mesmerized by one of a lone bull elephant in tall grass beneath a dust-orange sky. I wanted to be like him, the elephant: an immense presence, focused and intent, ready but still. I still regret not buying it.

But that's why I went. For the hidden treasures. For the surprises.

That's what I'm looking for when I hear a voice say, "You buy, Joe?"

I turn around. A half dozen Thai men have approached me and formed a semi-circle, blocking the sidewalk. Each of them has a different animal on a leash, which makes them simultaneously cute and unnerving. The one closest to me is in his mid-thirties and deeply tanned. He is maybe 5' 4" tall, holding out a monkey for me to examine. "You buy?" he asks again. I know better than to touch his monkey.

And obviously, I cannot buy the man's monkey. But I consider it anyway. It's what I do. Consider things I shouldn't. It's a practice that gets me in trouble sometimes. Like when I found out Kim was cheating on me the first time and I married her anyway.

It's such an incongruous offer that I say nothing. I turn back to my shopping. If I ignore him, maybe he'll go away.

He hands the monkey to a member of his sales team, then takes control of a large bird. "You buy hawk, Joe?"

Reality seems to have slipped out to sea, and where I'm standing feels muddy and surreal.

Too late, I stop being polite. I frown, wave him off, and begin to edge away, focusing my attention on souvenirs that can be more easily explained to the customs officials when we return to San Diego. Or, you know, won't need to be snuck past the quarterdeck watch and won't need to be hidden and fed for six weeks. I mean, if I bought the hawk, and fed it a mouse every day, I'd need to find forty-two mice for the trip home and somehow sneak *them* on board, too. And I'd need to feed them, too. I wouldn't be buying a hawk, I'd be creating an ecosystem from scratch.

"Then you buy my elephant, Joe!"

I don't think it's possible to keep your back turned when someone makes you an offer like that. When I turn around, he is holding the end of a rope leash, which is attached to the collar on a four-foot tall baby elephant. An image pops into my head: trying to coax a panicked, several-hundred-pound animal off a speed boat onto the accommodation ladder by which we get aboard the ship.

I look at the elephant again and my pulse quickens the way his would if I tried to get him onto the boat. There are leashes on me, too. I am afraid of the conflict awaiting me at home. I am afraid she will leave me and also that she will not. I am afraid of not knowing. I am afraid that she will have all the control and I will have none.

The elephant in that painting would never allow himself to be put in that position, would fight it with all that made him what he is.

"*NO!*" I shout. I look out to the bay, and there is my hazy gray home. Annoyed, I point to her and explain that there is my ship. I cannot buy the baby elephant because I will not be able to get it home. But then, for only a moment and just inside my own head, I imagine what it would be like if I did. Would *this* elephant be any harder to deal with than the thing I'm avoiding, even though I know I'm going to have to face it when I get back to San Diego?

"Hi, Honey! This is Norman. Yes, I named him after your mother…isn't that sweet? He can stay on the balcony, can't he?"

That's right. We'd keep him outside, where we wouldn't really have to deal with him. It's what we do. Like when we'd spent all those evenings drinking beer on the patio with the neighbor she'd slept with the first time she cheated on me. Or when she came home at four in the morning without any underwear and said she'd been out with the girls.

Animal Sales Guy tries to hand me the leash. He seems changed from a moment ago. His face has hardened, and there is desperation in his eyes. I don't understand why he doesn't just *take* my money. I don't understand the charade. Not his and definitely not hers.

I yank my hands clear of his and hold them up in a defensive gesture. No, I say again. I can't.

I begin to look for escape routes.

"Come on, Joe, you buy! Such pretty elephant baby. You got kids? Elephant good with kids!"

"What?" Half laughing, half panicked, I turn and walk away. Animal Sales Guy follows me. The elephant follows him.

I break into a trot. Animal Sales Guy breaks into a trot. The baby elephant also breaks into a trot, his head bobbing and swaying.

I cannot run from this any more than I can run from the effect of what she's done, what she's doing. I try anyway.

"You buy elephant, Joe! You buy!"

"No!" I shout over my shoulder. "I will not buy an elephant!"

I am certain, in this moment, that there are people watching who find our spectacle amusing, but it isn't, not at all. Even though I am laughing, it's for the same reason that I laugh when someone tickles me, because I can't help it, and also because I am terrified and angry and helpless and my life is hurtling out of control. The *here* and the *there*, Phuket and San Diego, have merged into a kind of existential hall of mirrors. Nothing is normal, and I desperately need to find the way out.

I got to the beach just as a few of my shipmates waded ashore. I nodded and smiled as we sat together on the sand, them donning their shoes and me removing mine. The water was heavy against my legs as I waded alone to the boat. I had the Chief's Mess mostly to myself that night. I listened to the sounds of the ship: the routine announcements, the distant door slams, the hiss of the air conditioning. I ate dinner alone, watched part of a movie alone, and went to bed alone. I slept like a baby.

When I got home, I still tried to ignore the death of our marriage. For a long time, I even gave her a pass for getting pregnant while I was away. Now and then, I'd tell the story of that time a guy tried to sell me an elephant in Thailand. I'd leave out how scary it was, so people would laugh and tell me what a great life I have. By the time the tsunami destroyed Phuket a decade later, my marriage had long been swept away, and what was left of me was still underwater. Even so, I thought about Norman, and the guy who tried to sell him to me. Did they survive? Was he still on that beach when the ocean rushed in? Norman would have been too big for the scam by then, but was there another baby elephant across the street from the beach that day?

I imagine there was; one thing I learned from my ex-wife's infidelities is that there is always another elephant.

Perhaps Animal Sales Guy was just a con man, a cartoon character half a world away, but the Phuket he lived in was filled with uncertainty wrapped in beauty. Just like here. Perhaps there were people he loved, people who loved him back. Just like me.

There are times when I'm so desperate to avoid rejection that I chase people down in the hope that it will make them love me. It never does. Sometimes, I just can't sell my elephant.

SAND LOVE

Ashli Taylor

got to Ft. Hood in January, went through in-processing, and was finally picked up by the sponsor. He introduced himself and let us know that we would be deploying to Afghanistan in 4 months. I got to my unit, 504th Military Intelligence Brigade, 509th Forward Support Company assigned to 163rd Battalion, where I would be working in a Standard Army Maintenance System office, better known as SAMS-E. The office had the regular smell of miserable married men, Red Bull, cigarette smoke and coffee. I noticed Aaron because he was the quiet one. The quiet ones were always attractive to me. He was an E-5 at the time I was a specialist. It took a while to do, but we exchanged numbers. I did it under the guise of needing help from an NCO, just in case my NCO wasn't around. Then it happened: we had our first personal conversation. He texted me.

> Him: Hey, how are you?
> Me: I am good. You?
> Him: Good. How are you liking it so far?
> Me: I don't know yet, but I feel like I won't in time.

Him: Well some of us are going out this weekend if you wanna come out.
Me: Oh OK, cool! I'm down.

That's how it starts, right? We tested the waters with a joke, we conversed about the "aintshitness" that wore rank higher than E-5, and we traded witty insults laced with sexual tension. Slowly but surely, the lot of us going out turned into just the two of us going on dates. The dates turned into nights spent together. Then he was draped in intimacies. Then I loved everything about him. Time flies when you're having fun and great sex. It flies even faster when you know you have a mission looming that is going to take you 7, 938 miles across the world for an entire year. That fact left no time for practical thinking or common sense. It left no time to sit and process the red flags that were evidently waving.

Statistics say that military members get married at three times the rate of civilians. I'm not shocked. I understood even before I deployed the feeling of loneliness, how tight it held me at night, woke up with me in the morning, and kissed me on the cheek before the sun even got a chance. I was motivated to hold on to anything and everyone that felt like home. I didn't want loneliness as my only companion for 12 months.

I heard what Aaron was saying and I heard what he wasn't saying. I heard him say I love you. I blocked out the "but," and the statement that came after it.

"I love you, but I don't want to rush."

"Rush into what? What is the problem with defining what we are doing?"

"Cause when you put a title on something people change."

"Oh, so you want the benefits, without the responsibilities…"

I wrote it off as fear. Young black men aren't often taught what love looks like. Young black men aren't often shown what affection looks like from an unconditional heart. They're taught to suck that shit up and provide; drive on, Soldier.

Before leaving West Ft. Hood for his own deployment, Aaron gave me a ring. It wasn't an engagement ring. It wasn't even a promise ring. My official unofficial boyfriend told me if we could make it through this year of being apart and re-adjust smoothly back home, we could discuss marriage. That ring was my carrot on a stick. I had sworn off the notion of ever getting married again, but Aaron weakened my resolve. The thought of him leaving pierced my soul.

When our time together in West Ft. Hood was down to its final month, reality started to kick in. How we would be deployed to different locations. How communication would be limited because of work schedules, tortoise-speed Internet, and phone card minutes we'd have to stretch. And the temptations that would be present. Down range conditions do not for logical thoughts make. All it takes is a missed call, a care package that doesn't come in, or the wind blowing briskly across nipples or testicles. Sand clogs everything, even the filters in the brain that would normally say, *You know damn well that ain't a good idea!* The fact that it would all be happening in a foreign and hostile area never set in.

Then it was time to board our magic carpet to Kandahar Air Force Base, kiss my family goodbye, secure properties and tie up any loose ends. Once there, I would have to perform my job with the expected excellence and accuracy that would ensure all combat vehicles were mission capable 24/7. Time to face the unknown and pray that God and His angels saw fit to push mercy a little closer to us. Up and off we go.

It didn't take long for things to switch on Aaron's end. All of a sudden, he wanted to "live life." All of a sudden, he wanted to "experience the world and travel."

"I hope you'll be there when I come back," he says.

The phone beeps to let me know that I have a few minutes left. I don't say goodbye in response. I just hang up.

I knew what he really meant. He wanted to be single and get the bachelor itch scratched. He had heard too many exciting and intoxicating stories from his army battle buddies, grandeur stories of Korean women that sleep with even the ugliest of men. You could be Flavor Flav and you would STILL get the cookies. He was told about the German women that sometimes had attitudes and bodies of black women, but more docile, and would do anything to become the wife of a military man. He had the urge to conquer.

Heartbreak in a foreign land is different than heartbreak in the homeland. At least when you're home, you can contact friends and family, pour some wine, put on some Mary J. Blige or Drake, and talk about how *he wasn't shit in the first place!* In a dry land I was dying for a drink. His name was Tyrone.

Tyrone oversaw the generator mechanics. He found reasons to come into my SAMS-E office every single day. He had the smell of sweat, hard work and cologne. It wasn't hard to know what we both wanted, the only issue would be keeping it all hidden from everyone else.

Aaron wanted his space. He wanted time to think. I wanted to feel better. Tyrone and I both knew what it was: he was married and I was a scorned and emotional ex-girlfriend. Even if it was forbidden, even if it was the most repetitive sin in the world, I needed Tyrone to be the Codeine, Vicodin or Percocet I couldn't get. I just wanted to feel numb.

Tyrone sneaks into my living quarters. Tyrone sits on my bunk and I sit next to him. I don't see Tyrone in this moment. I see the one who I want to want me, the one I want to call saying he has it all figured out, he knows what he wants, and what he wants is me. That doesn't happen. Instead Tyrone begins to do what men do to get a woman excited. But the kisses I feel on my neck are not from him. I imagine a different set of hands rubbing me in the places that matter most. The words he whispers into my ear are not his.

I am ready, he is ready. We do what we came to do. We do it quietly. We do it under the hum of the generators. We mix and mingle under midnight's blanket of darkness. I think we are both thankful the Middle Eastern sky seems a tad bit darker than usual. The strokes only lasted for so long. Which is disappointing to say the least, especially after making up my mind to do something like this. Not only am I a willing sinner, I am a disappointed one.

Tyrone takes the sheath off. I take it, put a knot in it, and walk to the bathroom to shower quickly and dispose of the evidence. I dress and escort Tyrone to the door. When he is gone, I lie in the sheets that smell like sex, hate, disappointment and self-loathing. I don't like myself in this moment, I knew better. Now I have to look at Tyrone every day and know he had a piece of me, and I him. It doesn't take long for him to act like I wasn't even a person anymore. I am just the 20 minutes he spent thrusting between my legs. I am the girl that ties the condom in a knot and flushes it down the toilet. Instead of numbing, it fully awakened my sorrow, and the realization that Kandahar wasn't the only threat to my well-being. The most hazardous combat area is inside of me.

EVERYONE'S POOP
Francisco Martínezcuello

Every day for seven months since arriving in Waleed, Iraq in 2008, I woke up in a fog of denial. My Z87+ polarized sunglasses failed to block the intense light reflecting off the fine sand, even early in the morning. I'd pretend the shimmers were ocean crests, frothy like boiling milk but with a shallow trough, but the wafting aroma of decaying organic matter never failed to burn the marine layer off my brain.

"Salaam alaikum," an ominous man greets me.

"Walaikum salaam."

Nosferatu isn't his real name, at least I don't think, but more like I never asked. He's tall, lanky, and bald with reddish tar-stained teeth. He finishes all his work right before sunrise, so I concluded he sleeps in a coffin within his home, a modular shipping container with a packing list that suggests it was shipped from the Balkans. He carries two hoses, one is a garden hose attached to a long metallic spray nozzle. The other is a large diameter hose that's connected to a silver bullet-shaped tank on wheels—a honey truck. The white crested waves in my mind dry up and reveal blue porta-johns.

At zero-seven-oh-five, all 150-plus Waleed occupants go inside to eat breakfast, and I wait outside for Nosferatu to clean all 35 of the porta-johns so I can have a bowel movement, a BM, or Bravo-Mike if you need to transmit over secure radio. The logistics of shitting in a combat environment are never talked about, but everyone poops.

The average deployed service members' shit-kit consists of baby-wipes, an mp3 player, and depending on what time of day it is, an outdated *Smooth*, *Curves*, or *Kings* Magazine—PX Porn. Once a month a mobile PX—a convenience store on a flatbed—would arrive with our resupply convoys. The contents are a fat kid's wish list—Oreo's, jerky, Doritos and men's interest magazines—soft porn. An Iraq afternoon average temperature is ten degrees warmer than a menopausal mother's hot flash, so you best believe I only urinated in the middle of the day. No one sprints at high noon in the desert unless they're getting shot at or they've got mud-butt. After a leakage incident, I learned quickly to never trust a fart in Iraq, so I held it in unless I was near a bathroom.

In normal kinetic combat conditions, service members are trained to maintain light discipline at night and strictly use Night Vision Goggles (NVGs) to conduct operations. In 2008, Waleed wasn't under normal conditions and at night, and from the four surrounding guard towers, I used the NVGs to observe servicemembers enter porta-johns, some with backpacks. While on watch, I imagined a laptop loaded with gigs of fetish porn, a tactical field expedient fleshlight—perhaps in olive drab or coyote tan—some astroglide substitute maybe. I chose to ignore it, so long as the occupancy for each porta-john is one—because the prohibited activities under General Order No. 1 states you can't have sex, but you're free to go fuck yourself.

I don't carry anything when I Bravo-Mike in Iraq, not even my standard issued pistol. I figure if I get mortared then a pistol won't save me, and if we are overrun by the enemy then he's more than welcome to join me in breaking General Order No. 1. I don't bring baby wipes either, because I don't like to leave my hole moist and smelling lilac fresh in a combat environment, so I stick to the Chuck Norris TP—cause it's rough, tough, and don't take shit from no one.

One day, my bowels moved faster than Nosferatu's cleaning and I decided I could not wait for him to finish his duties so I took my chances playing porta-john-roulette, not even stopping to do a customary search for scorpions, snakes, or a porta-potty-peeper with a scat fetish hiding in the tank. I was in mid flatulence when I noticed a footprint on each side of the seat with a smashed cigarette butt as if to welcome me—"Salaam alaikum." The interpreters defiantly rebelled against standard poop procedures by squatting over the lid. The dusty footprints on the tank were their sign of protest.

"The sons of bitches can't even shit right," I thought, dismissing the empirical evidence that elevating your feet during elimination is healthier than Western convenience.

But that's what war reduces humans to, believing one shit is better than another.

The sun bleached the outside walls of the porta-johns to a light cyan/aqua blend, but the inside color was ocean blue. The inner walls were pristine and lacked graffiti. No declaration that the commanding officer and sergeant major were gay lovers. No Sharpie illustration of ropes or droplets coming out of a giant mushroom head. No sketches of "Your Mom's Vag," or other derivatives. No stick figure rendering of Jody and your girlfriend in different *Kama Sutra* positions of penetration. It was as if Waleed wasn't worthy of it all.

The combination of waking up in Iraq and trying to eliminate in a porta-john after someone just smoked and squatted infuriated me. I was so angry I couldn't Bravo-Mike, I was instinctively driven to masturbate. But even my dick didn't feel like working, and after a few strokes of pulling taffy, I stopped self-soothing and cleaned myself up. The toilet paper cut my grundle when I wiped, which fueled my rage. I stormed out to project my frustrations toward Nosferatu. The spring that retracts the porta-john door caused a loud and delayed slam which caught his attention. Our eyes met through dark lenses, and he smiled as I stomped through the sand. It is impossible for someone to look tough while walking through sand.

He cleans the remaining porta-johns then drives the honey truck through the exit gate. He stops at the 400-meter mark, where engineers dug a hole in the sand—an expedient turd pool. Nosferatu reverses the pumps on the honey truck to expel the contents. It's so dry the sand absorbs the liquid instantaneously leaving only the chunky remains. I'm unable to Bravo-Mike, but I can't stop thinking about all that shit.

At dusk, Nosferatu changes vehicles and collects the trash from all four dumpsters. Tattered or unserviceable green undershirts, stretched out white tube socks, and veggie omelet MREs are just some of the dumpster contents. Garbage used to be collected in the morning after the wastewater removal, but because the Palestinian refugee camp kids would rummage through the trash without permission, I directed Nosferatu to collect it at night.

I'd like to think that by keeping the kids out I was "executing my duties as the Antiterrorism Force Protection Officer by reducing access to our perimeter, mitigating the possibilities of non-coalition forces to probe our defenses, denying the enemy the ability to gather intelligence, set up ambushes or plant fatal IEDs." At least that's what my award states—but that didn't make it true. Maybe I didn't like the fact the Palestinian refugees received so much attention that Angelina Jolie visited them and not the Marines. Perhaps I didn't know how to break the cycle of neglect and abuse I received as a child and I was perpetuating it by not sharing my leftovers and scraps with the Palestinian kids.

Looking back, I think they reminded me of my kids who were so far away, and yet the Palestinians were so close, but instead of providing them with compassion and love, I buried my emotions and discarded them like a case of expired ravioli. Maybe I stopped firing flares at the pack of wild dogs and let them feast on the trash before the Palestinians to establish the desert pecking order.

A few weeks later I walked the grounds to conduct inventory of food, fuel, ammo, and water levels. We were going over my water allocation. The last resupply was less than a week prior and it would be more than a week for the next one. I couldn't figure out how we went through so much until I inspected the tanks. The sand around one of the 500-gallon tanks was a different color than the others: it was leaking. I requested permission for a convoy, consisting of two up-armored Humvees to escort the silver bullet truck for a resupply at our logistics base, Korean Village—an hour-long drive down IED-riddled Route Mobile.

Weather operating conditions varied locally in Iraq, and we used the traffic light method, where if conditions were green, operations were permitted. Red meant conditions were bad enough to reduce visibility for pilots, causing aircraft to be grounded and unable to support troops-in-contact or medevacs. The air was literally red also, due to the sandstorm or haboob. There was a haboob covering Korean Village at the time, but after two days of red air we took our chances to conduct the convoy. But to execute the convoy I needed Nosferatu to drive the unarmored water tanker.

Gunnery Sergeant Hurst volunteered to serve as Nosferatu's protector and vehicle commander. We started off slow, conducting radio checks every 100 meters. It was difficult to see on MSR Mobile, it was like driving through a coastal brown fog with a glassy mist that cuts your skin. I asked if we could go faster, but Gunny said it was as fast as Nosferatu was capable of driving. Nosferatu was taught how to shift using reverse, first and second gear only. The speed limit inside Waleed was 10 kilometers per hour, so he didn't bother to learn or practice the other gears. At that rate it would take three hours just to make it to Korean Village. I made the call to return to Waleed. Nosferatu emerged from the truck like a vampire after being staked.

Water use was restricted until resupply. Tensions rose like the thick swarming sand clouds in Western Iraq. We took turns cleaning the showers. As I approached, a familiar air of decaying organic matter crossed my olfactory senses to warn me. Someone shit on the shower trailer floor.

I was confused as to why someone would defecate dead-center in between the row of showers and sinks. It was deliberate and untouched, not a baby wipe or Chuck Norris TP in the vicinity. The showers were all dry, so he didn't even have the decency to bidet his butt. I closed the shower trailer. My master sergeant voluntarily scooped it up with a trash bag like an experienced dog owner curbing their pet. Speculations swirled. Naturally we blamed it on the squatters—the interpreters. It was too skillful of an execution to be done by a non-squatting service member.

The resupply arrived two days later after the haboob blew through. Nosferatu's supervisor and translator arrived with the tank on the convoy. He explained Nosferatu wasn't a professional truck driver, garbage collector, or porta-john cleaner. He was just a man from the Balkans trying to provide for his impoverished family who jumped at an opportunity to profit from the global war on terror. He may have lied about his skillset or his company may have lied on his behalf, but I believe he was sent do a job he wasn't adequately prepared to do, like most of us in Iraq.

My decision to have Nosferatu drive the water truck in the convoy put him in harm's way, filled him with the very real fear of getting blown up so we could shower. The language barrier added to his frustration enough to act out, which is why I suspected he shit on the deck of the shower trailer and decided for once it wouldn't be his job to pick it up. I wasn't even mad. We all were cleaning up someone else's shit.

RICK'S LOUNGE
Michael Foran

J ust before Army Sgt. Jeff Duncan hopped onto the stage at Rick's Lounge, he turned to me and said, "Fuzzy, we gotta do something about this fucker NOW!" and with that he yelled "Hit it," a ritual we practiced while drinking and a tactic Jump School Black Hat cadre used on new Airborne recruits. *Hit it*, much like *drop and give me ten pushups*, was used to get new Airborne recruits to understand that that paratroopers had about three seconds to determine if the parachute on their back had deployed properly...we used it to down shots in beers... Jeff downed the boilermaker in a practiced three gulp move.

As with most weekends in garrison, many of our guys could be found walking around the 500 block of Hay Street in downtown Fayetteville, the city intricately tied to Fort Bragg, home of the 82nd Airborne, many of the Green Beret Groups and Pope Air Force Base. Fayetteville, or Fayettenam, as all of us called it, had the infamous Hay Street.

In the late 1970s, Hay Street was still home to a red-light district said to resemble the red-light district in Saigon at the peak of the Vietnam conflict. Establishments like Rick's, The Bunny Club, The Oasis, Seven Dwarfs, and Luck Saloon offered topless dancing and other various levels of debauchery and depravity to any GI with a paycheck. For the most part, these establishments were staffed by Asian girls, a nod to the Saigon sister city. Tonight, Rick's was packed with soldiers out of uniform sporting high-and-tight buzz cuts and out to blow off some steam. The alert had been in place for several weeks now and the inaction was creating small stress fractures in the psyche of paratroopers of the All American Division.

I had known Jeff since being assigned the 82nd Airborne Division's 1st Squadron 17th Cavalry Regiment upon finishing infantry and Jump School. I didn't know it then, but as Sergeant White, my first squad leader, said: "Cherry, you done hit the lottery. You in the Cav now, and if you ain't Cav in this mothafuckin' division, you ain't shit." What he really meant was every other 11B (Infantry) in the 82nd walked; we rode the UH1H birds.

When Jeff jumped onto the stage, it had just been cleared by the MC and the dancers were in transition. At the center of the stage, stood a microphone. Behind it, mirrors covered the back wall and a disco ball hung from above. All around the stage men sat three deep with their pitchers of beers and shot glasses, waiting for the next round of girls to be announced and paraded to the front. Grabbing the mic stand, he dragged the base along the flooring until he reached the edge of the stage.

"All you mothafuckers, shut the fuck up and listen. It's time to saddle up. We are the 82nd Airborne Division! Let's do our job and get those fucking hostages!" Jeff's voice boomed and the crowd of drunken troopers, silent at first, began to roar, not the new Army OORAH, but the old school animal ARRRAHHH! "Jimmy Carter is a fucking pussy! Let us fight! Carter is a Pussy!" He was screaming now: "PUSSY! PUSSY! PUSSY!"

As the crown started to join in, two Asian dancers burst out of the far end of the stage and charged him. And with that, it was over. Shoved from behind, Jeff was airborne for a second and then came crashing down on the front row of tables. Next the bouncers came, then more girls, and for the next full minute a melee followed that rivaled some of the best John Wayne saloon brawls. Bottles, chairs, fists and breasts were at the center of this vortex of built-up rage that each soldier felt as they waited to be called to end the Iran Hostage Crisis.

Of course, we know how that ended. Though on full alert for those 444 days, the 82nd was never called and Jeff and I continued to roam Hay Street whenever we weren't training in the field for the action that never came. We would also watch that newly created unit called Delta get caught up in the failed Operation Eagle Claw, where eight men died. I was home and discharged for three months when the remaining 52 hostages were finally released.

Jeff spent a few years after his active duty assignment in the reserves, and then following 9/11, re-enlisted in the Arizona National Guard and, as a 50-year-old infantryman, later deployed to Afghanistan. The last time I heard from Jeff, it was at 2:00 in the morning. He was calling from a bar in Phoenix.

"Hey, Fuzzy, you there, you cocksucker? Pick up the phone. I'm outside of this bar looking at all these bikes lined up in a neat row. I'm thinking of kickin' 'em over."

SLOWLY COMING BACK FROM CHAOS
Michelle Nielsen

was in my room getting ready for the evening shift when the entire room started to shake. At first I thought I was sick, because unlike earthquakes I'd encountered in California throughout my life, this one lasted almost five minutes. The longer it lasted, the stronger it became, until finally the ground stopped moving. My first reaction was to look out my window and check on Mount Fuji, because I was worried the volcano had erupted and when I didn't see smoke, I quickly picked my belongings up off the floor and ran downstairs to the parking lot for accountability. After they took everyone's name and dismissed us to go back to work I headed into the chow hall where I was temporarily working for that month.

Immediately after the earthquake the entire base lost power and we were running off of backup generators for lighting, but after twenty minutes they also lost fuel, and shortly after we had nothing. The entire country of Japan would be black that night, and our Japanese cell phones would have no service for several days. All civilian Japanese workers were sent home to their families, and it was starting to get dark. With no power, no one had any idea what was going on outside of the base.

I had been living in Japan for eight months, serving a year-long tour overseas for my last year in the Marine Corps. When I was first told I had orders to serve at Camp Fuji Japan, many Marines were envious of me, because Camp Fuji is stationed on mainland Japan at the base of Mt. Fuji, a short two-hour drive from Tokyo. It has no more than 100 Marines stationed on a base less than three miles around, in a town called Gotemba, that absolutely loves Americans. Camp Fuji has always had a good relationship with the locals. It is located at a higher elevation up the base of the volcano, giving Marines a dazzling view of Gotemba below. This prime location offers Marines the opportunity to travel throughout the beautiful country of Japan.

As I looked out over the town, I noticed how quiet the usually loud city was and how dark everything looked. I suddenly felt alone and isolated, and it was as if I was seeing my surroundings for the first time. Our base was on lockdown and we were to remain at work until every person checked in. Even though the chow hall was dark and empty, I had to remain with all the cooks huddled on a bench joking and laughing around a candle until someone finally managed to tether their American cell phone to a computer and connected to the Internet. In that moment the entire room fell silent as we realized with horror the destruction the magnitude 9.0 earthquake had caused and the devastating tsunami that followed quickly thereafter. Every page that loaded brought us closer to the realization that the earthquake we had felt earlier that day was much worse than we had originally thought.

Every Marine on base worked nonstop over the weekend. We set up beds on our base in case refugees were sent our way for shelter, and we gathered our gear in preparation for convoys that were going to Sendai Airport to help with the humanitarian aid. We were issued Iodine pills to take daily because of the radiation threat and warmer jackets because it was still snowing. We left as few people back on base as possible and headed out in two groups on Sunday morning and Wednesday morning with over two dozen trucks of Marines and gear.

I went up with the second group and we were first flown out in the morning on a helicopter, but were forced to turn back, because Sendai was in the middle of a blizzard and it started freezing the propellers on the helicopter. As we flew, I was able to see for miles where the ocean had flooded entire fields that were once dry. Trees had been ripped from their roots and lay scattered across the ground.

We were loaded onto a C-130 airplane in the evening with pallets of water for the Japanese people and finally landed at the Sendai Airport around midnight on Wednesday. We met up with the first group of Marines that drove up several days earlier and went to sleep on cots borrowed from the Army. The first group drove up with the bulk of the supplies and Marines, but due to the damage on most direct roads, they were forced to take indirect routes through the mountains, which made their trip to the airport just short of three days.

At night, we slept on the second floor of the airport, above the flood level, between the rows of chairs normally used by passengers waiting to board their flights. Whenever there were aftershocks, the glass ceilings would rattle and I always feared that the wobbling terminal signs would come loose and fall on my head. When the aftershocks were more powerful, we assembled on the second floor and waited until we received the all clear that there wasn't another tsunami headed our way.

For the first two days, we stayed at the airport and cleared debris off the runways so that more C-130s could land every half hour with supplies and military personnel.

I didn't know what I would find in the cleanup, and I was unprepared for the shock of seeing death for the first time as we uncovered the bodies of a horse, dog, and a bus with six dead people who'd been swept away by the water. As the runways were cleared, planes started landing every fifteen minutes. We sorted as many supplies as we could, then loaded them onto the back of our 7-tons and Humvees to take with us on our daily convoys to the people in the surrounding villages. Scattered across the tarmac were pictures and precious heirlooms. I realized that these were people's treasures that they'd probably never see again.

I was a Humvee driver, and the first time I ventured outside of the airport, words can hardly describe the chaos I saw. Trees were scattered across empty fields, houses were crumbling, cars were wrapped around telephone poles, and boats were planted miles inland as if picked up and thrown for us to find. The ground was covered with a black sludge of sand, mud, and dead fish from the bottom of the ocean left behind after the water receded. On the side of buildings that were still standing, we saw a mud line from how high the water reached when it swept through the cities.

We were required to travel with the Japanese military, so they could be our guides and translators, and so they could step in to handle the dead when we found bodies during our cleanup. I quickly discovered that when I told the Japanese where I was from, I could simply say "Hollywood" when describing California, and everyone knew where it was. During our chow breaks we would trade our Meals Ready to Eat (MREs) with the Japanese MREs. One day, a Combat Camera Marine took a picture of my sergeant trading his MRE and posted it in on the web. When we returned from our convoy that night, we all got in trouble. We were told, "MREs are government property and you do not have permission from the military to trade them away."

As I drove down the roads at night with my headlights as the only source of light, I wondered what the darkness hid from my view. The atmosphere was completely still and quiet as if devoid of any human life. I was forced to remain alert and drive at a slow pace, because within moments we might have to maneuver around an object blocking the road. My first convoy at night, I was driving to a school that the Japanese soldiers said was in desperate need of water. Initially, I noticed, the people were living on the upper level floors in case another tsunami came through. I also saw that the entire first floor had several rows of tarped bodies, recovered from beneath the rubble and waiting to be identified or disposed of. As I glanced at the dark windows that were lit up by the headlights of my Humvee, I grew uneasy whenever I saw a head pop up to look at us and then dip back down. It reminded me of all the horror movies I'd watched as a kid growing up.

After we offloaded the cases of water, nobody moved and I was angered that we'd driven so far and the Japanese weren't taking anything. We made this trip to their specific location at night, because we had received word they were in desperate need of water. The Japanese escorts assured us that after we left it would be taken and the people were simply being polite by waiting until we left. Sure enough, when we returned a couple days later to the same school, the water we delivered was gone and I was reminded of how resilient these people were to hold onto their manners when faced with such extreme circumstances.

We were required to carry our gas masks with us at all times and have our Mission Oriented Protective Posture (MOPP) suits ready in case the Fukushima Nuclear Power Plant exploded and covered us all with radiation. They also gave us little monitors designed to beep if the radiation levels climbed too high. It quickly became a game for us to guess who would get the higher radiation number at the end of the day since the machines were going off frequently.

We brought forklifts with us to help clear the heavier objects that we couldn't lift by hand, but were unable to use them at first, because the Japanese were afraid of what it might do to the bodies that were still buried under the rubble.

One morning we were tasked with helping to deliver fuel from one Japanese military base to a local town without any working gas stations. The Japanese had to use our Humvees because they were bigger and stronger than their vehicles; it was like comparing a Jeep to a Hummer. The towns that still had working gas stations had lines miles long, and it was not uncommon for people to wait for hours just for a couple gallons of gas.

In villages that were hit the hardest, the locals would gather in large public buildings (hospitals, schools, government buildings, etc.) because they were the only structures still standing that could be used as shelter after the water caused all other buildings to collapse. Whenever we entered a gymnasium or a large gathering room, I was always shocked to see how many people could live in such a small space.

Clotheslines would be strung up across the second and third floor, while the first floors were always full of white body bags. The children were always the first to greet us upon arrival with big smiles and completely unaware that their family had just lost everything they owned. I struggled to understand how the children could play games of soccer and laugh amongst each other while so close to dead bodies as if it was normal.

We always went out on a convoy with a specific goal but each time we ended up accomplishing additional tasks like passing out water, clothes, and toys to the children while others tried to clear debris from the schoolyard. We were given bins to put the pictures that we found in, and I always hoped that the owners of those memories would find them one day. We were instructed to remain inside the vehicles when we ate our MREs, because the civilians were starving and we didn't want to be rude by eating food in front of them.

On my first convoy out cleaning up a school's courtyard, I observed a family walk to a vehicle that was upside down in the mud. As the family rummaged through a broken window and grabbed things from within, I asked a Japanese soldier working nearby, "What are they doing?"

"That is their vehicle and they are retrieving what is left of their belongings," he said.

With arms full of their valuables, I watched silently as they carried off what they could and continued down the road to a house that was probably no longer standing.

One day, my buddies and I were trying to chop away at a roof that had been ripped off a house and we realized there was a vehicle buried underneath. As we began to push the roof off to the side to reach the car, a strong odor hit us and we fell to our knees sick to our stomachs. I had eaten a spaghetti MRE earlier, and to this day I am unable to smell spaghetti without being reminded of that horrible smell. Inside the vehicle, we discovered the body of the driver who had been trapped while the water swept the car away. I noticed that his back was twisted in an awkward position and his spine was protruding from his lower back. Everyone watched in silence as he was wrapped in a tarp. In that moment, it became clear that these memories would stay with me long after Japan was rebuilt.

As the day started drawing to a close, it started snowing on us and it was getting dark. We negotiated with the people to come back the next day and help them clear more debris. I was hesitant about coming back because I was scared about what else we'd find, but I knew those people needed our help. I thought of all the other overturned cars we'd casually driven by earlier that day that could be hiding more dead bodies from view.

The next day, we were sent back to the same school and were tasked with shoveling out an area so that we could put in portable showers for the civilians to bathe with hot water. My buddy and I were clearing the black sludge when we noticed several items of baby clothes buried within the mud. I saw the small arm of a little doll, so I picked it up. When I saw dried blood trailing down from her mouth, I realized it was a baby girl's body. Reacting on instinct, I dropped the baby.

We quickly called over a Japanese soldier and instead of coming immediately over, he brought over a younger-looking couple living at the school. When they saw the baby, they gathered her in their arms and fell to the ground weeping.

Baffled, I turned to the Japanese soldier who had a sad look on his face and asked him, "Why is the couple so sad?"

"That baby is their child and they were beginning to fear they would never be able to recover her body as she was swept away while sleeping in her crib," he explained with tears in his eyes.

I watched silently as the father quietly comforted his wife as she cradled the baby in her arms. After several minutes the father slowly stood and bowed as a sign of respect to my buddy and me. I still feel terrible about dropping the body of a family's beloved daughter.

The day finally concluded with new showers and hot water for the community. Back at the airport covered in mud, sweat, and dirt, I thought of all the families that still had loved ones buried out in the debris that hadn't yet been found. As I lay in my sleeping bag, I felt guilty for resenting the cold weather or complaining about the lack of power, because the people I visited everyday on my convoys had far less than I did.

After cleaning one building as much as we could, we would move to another building further down the road. The people in the next school had heard of our work and were extremely excited to see us. We were greeted with small cups of hot coffee as we got to work clearing large objects with our forklifts. A part of me felt guilty for accepting the coffee, because the people had so little to give and I was supposed to be helping them rebuild.

To lighten the mood during our breaks we tried to have some fun by playing games with each other and the civilian children. One day I got the idea to pin a dolphin hair clip to my buddy's shoulder pocket. It was located just out of his eyesight but in plain view of everyone else. Word spread quickly and for the rest of the day everyone asked him if he liked dolphins. It wasn't until the end of the day that we showed him the pin and we were still laughing about it days later when we returned home to the barracks on Mount Fuji.

I was impressed whenever we drove out on convoys by the fact that the Japanese people were not looting or stealing from stores that had been destroyed. The country was a collective band of people brought together by tragedy and trying to survive in the wake of nature's wrath. I was amazed when the Japanese people went out of their way to help each other and showed their humanity by allowing their elders to eat first whenever we brought food. I was touched at how positive they stayed even when all hope seemed lost. Helping in Operation Tomodachi was rewarding whenever we received the grateful smiles from the people that we were helping.

It wasn't until after I returned to base in my barracks that I struggled with what I'd seen and I started to have nightmares. I would wake up in the middle of the night and think there were rows of tarped dead bodies lying on my bedroom floor. I realized that the work I'd done in Japan would stay with me a lot longer than I expected, and I still get anxious whenever I visit the beach, knowing the ocean's capability for desolation. I struggled to connect with the civilians around me. As they complained about their petty problems, I carried the images of dead people in my mind. I now see the world in a different way and have become passionate about helping others. I am humbled by the power of nature and awed by the destructive force of water.

HURRY UP AND WAIT
Brooke King

We sit in the shadows of our Humvees, others stand or crouch, but never lie on the sand. We stare out across the desert, or at each other, or at nothing at all and wait, simply wait.

Though it has only been a month since they told us that we were leaving, our troubles weigh down our gear. We do not talk to one another. Some of us think of home, others of family. We pull drag after drag off a smoke stick burned ember red, hoping that by the end of this cigarette, the orders will be cast, and Kuwait will look like a dot connected by dashes on a map.

The younger soldiers pace back and forth, fidget, ask too many questions, and answer them before anyone can speak. The older soldiers, the ones who had been in the suck, they say nothing, look into the distance, stand with a lax in their back leg, as if to say, I've seen hell and that is where they're sending us. The young don't look at the old; their eyes stare down at the ground. They don't want to know what hell looks like.

It is here that they say a man may find himself, gain the true measure of what it is to exist, but here is nowhere; a place in the desert set up and held, all of us roped in like cattle waiting for the slaughter. Here, we cease to exist as women or men. Here, we are only the distant memory that our loved ones remember. Here, we are soldiers, and the remembering of training is of no consequence. Everything is now muscle memory, reactions, reflex, the texture of trigger pulls ingrained in fingertip feels and pressure points, the recall of radio 9 line medevac, call signs, and standard operating procedures.

And somewhere back home, someone is missing you already, and even though they can still smell your scent on the sheets, they grip the pillow tight every night for comfort. Some soldiers start to talk and it is then that they speak of home, of families, of too many nights wasted. The longing starts to creep in and someone quickly changes the subject. A deck of cards is produced with pictures of known Iraqi militants and leaders plastered on the faces. We play Gin, Spades, Texas Hold 'Em. We sing Lynyrd Skynyrd, rap Dr. Dre, and shout the lyrics to The Who's "Baba O'Riley." We talk shit about the newbie's ate-up rifle sling, point fingers and place bets on how many NCOs are coming home to an empty house. We clean weapons, fix trucks, talk more shit about the first sergeant's bitch of a wife. We wait, and wait, until the waiting becomes unbearable.

We don't want to go. We don't want to die, but they say that another battalion will take our place, that it won't be that long over in the box, that we might even get stationed somewhere safe, somewhere that doesn't see combat. They say to desert is dishonor, to stay and fight is courageous, but the young are scared and the old are restless, gun happy, and ready. But when the orders come down to push north, we all stand up and shout "Hooah" because we have chosen war and there is nothing more tempting than looking death in the face and saying, "fuck you."

THAILAND

Adam Stone

Phuket, Thailand.

For months we had heard stories from the old salty sailors and Marines. It was described to us as a land where all vices are catered to, a place of hedonistic behavior, where Eastern Europeans come to escape the winters and where the locals were more than willing to indulge one's deepest desires. Over the last six months, we dreamt of this land, talking of what we'd do once we stepped onto its shores.

During that time we talked about our prior conquests, sharing every glorifying detail of our own sexual exploits; what 19-year-old boys trying to be men do when they're in a combat zone. It was distraction from the world outside; our fantasies allowed us to escape, if only for a brief moment, all the suffering we were forced to endure and witness.

Now, here we were: the place we had been fantasizing about, salivating for. We had been crammed together for months in a floating city. Now, like sardines released from a can and dressed in Hawaiian print shirts and boardshorts, we rode in fifteen plywood speed boats, rented by the Navy to ferry us from ship to shore.

When the boats struck the sands of Phuket, my battle buddy, the guy that had slept in the bunk above me and who probably had more sex stories than anyone, jumped out of the boat, waded to shore, dropped to his knees, threw his hands in the air, and announced at the top of his lungs, "Before the night is through I shall bed you all!"

I placed my head in my hand, shaking it from side to side, laughing in dismay at his brazen declaration. He had never been one for modesty, so this was no different. On numerous occasions, I had been taken aback by his over-the-top personality. But then as I looked up, I saw *her* standing amidst the Europeans, the tanned skin on her long, toned legs a stark contrast to the pale overweight tourists that had beached themselves in awkward positions. Her belly button, playing peek-a-boo, was especially intoxicating compared to the large Russians that seemed to occupy most of the beach. Her pink bra strap, barely visible, causing my mind to wonder about her breasts, forming slight mounds under her shirt. Her black hair lay over her shoulders on both sides, framing her beautiful face. At that moment my vision of bedding European tourists and Thai girls vanished. All I wanted now was to know her. All I wanted to know was her name.

My partner in crime broke my trance by throwing his arm around me, "Come on man, let's go."

Still mesmerized, I said, "Hold on, bro. I'll catch up with you."

He tracked my gaze, looked back at me, grinned from ear to ear, and pointed his fingers at me. "OK man, but remember one thing: A French fry can only bounce so high."

To this day I still have no idea what that means. Only that it was his standard response to impossible situations.

I waded through the sea of pasty tourists baking in the sun and sat upon a wall separating the beach from the bars. I watched her flow from tourist to tourist, selling her wares of local fruits and homemade goods. Eventually she came to me and asked if I would like to buy something.

"Most definitely," and I bought two bananas and a sliced mango.

She grinned and asked, "Are you a Marine?"

"Yes Ma'am," I said.

"Are you drinking?" she asked.

Since I had just arrived I replied, "No Ma'am."

Her smile widened, showing perfect teeth, and her eyes appeared to glow a little bit brighter as they widened.

"Good. I don't like boys who drink," her slight accent tickled my heart.

I began blushing. Sensing that something might be there, I quickly asked, "Where can a guy like me go to relax and hangout for the night? That's kind of quiet, low key and not too crazy?"

She named off a few places, then after a slight pause she looked at me hesitantly and said, "I go to the Blue Parrot, and if I see you there, it would be nice."

I smiled a smile so wide it would put any Kodak commercial to shame. "I will definitely see you."

She smirked and said, "Maybe," then walked away, continuing her duties.

I jumped off the wall, found my friends and explained to them that we WOULD be going to the Blue Parrot that night, primarily for moral support but also if I had misinterpreted any signs, they could at least buy me a few drinks to ease the pain.

When we walked into the club that night, she was standing there—not in the middle of the dance floor with the spotlight on her like in some cheesy 80s movie—off to the side by herself, swaying her hips to the music. She looked amazing, soft, and delicate. I summoned my inner strength and walked up to her.

"Do you remember me?" She smiled so brightly that it lit up the room, lifting any trepidation.

The energy between us was so high we didn't leave each other's side. We danced a lot, talked about everything and anything that peaked our interest. We walked on the beach holding hands, listening to the ocean waves, gazing at the stars, and finding moments of serenity in each other's arms. When it was time for us to say goodbye for the evening, we made plans to meet at the same wall where we first spoke.

For my three days of liberty in Thailand, we spent every waking hour with one another. She took me to places only the locals knew about. I rode elephants, her sitting between my legs, teaching me to steer the pachyderm by pressing my toes behind its ears. We played with monkeys, hiding pieces of fruit on one another so the simians would have to tickle to receive their rewards. We took moped taxis everywhere we went, playing a game of high speed cat and mouse, tipping the drivers to go even faster than the other. We ate at small restaurants, down back alleys, where only two choices were listed on a hand-written menu.

On my last day in Thailand she invited me to come meet her family, and I accepted. When I arrived at her home her mother wrapped me in her arms, embracing me like a lost child who finally made his way home. We sat around the table that night passing homemade Pad Thai, rice, and fresh fruit as we talked and laughed. I played with her three younger brothers in their small home; I wrestled with them and won, then they practiced their Muay Thai on my shins, and they won. That night they showed me that family is family no matter where in the world you are. In turn I showed them that not all Americans are "James Dean Cowboys," as her mother put it later in the evening, as we said our goodbyes.

She escorted me back to the beach where I had first seen her, and we walked upon the sands now void of tourists, speckled only with lovers finding private moments in each other's arms. We sat upon the wall that I first watched her from, and under the moon, I slowly leaned in and we kissed for the first time. It was that kind of kiss I saw in fairy tales, where lights flash, fireworks went off, and Kenny G played in the background. Then out of nowhere it abruptly stopped, and she pushed me away.

She closed her eyes and said, "Hold on. I have to tell you something."

In a flash, everything that could possibly be wrong at that moment rushed through my head: one of the little brothers I had met early that night was really her son—I never asked, I just assumed. She has a boyfriend, no wait, a husband. What else could it be…She might have AIDS; it was the early 90's.

She looked at me with wet eyes, reached up and began to stroke the crucifix she wore around her neck.

"I'm really a boy."

I was shocked and confused, and I'm sure I had a look of dismay on my face. Again in a split second, every emotion that could run through my mind did, except for fear, or anger, or hate. However I still said one of the worst possible things I could have said at that moment, with her vulnerabilities exposed.

"How…interesting."

As soon as the words escaped me, I saw the weight of the world crash down upon her. She placed her hands on the wall, pushed herself up, and began walk away, murmuring in an almost breathless voice, "I understand."

I immediately reached out, grasping her wrist, pulled her back and as coherently as possible tried to explain that wasn't what I meant, that what I meant to say was I have had the best time in my life. I admitted that this was not how I saw my future, but I had loved every minute spent with her, and I didn't want it to stop.

She gave a slight smile, wiped away a tear, and sat down once again beside me where we talked for the rest of the night. We talked about her, her true self. We talked about the internal conflict she faced growing up, not knowing what was right and what was wrong. We talked about her struggle with her religion, of it not accepting her for who she really was. We talked about her coming out to her family, the family that I had just met hours before, how they embraced her with love, understanding, and acceptance just as they had done with me when they welcomed me into their home.

Her head resting upon my shoulder, her arms wrapped around me and mine around her, in a moment of silence watching the moon cascade across the bay she looked up at me, her eyes wide and innocent. I leaned in and kissed her once more.

When it was time for me to head back to my ship, we walked together hand in hand. At the boat launch we embraced one last time, not knowing when we would see each other again, if at all.

She leaned in and whispered in my ear, "Thank you," and my reply was simple. "No, thank you."

As the boat separated us, all I could think of was how just months prior I was in Somalia, watching that world fall apart to genocide and tribal conflicts. I saw death everywhere I turned, even on the faces of the living. Now, even as my heart was sinking at our separation, I felt a lightness about me. She showed me that the world is a much more beautiful place than I had come to believe.

After many years when I returned to Phuket, I looked for her and her family. I would walk the beaches expecting to find her selling her wares. I went to where they once lived, but nobody knew who she was. I would wander through the bars looking at the bar girls and ladyboys wondering if that was where she wound up. Every night I found myself at the Blue Parrot, hoping that I might see her once again standing to the side, swaying her hips to the music. I don't know what I would have said or done, just that I always carried the desire to see her again. To touch her one last time. To wrap her in my arms, look into her eyes again, and possibly kiss.

In 2005 when the tsunami struck Phuket, I found myself watching the news continuously, hoping to see a sign of her. I needed to know she was OK, that she survived all the death that had occurred, to catch some glimpse she was alive and well. But I knew in my heart I would never see her again, and the smile I looked for was lost somewhere between my memory and a vast, raging ocean.

NEW TRADITIONS
Delia Knight

The plane touches the tarmac and I drum the back of my nails against the window as we come roaring to slowness.

Please.
Keep.
Him.
Safe.

One finger for each of the four years of active duty.

I turned quite superstitious after my brother's enlistment in fall of 2001. Superstition included convincing myself of taking the same way to work every day, sitting in the same row at church, and saying a prayer when I am stopped at a red light. I've turned certifiably nutso after his deployment in March. Certifiably nutso has included (but is not limited to) halting anything I'm doing every time I think of him (which is more times than I can count in a day) and counting 10 hours ahead—Baghdad time—then saying a prayer for whatever he's doing in that exact moment: eating a meal, cleaning his weapon, going outside the wire. Convinced that if I just keep up with all these tiny rituals, it will amount to his safe return. So far, it has worked.

It's Christmas Day 2003 and my mom, stepdad, and I fly from San Francisco to Phoenix. Home to my future sister-in-law and her mother. We are here to celebrate the holiday. Jan is between deployments, having arrived home in September. His first Christmas home from war and he left a Middle Eastern desert to celebrate in a Southwestern desert.

He meets us at the airport and I can tell something is wrong. He looks more tired than usual. And rough. Not just lack of sleep rough but battling demons rough. Probably a long night the night before. One of our childhood friends who is also in the Marines got a 96-hour libo, drove over from Yuma, and is celebrating the holiday with us. I am positive that they were drinking last night, swapping stories of time in-country and idiot things they did as kids. They probably ushered in the sunrise, stumbling to bed in the soft light of morning.

I hug Jan. He tenses up. Something is definitely wrong. I feel it in the thudding hand on my back. He's compensating, trying to make us all feel at ease when I know he's not at ease. And he knows I know. It's the result of years of terrorizing each other as children and becoming best friends as adults. I know him like I know myself. Something is wrong. He smiles a don't-worry-about-it-everything-is-fucking-peachy smile. I nod and accept that. Even though I can smell the whiskey and beer wafting off of him.

Being between deployments is a limbo time where you're not home long enough to talk about much and so you carry it with you. No matter how heavy it is.

First stop: grocery store. Beer. He has the distant eyes of someone who has seen too much. After the previous night of binge drinking and the whisper of a hangover he had to start drinking again. Running out of beer meant sobering up and sobering up meant answering questions. He needs to be well on the way to being drunk. He needs cigarettes and beer. Cigarettes and beer. Ever the prepared Marine, he was gathering what he needed before entering battle. Something to keep him busy. Something to keep him numb.

I stare out the window on the way to the house. Instead of lawns there are rocks, in the place of trees with leaves blowing in the breeze there is cactus. Immovable and prickly. There is both a stark beauty and a sense of desperation. Our bodies know the hazards of the desert. The lack of a water source, food and shelter. We instinctively know that if we don't act fast, we're going to die.

We arrive at a one-story tract home that looks like every other house in the neighborhood. Jan cracks open a beer. The cracking open of a can usually sounds refreshing, an exciting start to a party, unlimited fun. But it's not. Not now. The opening of the can is a warning shot.

The house is beige, white trim, rock and cactus in the front yard. The house is more formal than comfortable. Very few chips in the paint, scuff marks on the floor and any of the hallmarks of a well-worn and well-loved home. This is just a house. A house where people live.

Dinner is polite. No one speaks of politics or religion. We chew our food, eat slowly and smile. The sound of more beer cans opening, forks scraping plates and the occasional murmurings of "this is delicious" and "thank you."

Clean-up is all the ladies in the kitchen searching out containers to put leftovers in and gingerly handling the china in hot soapy water. It is also polite. A lot of "such good food" and "I appreciate the effort."

Christmas in the desert is a long fuse. It is lit and I have no idea when it is going to explode.

As the dishes sit in the drying rack, we sit in the living room near the front door, watching television. Something holiday, something that has the potential to please everyone. I hear an argument. Muffled. Someone trying to hide something that can no longer be hidden. Demons may live in the darkness but they make a play for the light. They crave being heard and it's easier to penetrate boundaries when you've been drinking.

Jan storms past us, shirtless, his clothes spilling out of his duffel bag. I feel an alarm go off in my head. He loved his clothes. He took great pride in them, picking them out, matching them. He'd lost weight in boot camp and during his first leave he started buying clothes that fit his new body. There were many points during the day when I thought things weren't right. Comments made, facial expressions that were supposed to be funny or entertaining, but only belied a deep pain. They were things I could second guess or convince myself I was being worried about, or being an overprotective big sister with an overactive imagination. Seeing clothes drag across the floor, trailing behind him like a child trying to keep up with a swift moving parent, is something that makes it real. The complete disregard of the things he treasured sends a chill up my spine. This isn't him. He no longer has the energy to keep up the facade of a stoic combat veteran. His crumpled clothes are his tell.

Recipe for disaster: one part politeness, eight parts domestic beer, three parts whiskey, one part horrific events you have not yet developed the language to tell.

My mom and I look at each other and go chasing after him. It is still hot and we see my brother fumbling to get into his car.

"Where are you going?" my mom screams.

"Leaving this house." He is trying to keep it together. A barely held together rage.

"You can't drive, Bud. You've been drinking," my mom says, approaching the driver's side of the car.

With that, my brother hurls his keys down the street. He throws them with such force that I'm convinced he doesn't want them to be found. Seconds later the keys hit the asphalt; the sound is empty. My mom turns toward the sound and runs towards it.

My brother storms up to me in the driveway. He is screaming in my face. "I can't stay here," he spits out. Tears fill his eyes and he is clenching his teeth.

I do the only thing I can think to do. I throw my arms around him and put my ear to his chest, listening to his heart thump wildly like a caged animal trying to get free. He pushes against the top of my shoulders, screaming, "Let go of me, Del!" My grip tightens. The harder he fights, the harder I hug, not saying anything.

"Fuck you! Let me go! Let me fucking go! I want to leave! Fuck you!"

I say nothing. I just hold on to him. I feel the anger and rage and guilt and shame pulsing through him. It's alive and separate from who he is. He brought it back from this deployment. I wait, hoping that I can outlast the episode.

My mom comes running up the driveway and throws her arms around both of us. My brother no longer has any fight. He collapses into us, sobbing.

"I just want to die," he repeats over and over again. A mantra of release as my mom holds him like she has held both of us since birth. Her hands running up and down his back. "It's okay, Bud," her mantra in response.

We are sitting on the back patio in silence. We wait for someone to speak. Jan is the first to break the silence.

The sound of a cap being twisted off a bottle and flung onto a glass table top. The sound of a pack of cigarettes being tapped against the inside of a wrist and the flint striking steel of a lighter producing flame. A deep inhale and the rosy glow of a lit cigarette.

"I've killed men, women, and children."

My breath catches, and I have to take a swig of beer to swallow down the lump in my throat.

My brother no longer has the capacity to keep the awful truth in. He is too tired and too drunk. He forces it out on an exhale, no longer wanting to carry the burden of this himself.

"I was in a convoy and there was a guy with a gun on a roof. I took my shot. I hit him and he tumbled off the roof and as I watched him fall I realized he couldn't have been more than fourteen or fifteen." He shakes his head and takes a long drag. "I just wished he hadn't picked up a gun that morning. I wished I could have told him to just go home. You're a kid, go home and kick around a ball. Just don't pick up the gun."

I shift my weight. This is what I waited to hear. What I prayed my superstitious routines would yield. This is what I knew was coming, forced over teeth and lips in the exhausted exhale of smoke and awful honesty.

I prayed every Sunday at church for God to bring him home safe and if that happened, then I could handle anything. I could handle any story, any injury, anything, just bring him home. I waited to hear this. And when I do, when I hear it, when I realize what is being said, all I want is for it to be taken back. I've never been so grateful for darkness and drunkenness, easy hiding places. It is a cloak I can use to disguise my inability to handle everything I promised I was able to handle. I promised anything before I fully understood what anything was.

"People aren't on this planet anymore because of me."

We all sit in silence. The air sucked out of the space. While some families might be singing Christmas carols gathered around a fire and sipping hot cocoa, here we are: telling ghost stories around lit cigarettes with warm beer. It's what people do in the desert. They tell ghost stories. They tell how people survive and how others don't make it to see sunrise. Ghost stories highlight what we're afraid to become, what we know without saying, that if pushed we will do anything to survive. That all the politeness will not put the genie back in the bottle. No amount of Christmas tradition and civility will erase what we all now know. People are no longer on this earth, at the hands of...

My mom finally calls it. "Let's go to bed," she announces.

Before too many questions can be asked. Before the sun rises and we have to usher in the day with that truth. We shuffle off to bed.

I catch my brother's arm as he is going through the sliding glass door.

"I love you, Bud." I attempt a smile and throw my arms around him.

"I know, Del. I love you too," he says, his chin buried in the top of my shoulder.

The next afternoon, Jan decides he has to leave. I'll drive him from Phoenix to northern California. When he gets in the passenger seat, I start the car. My mom knocks on the driver side window, her hand, two fingers extended, one to the ear, one to the mouth, the universal sign for, "Call me when you get there."

I nod. She steps back in the driveway and waves.

I turn toward Jan. "Home?" I smile.

"Home," he exhales.

SMOKING WEED WITH THE TALIBAN
As told by Dan Lopez to Justin Hudnall

DAN LOPEZ:

So anyway, here we go:

I've been getting roughed up like, man, since I was six.

I grew up in northeastern Colorado—parts where nobody talks about Colorado, the plains. We grew up on a farming ranch, we had cattle, we had horses, we had more crops than anything. I mean there's more cows where I grew up than—we graduated 13 kids in my senior class.

The connection to this whole story is just the kind of lifestyle I grew up in, and it was just very relatable to what we're about to talk about.

My uncle was a Vietnam vet, he was with 1/1 Delta Company, man.

He said, "They called us Dying Delta."

I always looked at him like the manliest man because my dad, he was never around. So I grew up just outside of jail either in social services, foster care; got emancipated, got back and then stayed with my mom for a little bit. Got in a car wreck right after

I enlisted in the Marine Corps, dislocated my hip and jacked up my leg pretty good, so that disqualified me for two years. After I got out of that, foster care dropped me.

So I was just like, "Oh man, what am I going to do?"

I was reaching out to my recruiters.

"Hey you still want to get in?"

I said, "Yeah!"

He goes, "They're taking dudes with pins in their legs."

Because that's when Iraq was just—that's when Bush was doing that surge, man. And I'd just gotten a DUI and I had gotten so many minor in-possessions or whatever the hell it was. Next thing you know, we're in Iraq and we're doing the first bump, doing the second battle of Fallujah. Phantom Fury, man.

Then Haditha happened. We all know what happened in Haditha. That rock and roll show happened, lost my closest friend there. After that, guys got out, guys lost it. Guys took their lives. Guys overdosed. We all shotgunned everywhere, man.

I was like, you know what, I'm gonna take a time out. Got married and had a kid and kind of took in my other son. You know, I got two boys—I've got three boys now, gosh dang it.

Iraq was a bitter, bitter beast for me, man. But I loved my job. I was a squad leader, infantry squad leader dude, how much more could you ask for?

JUSTIN HUDNALL:

What did you like about it?

DAN LOPEZ:

Oh My God! It's your guys. When you're away from everybody, you could run it how you want it and you can build the leadership how you want it, and you could filter all that stuff from higher ups, and you can take care of your guys the best you could.

They know that you're going to have their back no matter what. If you're going to go to bat for them like this, they gotta know you're gonna have them there. Taking care of them, you know? They're yours.

You know, man, I just grew up with such a variety of people. I mean, I was a knucklehead growing up too, so it was easy for me to relate to these cats. There's so many guys who would just snitch on their guys. It's like, why would you do that, man? Keep it at your level. If it becomes a problem, if you warn this guy enough and he doesn't want to listen to you, and it's going to cause problems for you, then it's a problem. Take care of it that way, but in the meantime, if you can't handle your boy? Then man, you don't deserve the position.

JUSTIN HUDNALL:

So after Iraq you become an instructor at the school of Infantry for how long?

DAN LOPEZ:

A year and a half. Two years almost. And then somebody said, "Well, if you don't want to extend to reenlist you're going to go straight to Afghanistan with 2/1." And I was like, "Guess who's gonna wait out your little gun show, man?" So next thing you know I'm getting sent over to 2/1.

JUSTIN HUDNALL:

So tell me about the deployment to Afghanistan. Where was your first landing?

DAN LOPEZ:

We went to Helmand province. This was in the winter, so it was kinda cool. There wasn't a lot going on, you know. A lot of stuff was blasting off down south, though. I mean it was wild, wild west. These guys fought the Russians, you know what I mean? I have a lot of respect for the Afghani people in general, man. There's some places in Afghanistan that have never been conquered by anyone.

It is just insane the strength that these people have. It's respectable, man. You gotta respect that. True-blooded warriors there, man. You got the Kuchi tribe there. They're traveling in the desert people. Crazy, man. Camels, man, still like biblical style people, man. They live in these dome tents, made our camel skins and they just travel north to south through the desert.

I saw these people. We hung out and I drank some goat wine. It messed me up. It made me sick and holy cow and I drank it again because it made me feel so crazy. It was great, man. I was having a blast out there, man.

Everybody's like, "Careful what you eating," and I'm like, "I eat everything, Sir."

They're like, "You're going to eat something, they're going to poison you."

I'm like, "Well, if they're going to poison me, they're going to do it. I haven't found anything to kill me yet. Let's see. Party on, man."

If it's going to be poison, it's gonna be some hard drug that's going to just send me for a trip. Threaten me with a good time, you know what I mean? Would you poison everybody you meet? God, would you just treat somebody like they're a human being? It makes me sick.

JUSTIN HUDNALL:

What's your patrol route or your mission when you're in Afghanistan?

DAN LOPEZ:

We're holding, we're just holding this land. This is already taken ground. There's a lot of IED problems there, guys getting blown up left and right. The Holley Stick was created there, named after Gunnery Sergeant Holley: the longest bamboo stick you could find with this little sickle, you know what I mean? That we used and we bent, 5.50 corded, duct taped it, whatever. And that was our IED finding tool.

The first patrol base I get was just called "Wardak." It was just named after the village it was next to, and I made friends with everybody over there. Good friends, we were playing volleyball with those cats over there, man. We were having such a good time.

Posted security and I was like, "You mind if we just watch you guys play ball, man?"

They were like, "No, go ahead." And after a while it'd be us against them. It was good. It was community, man.

I was like, "Hey, I'm not like those guys," and they're like, "We know."

I started asking my wife at the time, was like, "Hey, can you get me a volleyball net, we need another volleyball." They stretched it out, looked awesome! Later on, some other kids stole it from another village.

I went and patrolled over there: "Hey, gimme my volleyball net back."

And then where I was at, was exactly the kind of place that I grew up in, man. Farmland, guys just trying to, just scraping their backs, making a dollar. Granted, it's pot and opium, hey, that's their crop. It's how they're making money. That stuff grows in the sand. Hey— they told us to go there and chop down their fields and tell them if they want to grow something, to go get wheat. Really? Really dude? Go get wheat? Deliver this stuff to them. You want us to chop it down, man, let them harvest this stuff and then when they go get their new seed—oh man, it made me mad.

So I was going around and telling dudes, it's like, "Hey, you guys can't have it outside. Alright, harvest what you can right now. I'm not going to chop it down. If you guys got a little dumb little thing, I'll stomp on some stuff just to feed the bear if I got some kind of commander with me, but I'll patrol them away from all the fields."

Because I knew where everything was at, and they were telling me I wasn't patrolling my AO because they kept on finding all the poppy and all that. Let 'em make a buck, man. They're poor, man. They need to make some money.

There's so much pot out there. So much pot that you couldn't come back from a patrol without the stuff being in your dump pouch. If you're a gunfighter, you know what a dump pouch is, it's where you toss your empty mags because it's not like in the movies, you just don't leave mags on the ground. You've got to keep that stuff because later on you're going to get another gun fight and got to reload those things. Those things don't just fall from the sky or whatever. But you couldn't come back from a patrol without having buds in your dump pouch, man.

I was like, "Shoot, I got papers, I got spliffs, I got buds. Come on, let's see what Afghanistan is all about." I grew up in Colorado, man. We smoke weed.

I got sent over to this other spot called "Kojibad." I shouldn't be saying these names, I'm going to get my head chopped off.

It was a good village man, but these dudes, man—there was a doctor, a dentist, a shopkeeper, and this sneaky schmoozy dude. He hung always in the back. Cool cat, but he never said much, you know what I mean? After every patrol, I'd always be like, "Hey guys, let's stop by the shop. Let's see if they got anything you guys want." And I'd sit down, we'd just smoke cigarettes and I'd have my interpreter there, and we'd all just talk.

Some of my guys, hey, I told them, I said, "You guys can bring whatever you want. I'm going slick because I want to show them that I trust them."

It's a familyhood thing, you know? We're neighbors. They had their AKs. I don't give a damn. You got a gun, I got a gun, right? We're outlaws, brother, what's up?

The old man started talking to me about when he fought the Russians. Man, it was so much like when I was talking to my uncle, dude. He was talking about stories fighting the Russians. He showed me some bullet holes. He had three crazy bullet holes down the side of him and I was like, oh my gosh, man. All those guys were his sons: the shop owner, the doctor, the teacher, the dentist... and the other cat was Taliban, man.

After a while, that guy that always was hanging out in the back started speaking up. I remember there's one time he goes, "Why are you here?"

And I was like, "I'm here for a job, man. I'm getting paid to do this. I wanted to do something for my country. Military was what I wanted to do. I wanted to be a fighter."

Because I knew exactly who he was. Growing up, man, I've seen enough dudes that love who they are and just don't care. Hard hitting dudes, man. I've seen some meat grinders growing up, man. I knew he was one, man. I could just tell, just the way his demeanor, the way he just hung back and just read everybody. He's just reading my man card basically.

JUSTIN HUDNALL:

Do you think he read in you what you read in him?

DAN LOPEZ:

Yeah, we talked about it.

JUSTIN HUDNALL:

Yeah? How'd it go?

DAN LOPEZ:

It was pretty good. I was like, "Hey man, tell us what you know. I know you know something. What's up, dude? I'm going to keep hassling you."

I kept on hassling him because I knew who he was. I was like, "You know who we're looking for. You know some of these guys. We came across a couple of them, we got pictures of these guys. I'm tired of just giving you guys contracts. I'm hooking up your villages. I'm doing all this stuff. I'm not gonna mess with you guys. I'm not going to do some dirty stuff. I'm not going to tear your stuff apart. I'm here to help you out, man. Be open with me."

He goes, "Some of these guys are my friends, some of these are our farmers." He goes, "We're all just here living here. Yeah, I made my living off of poppy and pot. Yeah. Yeah, this is me. Yeah, this is my palace in the middle of nowhere. What do you expect me to do?"

I said, "I don't expect you to do anything different, man. I know exactly what you're talking about, man. I get it, dude. Don't blow us up. That's all I'm asking. Don't blow us up, dude. Stop killing Marines."

He goes, "Then what's wrong with them over there?"

Talking about the other squads! I was like, "What are they doing?"

And he goes, "Go over there. Go over there!"

And I was like, alright, cool. Screw it. And I think that was kind of his like, "What kind of man are you? Are you going to listen to me? Or are you just going to sit there and just tell me I'm some dumb Afghani, some dumb sheep-humper, whatever." You know what I mean? Some kind of stupid, ignorant thing that they always hear.

We got back from that patrol and one of my team leaders, he goes, "Sergeant, I didn't know which way that was going to go." He goes, "I felt we were going really close."

I was like, "Hey man, that's why I had you guys there, man. I'm not going to go solo." And I said, "If stuff would have popped off, we'd have killed them all."

I patrol over this other spot, man, and I'm like, "Hey, can I just kind of scramble around? I just want to go for a walk. I want to check out all the AO, I'm hearing all these great things. I'm hearing about these elders over here that have great food."

And I'm seeing how these guys are going. I'm looking at these locals, and like everybody's going inside their houses. It's like, what the hell is going on here, man? What are these guys doing?

When I'm patrolling around my neighborhoods, they're coming out and they're grabbing me by my arm and pulling me in the house so we can have chai, eat candy, we can talk about ditches, we can talk about building bridges across canals and stuff.

These other squads were going in there, wrecking houses, putting cigarettes out on dudes, kicking them around, ripping families apart right in front of the kids. It's like, what are you doing man? Have some respect. Don't zip tie the dude in front of his family, in front of his kids. Oh my God. It's... It's ridiculous, man. No wonder why they hate us.

It hurt me because it's like, I know there were good dudes in those squads getting messed with. One dude, he's messed up. Nineteen years old, man. Nineteen years old. Just got hit with a roadside IED. Roadside bomb just knocked this kid, knocked him out cold, come back shaken. Just saw somebody get blown up in front of him. Called in a hit that just happened on his squad to make sure everybody else is okay. He didn't know what happened. He just knew he got hit and he knows there's a guy dead in front of him. He got on the hook. Nineteen years old, man. Got on the hook and did that. Nobody thinks about this stuff, man.

And then you got poor leadership in front of them, dragging these solid kids, man, smart kids through hellacious thorn storms like that, man. And it's just like, what are you doing man? Take care of them. You bring them through this stuff, imagine what they can become, man. Can you imagine that?

And they're just dragging, it's like, "You're just a dumb boot!"

And it's like, oh my God, I'll kill you right now. I'll do the job for them, man. No, dude, if you're going, I'm not going to be the one talking to your mom. If you get blown up, I'm getting blown up with you, man. I'm not... Hell no, no. I'll let somebody else box us both up and pick up our pieces.

JUSTIN HUDNALL:

So after you went up to the other AO and you kind of see what this dude was talking about in terms of like, the disrespect, did you get to have another conversation with them? After that?

DAN LOPEZ:

We had a lot of conversations after that, man. We became boys, man. We understood we're enemies, but we don't want to fight each other. We would wreck each other's lives. More than likely, we would destroy each other's families before we'd destroy each other, because that's how we fight. He would attack my squad, he would let me watch my guys get shredded. I'd make him watch me destroy his villages. We knew what each other were capable of. We knew it, and we respected that. A whole little thing was starting to blossom, dude. I'm not gonna say his name. He's on an HVI list.

And then after awhile I was hanging out at his brother's shop and he came in over there. It was one of those times where I was patrolling. I just told my guys to go ahead, and we brought out the hookah, threw on some herb, man.

And I was like, 'cause we started asking, it was like, "Do you guys smoke any of this stuff?"

And they were like, "No. We don't do any of it."

And I was like, "Bull! There's no way! How come I keep on rolling up on you guys around the corners, like sneaking this stuff in your, like,...." Dude's high. Just high.

I feel like all my guys came back because I smoked pot with the Taliban, man. It was just, it was there dude. I mean *it was there*, man. And when we got back from patrol, we were kind of debriefing.

I said, "Boys, I don't think we got to worry about anything. I think we're good."

Every single one of my guys came back without a scratch, man. Every single one of them, dude.

I love my boys, man. I got three kids, man.

Every single guy I ever had under my command, I've always tried to treat him like a son of my own.

Nobody's going to understand that, man. Ever.

PERCEPTION IS REALITY

Tenley Lozano

erception is reality. The phrase was repeated to us over and over until it seemed more like a joke than a cautionary warning. We were separated from the male Coast Guard Academy cadets and told to look out for each other, that the enlisted men would try to make us their conquests. We'd heard rumors about female cadet "sluts" caught sleeping around during their summer assignments. These so-called "promiscuous women" were ostracized for their illicit relationships, formally punished, and restricted to base when they returned to the Academy. Whether the rumors were true or not didn't matter. A military woman's reputation was everything. Professors, male officers, female officers and senior female cadets all told us so. Perception is reality, they said.

My first experience on a Coast Guard cutter was the summer before my senior year as a cadet at the US Coast Guard Academy. I was assigned for an 80-day patrol to the US Coast Guard Cutter *Morgenthau*, a 378-foot ship with a permanent crew of 162 and an additional 13 cadets for the patrol. All of us cadets were to be fully integrated with the crew for the patrol in the Eastern Pacific Ocean on a Counter Narcotics mission.

The engineers did their best to make me feel welcome and put me right to work. As the ship sailed off into the Pacific Ocean on that first day, I was happy doing the simple task of cleaning thick black gunk off a piece of machinery to the comforting rumble of the giant engines, muffled by the double hearing protection of foam inserts and big earmuffs. I felt optimistic about the patrol and excited to be part of the crew and to learn everything I could about the ship.

That night, I was walking through the labyrinth of the ship's passageways and stairwells with one of the male enlisted crew-members, completing a task from my Academy summer checklist. He was bringing the Captain's Night Orders to each of the night watchstanders for them to read and sign. The hallway's fluorescent lights were turned off and replaced by the dim blue bulbs of a darkened ship after sunset. People heading to and from the outer decks couldn't risk having their night vision ruined by bright lights. We climbed deep into the steel belly of the vessel to the Combat Information Center.

Inside, the CIC was lit with the same faint blue lights and everyone was dressed in dark blue uniforms. I could tell where the watchstanders were only by their silhouettes against the glow of computer and radar screens. The man who'd let us in the door signed the Night Orders and asked the watchstander who'd brought them, "So dude, we got a bunch of female cadets onboard now. You fuck any of them?"

I spoke from out of the darkness, a disembodied voice, overly cheery and distinctly female, "Not yet! Just give us a few days." I couldn't believe the ship's crew had not even lasted 24 hours before making jokes about us.

The man spit out a few curse words and stuttered a hasty apology.

The next day he found me in the hallway in front of my living area and apologized profusely, repeating, "I'm so sorry, Ma'am. I shouldn't have said that. I would never have said that if I knew you were there." He was terrified I would report him. The entire crew had been given a Cover Our Asses sexual harassment training in preparation of the female cadets arriving. It would look bad for the command if anything happened to us cadets while we were stationed onboard the ship.

I decided not to say anything about the incident, knowing that the whole crew would treat me differently if I did. I already felt unwelcome in my berthing area, bunking with enlisted women who were a few years older than me, worked in different departments, and scolded me for bringing oily boots and uniforms into their sanctum. Even the engineers who were beginning to act like I was one of them would quickly label me as "overly sensitive" and be cautious of every word they said around me. I didn't want to be known as "the girl who ratted guys out," so I laughed it off and accepted the apology. I decided that his comment had annoyed me, not offended. I wanted to be part of the crew without attracting any extra attention.

The next night, the women officers gathered the female cadets in their stateroom to lecture us about interacting with the mostly-male crew. They told about the time they'd gone dancing at a popular bar in Costa Rica on a port call and had a few piña coladas with some of the crew. Before their hangovers were gone, ugly rumors had begun to spread across the ship the way a drop of diesel spreads its polluting rainbow the moment it touches water. They reiterated the cautionary phrase—"perception is reality"—and told us they had begrudgingly accepted that they couldn't hang out with anyone but the other officers in port calls.

After that meeting, the other female cadets and I made a pact: we would enjoy the patrol, make friends, and look out for each other. I refused to believe that perception was reality.

Two days later, the highest-ranking engineer onboard, the engineer officer or EO, took me aside. He was concerned, he said, that I was already getting a reputation for being too friendly with the men. I'd been seen in a public area talking to male enlisted members. Because I was working in his department, he felt responsible for ensuring I wasn't fraternizing with enlisted men. I told him, "Sir, we were sitting on the Mess Deck together because they were helping me study firefighting equipment. All of the engineers are men except one, so how can I learn the job without being seen talking to men? I would think it'd be more suspicious to study in secret."

"It doesn't matter what you were working on," he said. "You need to be more careful about who you are seen with and how you are perceived." I ignored his advice, continuing to study and work in public. The male cadets hadn't received any of these lectures about how they were perceived, so I saw no reason why I should act differently. I knew I wasn't doing anything wrong and wouldn't let the EO's wild imagination stop me from becoming the best engineer possible. I knew what the mechanics said about the EO behind his back: he read the equipment manuals from cover to cover but couldn't turn a wrench to save his life. I did not want to become an officer like him.

Onboard the *Morgenthau*, I sketched system drawings by hand, memorized operating parameters, conducted maintenance, and passed an oral examination in order to earn the qualification of Generator Watchstander. In four-hour shifts, I oversaw the six-foot tall diesel engines that powered the electrical system of the ship. One day near the end of the patrol, one of the ship's service diesel generators had been shut down for routine maintenance and I was told to start it back up. Two of the other female cadets came to the engine room to watch the procedure. I climbed on top of the machinery and pointed to a lever as the EO walked into the engine room, right past us and into the soundproofed control room.

"Is anyone out there even qualified?" he asked the head engineer on watch, a bald chief with a bushy mustache.

The chief replied sarcastically, "Well, Sir, occasionally we have qualified watchstanders." Then in a more serious tone, "She passed her qual board and you signed her letter. Did you think we wouldn't let her stand watch on her own?"

The EO left the engine room while I completed the starting procedures for the generator. When I returned to the control room, the chief was angry, defensive of my abilities, and in disbelief that the officer would treat me that way. But after two months at sea, I was more surprised by the ferocity of his defense of me than I was of the EO thinking I was incompetent.

By the end of the summer, all the female cadets were friends with crewmembers and many were rumored to be sleeping with them. It felt like if we had any casual conversation with a crewmember, let alone a friendly relationship, we would be judged as sluts. One female cadet told me before our last port call, "Everyone already thinks I'm fucking Mikey, I might as well have some fun."

After 30 straight days at sea, the ship pulled into San Diego for a final port call. The school year at the Academy was scheduled to start in a week and a few of the cadets had decided to spend a couple days in the city before heading home for a short vacation. As the cadets and crew walked off the ship, I noticed all the female cadets staying behind had paired up with enlisted guys we'd worked with for the last two months. I'd spent the entire patrol fighting for a good reputation as a woman engineer. I was frustrated with how poorly I'd been treated by the officers onboard and I knew that I no longer cared what they thought of me.

I stood on the pier by the ship and watched as my friends, enlisted and cadets alike, began walking toward downtown San Diego. In a spontaneous decision of rebellion against the expectations placed on me as a future officer, I ran after them, not caring who saw me. When we all ended up hanging out at a hotel, I picked a mechanic who was decent looking, then I got drunk and spent the next two days having my way with him. He was a few years older than me, more experienced, and more mature than most of the single guys from the ship. That was the first time I'd ever had sex with someone without having an emotional relationship first.

After that, I returned to the Academy for my senior year. None of the female cadets on the *Morgenthau* told anyone else about our illicit relationships with enlisted men, no one found out, and no one at the Academy called us "sluts." I was proud of the bond we'd formed on the *Morgenthau*. But the women couldn't tell anyone else or risk all of us getting a bad reputation. I wanted to believe that I hadn't let those onboard the ship dictate what I could or couldn't do. But the truth is I wouldn't have fucked that enlisted guy if the officers hadn't tried to isolate me from the crew.

I did it because I knew I wasn't supposed to. I wanted to forget about my future career as an officer—to just spend a couple days hanging out with my friends and having sex with a guy I'd never speak to again.

Their perception was NOT my reality.

BURN PITS AND PORN

Sylvia Bowersox

t was cold as hell that morning at Q-West Airfield in the North of Iraq. The rest of my unit stayed in Baghdad and I got sent up north with my squad leader and a tech guy. They put us up in a converted barn with four bomb disposal guys who didn't like us. It was December, and I was trying not to be miserable, but they had just captured Saddam and I was stuck in a place where the air smelled like smoky shit. It felt like it was attacking my lungs, shortening my life—sweet Jesus. For a while, I tried breathing through my mouth to keep the air from giving me a sinus infection, but it dried out my throat and made me choke. Go figure.

I was in no mood to start another noxious day, but I needed to get up; couldn't be late for the war. I shimmied out of my mummy sack, sat up in my cot—without tipping it over this time—and leaned against the plywood partition separating my floor of dead insects from the guy-next-door's floor of dead insects. I stretched and said good morning to the picture of my darling son without any tears. My sister sent me that picture. She sends me monthly care packages full of cans of tuna, chocolate, Top Ramen and lots of pictures of my son. Only then did I take a deep whiff of the poisoned air.

"They're burning the shit early this morning," I said, hoping one of my buddies would say something in solidarity, maybe even a "we're all in this together." But instead, somebody bellowed, "SHUT the FUCK up." The situation was so ridiculous, the bugs so plentiful, my son was so far away, and the enraged voice was so angry that the whole thing got me giggling, and my pathetic attempts to scratch the bites some crawly thing left on my back only made it worse. By the time I realized I woke up too early, and it was black-hole dark outside my window, I'd lost it, and was laughing uncontrollably with tears running down my face. The only thing that made me stop was the thought of the freezing private who must have been on shit-burning detail that morning. That and somebody else screaming, "Shut it NOW, Sergeant!"

I knew all about the shit-burning detail because I was an Army journalist. About a month before, I wanted to do a story on the burn pits and what the hell they were burning—besides the shit, I mean. I even read a technical manual on the subject, and it made burning shit and garbage and who-knows-what-else seem so simple and easy—Insert Tab A into Slot B, and everything will be all wrapped in plastic and perfect; it didn't say anything about the smell or the dangers. I wanted to know more. But my assignments editor, who was really my squad leader, killed my story idea. According to him, nobody wanted to hear about burn pits or shit or anything else on fire, unless it was one of the bad guys.

But once I've got my mind around a story idea, it haunts me. And it didn't take much for this one to haunt me because they kept burning the shit, and sometimes it smelled like they were burning plastic too, and other dreadful things, like rotten meat and old tires and who-knows-what. We made all kinds of jokes about what they might be cooking in those pits, especially when the black smoke settled into a grimy film all over everything. I needed to find out and I did it by tapping into the time-honored Army ritual of cigarette smoking.

But on that particular morning, the smoky air at the airfield made me feel nasty and filthy and used up. It felt like the smoke invaded my skin and broke down my body, making me old. I knew I was going to shrivel up and blow away, like a vampire left out in the sun, if I didn't do something about it quick. I had to get the microscopic ashy shit off my skin. Since there wasn't any water in the female showers—and I couldn't face wiping down my "tits and pits" with baby wipes one more time, I snuck into the headquarters' all-male showers.

I took a nice, long shower, and enjoyed the hell out of it. Later, when I was clean, dressed, and brushing my teeth at the sink I saw something weird on my face. I looked closer, patted my cheeks, and pulled the skin next to my ears like I'd seen my mother do. There were new lines gathering around my mouth. Without thinking, I told my reflection, "Goddamnit, the air is making me fucking old, shit."

The guy who heard me, and cared, wore a towel around his waist and shaving cream covering his head. He demanded, in an I-am-going-to-fuck-up-your-life voice, that I move away from his space at the mirror and get the hell out of his showers.

Since the man sounded like he outranked me, I took my boots, my mouth full of toothpaste, and my hygiene bag and went outside. The toothpaste and spit went into the sand; my boots went on without securing the laces. I put my bag under my arm and went to get in line for the phone. I had to tell my sister about the lines in my face and all the shit in the air making me old and getting kicked out of the shower and everything.

Instead of the phone, we could use the email at the haji Internet café after work. It cost about two dollars an hour, which wasn't much, and even though it was a great place to get information for stories, I didn't like it there with all the guys and the porn. All those guys watching the naked girls—bouncing around, eyes-glazed-over and frozen, with their armory spread out, either in their laps or within reach at their feet. There was enough firepower in the room to kill a whole lot of people, and that was the way of war. But the rows of young men shifting in their seats, moving their groins in such a private way, keeping time with the rhythm of barely audible grunting and tinny porn movie music, was comical and sad and too many things to count. And fuck, I was lonely too. But now I would stay lonely because nobody would ever want me again because the shitty burn-pit air made me old, giving me lines all over my face.

I was lucky that morning, because it was our only day to use the phone barring any family emergency. Then somebody from headquarters would hunt you down, and you could use the phone no matter what day it was. Of course, your family could call the Red Cross, as they did in other wars, but that took time. Sending an email or calling headquarters was faster.

I had to hurry and get to my phone call because today we were going out on a mission with the PsyOps guys to some village to hand out flyers—or going to a meeting with village elders, or to some office in town to hang posters, or maybe we were winning hearts and minds by passing out peppermints and butterscotch candy in yellow wrappers. I didn't care; it was vital to tell my sister about how I was here in Iraq, getting old, getting yelled at, with lines forming around my mouth, and how young men who would never want someone old like me were watching porn right in front of me. She would understand what I meant, even though I didn't know yet what I meant. I needed to hear a voice from somebody a million miles away who would make it all better.

Just the night before, I discovered that the guys on the burn-pit details spent their off-time at the haji Internet café watching porn—right in front of everybody. And it wasn't just the shit-burning soldiers, it was infantry guys too, and I'd bet even personnel specialists and the cooks. Males in uniform were always sitting in front of the rows of computer screens, staring at porn. Screens and screens of writhing females, bright with prices and promises in gilded lettering. Each screen shimmered extremely bright red, white and blue graphics, and I couldn't keep from staring, while I was waiting in line to check my email. But that day, I couldn't take it anymore. I marched out of the café and, as fate would have it, into a group of the shit-burning, porn-watching, soldiers on a smoke break.

I lit a cigarette and joined their conversation. Of course, I sort of flirted, to get them to talk to me, to fit in—I was a journalist, for Christ's sake—and although I avoided the porn topic like the fucking plague, they didn't. But eventually they discussed what they did every morning to make the air smell so bad everywhere, especially in my quarters. By my fourth cigarette, I had learned they were burning arms and legs along with the shit. Amputated limbs all mushed up and useless, wrapped in heavy-duty black plastic, cut off of who knows who.

If I showed up for duty one day to a pile of severed arms and maybe a lonely leg or two waiting for me to throw them into the burn pit, and it was my job to toss them into that fire, I couldn't have done it. I mean, those things had once been attached to human beings, for Christ's sake. I'd be afraid that the arms and legs would come alive somehow and come after me to extract some kind of revenge. When I go to funerals, I'm always certain that the guy in the casket will open his eyes and grab me around my throat in a "you're coming with me" moment. It's got to be worse with angry limbs.

When I was in Baghdad, I saw a severed arm once and it was enough for me. Our convoy was coming back from the airport when a haji car exploded up ahead of us. We swerved through the debris that just landed on the roadway when I saw it. Something that looked like a charred log lying on the ground next to the smoldering metal skeleton of what had been a car. The longer I stared at it, the more I recognized it, and the more I recognized it, the more I feared it, and just before we took off, the words "Oh God, it's an arm!" flashed in my brain. A human being had been a part of that blackened thing and used it in all the strange and beautiful ways that humans use their hands and arms and fingers.

But at least I didn't have to touch it, throw it into the fire, build a fire to burn it, or monitor the burning. I just breathed the air that floated over to my side of the base when others did those deeds. The Army manual recommended the use of gasoline, diesel oil, or even jet fuel, to get individual pit fires burning. The soldiers were required to stick around to monitor the fire and breathe the toxic shit for who knows how long to confirm the arms, legs and everything awful was completely burned up and gone. Talk about building your tumors. Sometimes the mess would have to be burned a couple of times to get it down to the regulation consistency for burial. And that made it a "here and now" kind of dangerous.

I once sat and listened to a former Army doctor who'd treated soldiers hurt in burn pit accidents. I had been home from Iraq for about a year when some friends convinced me to go to a local bar with them. We met up with the doctor at this place in Georgetown. He was sitting at a corner table, with a bottle of wine and a couple of abandoned glasses keeping him company. He was clearly upset about the soldiers getting hurt, and even though I didn't understand the technical aspects of his argument, I did understand this: it was common for soldiers working the burn pits to get hurt and hurt badly. He kept repeating, "Nasty; it was nasty. Nasty."

When it was finally my turn at the phones, I called my sister and cried into that receiver for all I was worth. I was standing outside the headquarters building with the Division logo painted on its side—talking and watching soldiers in flight suits, trucks and Humvees throwing sand around, and Blackhawk helicopters coming in for landings and taking off again. Another Army sergeant was waiting to use the phone. He looked prepared to take it from me by force. But it was my turn, so he could go to hell.

"I am getting old, I have lines around my mouth, and I miss my son. I hate it here, and there's porn everywhere," I announced to my sister before she could say hello.

"Honey, calm down," she said in a motherly tone. "It's OK you have lines around your mouth. They match the crow's feet around your eyes."

"What are you talking crow's feet for? Didn't you hear me? I'm old and ugly, and I miss my son so much, what do I do?"

"I'm watching him, honey, don't worry," she said. "And you know what you could do? Gain a little weight, and then your face wouldn't be so liney."

I laughed, and then she laughed, and everything was all right for a moment. Nothing had changed: they were still burning arms and legs, and the air still smelled like burning shit, melting plastic, and dead things; the soldiers waiting for their fifteen minutes on the phone still shuffled with impatience; and the Blackhawks still took off with regularity, hanging for a second in the cloudless sky of Northern Iraq like a crayon drawing done by a fifth grader, before disappearing toward the day's mission, to be erased from our collective memory like so much gossip.

And that was Monday.

ALLIED WEAPONS SYSTEMS
FAMILIARITY TRAINING

James Seddon

Let's say you're in a ship with catastrophic flooding," said the
real naval officer sitting across from seventeen-year-old me.

"And you'll have to seal this hatch to save the ship. Yet,
there are still sailors below the hatch that could be saved
from drowning if you kept it open. What do you do?"

This ROTC scholarship interview was my first interaction
with the Navy and the first step to become a naval officer. I was
awed and impressed by his uniform.

Even idealistic seventeen-year-old me thought it sounded like
a movie script question, though.

"I'd close the hatch. After all, if the ship sinks, we'd all drown."
I said it with all the conceit of youth's firmly held belief that the
right path will always be clear.

"Yeah, that's great," he said, looking down with a slight sigh,
tapping his pen.

Then he leaned in, set the paper down, and looked me in the eye.

"The hard part isn't making that decision. It's doing it without
knowing whether the ship would *really* sink if you don't seal the
hatch. Doing it without knowing whether the sailors could *really*

be saved by keeping it open. You'll be paid to make decisions without the information you want."

At that, all sense of movie stereotypes, along with my confidence, were gone.

I discovered early in my career that truly dire situations were not the only ones that demanded decisiveness without knowing the consequences.

Five years later, twenty-two years old, in 1995, I was in the Northern Arabian Gulf, the NAG as it's un-affectionately known, roaring across the oil-polluted waters in a vessel under my command. Her haze-gray sides and powerful engine sent us planing over the gentle swells. It was a vessel of the class RHIB, pronounced "rib." Rigid Hull Inflatable Boat. What civilians might call a "rubber boat." She was a real beauty. The radio call sign of this mighty instrument of national defense was Steel Hammer One. Really.

As long as a small car, she had a fiberglass hull and inflatable sides. Fill the sides full of bullet holes? She'll float. Drill holes in the rigid bottom? Yep, still floats. She was indestructible. The only thing the Navy entrusted to the command of a brand new officer, an ensign, like me.

My crew consisted of a seaman and two petty officers; which oddly was the name of enlisted ranks in the Navy, not officer ranks. I was the only officer in the boat. The seaman, the boat's bowhook, was the only one younger than me and on his first deployment. The other two, my coxswain driving the boat, and the engineer keeping it running, had been in the fleet and actually deploying, while I was chasing girls and doing homework in college. These sailors had flushed more water than I had sailed over, and everyone in the RHIB knew it.

I *so* wanted to earn their respect, and become like them—experienced, salty, competent. I strove to be their ideal officer—by the book, but not too much, whose sailors looked up to, and related to, and followed to the ends of the earth. I knew I had a long way to go.

My ship's captain was another story. He didn't suffer from an overabundance of reasonableness. He had published a twenty-six-point memo listing, literally A to Z, the ways we officers on our ship were messed up, calling several out by name. Screaming in faces was how he expressed his preferences. After a flag that was not my responsibility—and had nothing to do with my watch—wasn't displayed properly, he had ripped up one of my formal watch qualifications. He loved making examples out of people.

1995 was a tough time in the NAG and not just because of the captain. I averaged four hours of sleep a night, split into separate two-hour naps. My ship was busy. Enforcing a blockade against Iraq. Escorting aircraft carriers for a no-fly zone. Spying on Iran and anxiously watching Iranian military units as they harassed us. Guarding other navy ships while they were at anchor. And my part, practicing firing dozens of Tomahawks into Iraq. The probability of a real order to do so was high. Today's mission was to deliver my friend Cunningham, the commo (communications officer) carrying secret radio codes, from our anchored American destroyer to the British frigate anchored nearby so we could do an exercise together and demonstrate international resolve. I was overwhelmed. And I felt lucky to be doing it all for real!

"Gladiator, this is Steel Hammer One. Request permission to come alongside," I spoke into the model PRC radio, pronounced "prick."

"Steel Hammer One, this is Gladiator. Permission granted," came the reply, the voice sounding like a Monty Python character. I handed the handset back to the bowhook, who normally used the radio. I wanted to make the call to the Brits. It was a cool Navy thing to do.

The coxswain spun the RHIB to a stop within reach of the frigate's stern, on the first try, and made it look easy. If I was at the wheel, we would have rammed her. My bowhook heaved up a line to a waiting British sailor who made it fast to the frigate's deck.

"Ensign Cunningham?" A British officer was looking down. "Follow me, please. I'll take you to radio central."

The commo stood on the inflatable side of the RHIB, took his hand for an assist, and climbed up on the frigate's stern. She stopped and looked back down at me.

"Back soon," she said, as the British officer escorted her through a hatch.

"We'll be here," I replied.

The British sailor who had tied us up leaned in the shade of a nearby overhang and lit a cigarette. He was there to stand watch, and make sure we didn't just go romping around his ship.

The early morning sun was burning through the powder-like dusty haze, warning of the hellish heat to come.

The downtime waiting for the commo was welcomed. I had no duty to perform other than to stay with the RHIB until she returned. I knew I could get that right.

The sun felt warm on the dark blue uniform coveralls I wore, and I pulled my ship's ball cap over my eyes. This uniform, designed for boat and boarding operations, perhaps on unfriendly ships, was plain, with no rank insignia or name on it.

I was amused at the thought of getting paid to sit there with my eyes shut. I imagined Uncle Sam with a radio voice announcing, "Son, your country needs you…needs you to sit in the sun. Do it for Mom, for your sweetheart, for Jody and apple pie!"

My crew were chatting quietly. I kicked my steel-toe-booted feet up when a charming and delightful British voice, what I imagined I'd hear at a stereotypical pub, interrupted my daydreaming.

"I heard the Americans had landed. I wanted to come see for myself. You don't look so scary."

I peered up under the lid of my ball cap at a short, stocky, young British sailor, with a smiling broad face. He was wearing dark blue coveralls with a petty officer's insignia and had his hands in his pockets.

"You haven't seen us on liberty," my coxswain countered.

Some banter ensued between the Brit and my crew, but I stayed out of it. Officers could shut down conversations with their involvement. So I kept my relaxed pose, hat covering my face, and listened.

"So it's true you're not allowed to have alcohol on board?" the Brit asked.

"Yep. Sad, isn't it?" my coxswain said. We were aware that British ships served alcohol.

"Well then. Want to come have a beer?"

My eyes widened.

"Yeah, right," said my coxswain.

"Seriously. I'll take you blokes down to the Petty Officers' Mess and show you how Her Majesty's Navy does things. This chap here can watch your boat for you," he said, pointing to the British sailor standing watch.

My sailors in the RHIB slowly turned their eyes on me. Their faces told me what *they* thought the answer should be.

The heavy weight of command settled on me.

First off, a beer sounded really good.

Secondly, a beer sounded really good.

Thirdly, getting a beer would score serious points with the sailors. Movies portray military officers barking orders to instantly obedient subordinates. In reality, it's a complex relationship. There could come a time when these sailors would be able to cover for me, save me from making a terrible mistake, or otherwise help me. Whether they would depended on far more than the rank I held. The time might come when I'd have to order them to do something extremely unpleasant or even dangerous. Rapport built up prior to that situation could be crucial.

Yet, I would be violating naval regulations if we had a beer.

Commanding Officer Standing Orders, Operational Navy Instructions 5350.4, and 1700.16, and Uniform Code of Military Justice Articles 92, 133, and 134. They all forbid leaving the boat un-crewed, drinking on duty, drinking aboard a ship, conduct unbecoming a gentleman, conduct bringing discredit, and failing to obey an order. They all ended with the word court-martial.

Court-martial. Career over. Since I was fourteen, all I wanted to do was be a naval officer.

The ship wasn't sinking, but that officer recruiter told me there'd be days like this. Only I could decide. I had no idea what would happen with either choice. Yet, I was compelled by tradition and duty to decide. To beer, or not to beer. It felt as though my career might already be at a turning point.

What were the risks of getting caught?

My ship could call on the radio for something and we wouldn't be there to answer. I could leave someone behind with the radio. But then someone would be innocent. No, best that we're all guilty.

Stay behind myself and send my crew for a beer? No, I wanted to make sure the drinking didn't get out of hand. Plus, that would mean no beer for me!

One of them might brag about the beer back in the berthing compartment. Word would seep out like a slow leak. The command master chief, the top enlisted member of the ship's crew, and a close advisor of the captain, had a knack for sniffing out that kind of thing.

If we got caught, I'd have to frame it as a bad judgement call. "We were sustaining NATO operations through diplomatic means."

Ensigns, as brand new officers, were well known for terrible decisions. I could roll with that.

I could say no to the beer.

I would be branded as an uncaring stiff by my sailors.

No court-martial, though.

No beer, though. Beer! I hadn't had a beer in many, many, weeks; a good beer in many months.

Beer is cold.

Beer builds camaraderie.

I missed beer.

Careers, court-martials, and beers swirled in my head.

I thought about my future self. *Which story would I rather tell after I got out of the Navy?*

"Hand me the prick," I said.

My sailors shifted with suppressed grins. I guessed they were thinking, "Didn't they teach officers the only prick they should handle is their own?"

The bowhook handed over the radio. In the name of leadership, I would lie. I called our ship.

"Steel Hammer, this is Steel Hammer One, over."

I told our destroyer that we were going offline for training, implying it would be on navigation, or safety, or engine maintenance or something. It would cover if they called us and we didn't answer.

"This is Steel Hammer. Roger, out," came the reply.

Smirks turned into smiles, even on the face of the stocky British sailor standing watch over us.

I said, "Sure, let's go. We'll call it 'Allied Weapons Systems Familiarity Training.'" The previous half-minute of awkward silence morphed into decisiveness.

The inside of the British ship looked like an American ship. Linoleum-like decks, white painted bulkheads, hatches, knee-knockers, fire stations, uncountable wires and pipes, emergency power connections, battle lanterns.

The Brit opened a hatch and we stepped into the Petty Officers' Mess. It was the size of a couple of office cubicles put together and was the lounge for enlisted sailors. There were bar stools along one bulkhead. Along the other bulkhead was a beautiful dark wood bar, just like you'd find at a pub in England, only smaller. I'd never seen anything like it on a ship.

We settled into the seats and the Brit stepped behind the bar. He started pulling beer glasses out of the holders.

I realized how far from the boat and radio we were.

"Remember, we have to be back at the boat before the commo is," I said.

"Just a quick beer," the Brit said.

"Wow, this is real nice," said my coxswain. "The petty officers don't even have a mess on our ship. The officers have their wardroom. The chiefs have one. Nothing for us."

At that comment, I realized I was in violation of another directive—this one far older. I was an officer in the enlisted Petty Officers' Lounge. Officers were allowed only on strict and rare invitation. It was important for crew sanity to have areas where enlisted members could gather without fear of an officer barging in. This was theirs. I forgot about my lack of rank insignia on my uniform and I was probably the first officer ever to set foot in here.

"Thanks," said the Brit as he started pouring beers. "We're proud of it. We think it's as good as the Chief's Mess, though they'd never admit it. But compared to the wardroom…well, you know officers." He rolled his eyes.

I didn't hesitate. "Yeah, fuckin' officers."

My sailors laughed hysterically. The Brit chuckled, without really getting the joke, and handed out beers.

I stretched my arms out, smelled the dark beer, felt the carbonation tickle my nose, and listened to the sailors talk. The beer was brown, foamy, and luscious. For the moment, I forgot where I was. It was relaxing. I lost track of time. There might have been refills.

It was good. No, it was better than good. It was "I'm stuck in the NAG for months, and the last beer I had was 5,000 miles ago in Singapore, and the beer in Singapore sucked, so to hell with the captain and fuck those regulations, it's eight in the morning and I'm drinking on duty" kind of good.

The voice of God, coming from a wall speaker, slammed me from my bliss down to the deck.

"Ensign Seddon, please contact the bridge."

My sailors turned and looked at me.

"Who's Ensign Seddon?" asked the Brit. "Is that your commo?"

My crew went silent. My engineer sipped his beer and looked sideways at the wall.

"Ensign Seddon, please contact the bridge."

I pursed my lips. "Shit." I pulled a wall phone off its hook.

"What's the number to the bridge?" I asked the Brit.

The Brit's smile was gone, his brow was furrowed, and he answered slowly, "47999."

"This is Ensign Seddon," I said when the bridge answered my call.

"What the hell," the Brit said, realizing at once that an officer was in his Petty Officers' Mess, and that he was helping the American sailors break regulations in front of an officer.

On the phone, the commo was wondering where we were after having gone down to the boat to find it unattended. I said, "We'll meet you there."

I turned back to the Brit. The confused and hesitant look on his face made me think he couldn't decide if I was in trouble with him, or if he were in trouble with me.

"Thanks! This was very awesome, but duty calls." I extended my hand. A moment passed.

"Oh, what the hell, come back any time." He shook my hand, beaming.

At the stern again, I was glad to see the RHIB right where we had left it. And horrified to see that the British sailor who was supposed to be watching it was nowhere to be seen! But since it had not come untied or sunk, it was one bullet dodged.

When the commo appeared from the hatch and jumped in, and I explained our absence from the RHIB, she was pissed. It *was* totally unfair that I was having a beer while she worked.

On the way back to our ship, I said, "I think you all saw those bad teeth back there. Let that be a lesson to us. I think it's probably a really good idea if we all brushed our teeth as soon as we're back aboard and before talking to anyone."

The coxswain replied, "Aye, aye, sir. Dental hygiene is very important."

The commo never ratted on us, of course. We junior officers were a tight group and always had each others' backs. And there was no squealing from the seaman or petty officers who manned the mighty RHIB Steel Hammer One that day. We never even spoke of or acknowledged it, aside from looks that only secret confederates can give.

Buoyed by my success, minor though it was, the rest of my deployment seemed a little less daunting. Passing a strange version of the recruiter's test, I had been decisive amidst uncertainty. Not all heroes save sinking ships.

PHARMACOLOGICAL DREAM OF TRAVEL THROUGH TIME AND SPACE
Jonathan Travelstead

1.

So much to worry with the math.

The extra two hundred-a-month hazard pay volunteering for high-risk duty. At Scott Air Force Base, droning through ten hours of briefings and out-processing. Twenty-two-hour flight. Can't sleep. Next to me, Fryman watches a movie on his laptop. Jack Nicholson is dying. I down twelve airplane bottles of Jim Beam—now forbidden in this airspace—I count by the diminishing sum in one cargo pocket, and the rising, empty lump in the other. Enough heart medication knicked from my grandmother's medicine cabinet to trip across the sky and back. Another movie in which the main character is disconnected. Tom Cruise, or Hanks—I don't know which—talks to Wilson and we're both missing something in our lives, but Fryman says I'm ok. The lacertilian stewardess slithers by. Now I know exactly how long my mother has left to live.

2.

Kuwait.

What year—which version of me files out of the plane, then takes his place in a line which fills the charter bus? Windows curtained with black felt, the bus hisses to a stop and we dribble onto the tarmac two by two. The captain barks and we form up in this Martian light. Tallest airmen front left, shortest, opposite rear. How in god's name did I get here? One duffel on our backs, another hoisted over the shoulder in a fireman's carry. I feel sick. Remember where and when home is, that it will take a funeral to get me back to the present. Surely there's something I can take for this. Sand storms around us. Creases in our skin and the night sky fill with the base's alkaline light. Sober, I no longer trust my calculations. *How many seconds is eighteen weeks? Two bottles of Ambien. One-hundred twenty Adderall.*

BEEF
Jim Ruland

A t 0400 hours on the day my life changed forever, I was standing at attention with a dozen shivering recruits inside the largest meal-producing facility in the universe, awaiting orders from a gangly, nineteen-year-old sailor in a white t-shirt and a paper hat. The harsh fluorescent lights seemed to reflect off a zillion stainless-steel surfaces. My hands were numb, my body confused. I was groggy from lack of sleep, but thrilled to be inside the galley at Great Lakes Recruit Training Command, away from the wind whistling off Lake Michigan.

As the baby-faced autocrat went down the ranks, handing out work assignments, the realization started to sink in that I'd be on my feet and working my ass off for the next sixteen hours straight.

"Bakery…Serving line…Scullery…Deep sink."

They were the lucky ones.

I was dispatched to the ovens to work with Mike, a foul-tempered brute with a complexion like wet dough and circles under his eyes that were so deep and dark he looked like he'd been up for days. He kept his long, greasy hair in a net. His arms were clotted with terrible tattoos. His teeth inspired nightmares.

He was the kind of guy who said things like: *Old enough to bleed, old enough to breed.*

The work was simple but dangerous. Everything was hot, slippery or sharp. Before breakfast was served, I managed to remove a hundred trays of bacon from the massive ovens, drain off the crackling grease, and stack the trays in a rolling meat locker without burning myself.

After a couple of hours, Mike opened up a little, started cracking jokes he'd probably told a thousand times before. His comments were crass, his sense of humor profane. I wanted no part of it. I kept my head down, and my mouth shut.

After lunch we switched from bacon to beef.

It went like this: I took a tray out of the oven, speared a roast with a long fork, and placed it in a stainless-steel bin. When the bin was full I brought it to Mike, and he pushed the roasts through the meat slicer.

We were in a pretty good rhythm when it happened.

The blade got snagged on a piece of gristle and the roast shot into the air and stayed airborne for a few spectacular seconds before it hit the deck.

Mike and I looked at that hunk of meat for a long, long time, studying it, you might say. There was a puddle where the blood had squirted out and the roast was coated with grime.

I was pretty sure Mike was deliberating whether or not he should put the beef back on the slicer. I wouldn't have said anything if that's what he wanted to do. I might have volunteered to rinse it off first, but that's it. I didn't care one way or another.

But Mike had other ideas.

"You wanna fuck it?"

It took me a moment to process this ungodly solicitation.

I thought he might be joking. I *prayed* that he was joking.

He wasn't joking.

"I'll drill a hole in it and you can take it back to the cooler before it gets cold. What do you say?"

Now I was many things: the son of a naval officer, a slacker, a punk—but I wasn't someone who did unspeakable things to inanimate objects. Not yet anyway.

"Come on," he pleaded. "I know you ain't getting no action in them barracks. Plenty of brown eye though…"

That's when I understood that Mike, a federally employed wage slave in the food service sector, wasn't just offering to drill the hole: he *wanted* me to screw the meat.

In the gospel according to Mike, anyone who declined his invitation to have intercourse with a hot bloody hole in a cow carcass must be gay, which was the *worst* thing a sailor in Ronald Reagan's Navy could be.

I shook my head.

"What a shame." Mike said as he kicked the roast with the toe of his boot before picking it up and tossing it in the trash. "It's still warm."

We finished slicing the rest of the roasts. I stacked the bins in the meat locker and wheeled them up to the serving line. When it was time for my break, I got in line and stared at all those mounds of rare roast beef.

My heart started racing and I broke into a sweat. The drugs the Navy supposedly put in the pancake batter to suppress our animal urges weren't working. Somewhere in the soft, pink folds and shadowy dimples was my meat friend.

The association had been made and nothing could unmake it. The meat was making me *horny.*

And it will be the same for you. The next time you're standing in line for a buffet at a birthday or wedding, and the server forks a glistening slab of hot, bloody meat onto your plate, you will think of me, you will think of Mike, you will think of our lost innocence.

WE'RE ALL DOING IT

Sage Foley

The first time I reached into an abdominal cavity to hold a uterus steady, my hands were trembling. The first time I held the needle driver and slipped the needle through the soft flesh of fallopian tube, I was nervous as hell. She was close and watching intently.

"Be gentle, Foley. Make sure you bite a big enough chunk so it won't tear."

Her hips were snug against mine. She towered over me. I dominated her wanting. She could feel the way I was pulling her and I knew it.

I was effortlessly talented with a stitch, better than most surgeons stationed in the hospital. I was just a tech. I was enlisted, low ranking United States Navy. She was about forty pay grades my superior. She was my direct chain of command. She was out of bounds, out of reach, both of us out of a job. Dishonorable. Discharge. These were the threats that circulated.

She was soft and gentle and when I laid her down and kissed her thighs, she was only human. She was the only human I wanted. The human that wanted me; my hips reaching up to her.

*

The first time I saw her, she was in full surgical gown with mask and goggles. Splattered and bloody and concentrating.

"I'm Foley. I'm your new tech."

"Have you scrubbed an abdominal hysterectomy yet?"

"Many."

"Scrub in, I need your hands." She didn't look up, her ears the only body part visible. Adorably floppy and just the slightest bit big in proportion to her head.

I walked out the negative pressured OR door to the sink outside. I scrubbed every finger, 30 seconds each. The forearms up to the elbow. If strictly followed, it's a 5- to 10-minute discipline. I shoved my back against the door and pushed, hands free and theoretically sterile. I slid into my gown and gloves and squeezed my body between the table of instruments and her body.

"Do you know how to vaginally assist?"

"Yes, ma'am."

"Good. Reach in the patient and encourage the uterus proximal."

I did.

"Hold it there."

I did.

"Turn it up, please," she demanded. The circulating nurse found her way to the iPod and swiveled the toggle.

"*An angel kissed my lips as I slept last night. And her rhythm broke my hunger, and I died a little less,*" I mumble-sang along without even noticing.

"You know Tegan and Sara?"

"I do, ma'am. Like a religion, I know them."

"That's a religion I could get behind."

"Do you have a favorite song?" I asked in excitement of prospect. In a time before the social acceptance of gay culture, we relied entirely on cues and hints. I kept an eye out for Tracy Chapman and Tegan and Sara fans.

"Ocean."

Fuck. I'm going to love this woman.

*

"Foley, get in here, I need to speak to you."

The softest part of my bicep was stunned by the strength of his fingers. He directed me into his office. The space was tight, restricting our movements. The door was closed, gently, the tiny space beginning to morph into a closet, squeezing our tense energies, forcing them against each other.

"I know," he said, authority and disgust dripping from his vocal chords. "She flirts with you in broad daylight, she grabs your hips in the hallways of my surgical department. This is my fucking department, Foley. You seem to be very confused about that. So I'm going to clear it up for you."

His head lowered, his eyes at my chin, he cocked his head provokingly, "Are you listening? Fucking pay attention. How you choose to walk away with this information will determine the outcome of your future. A few words to the right people and I could throw you off this island with a Dishonorable Discharge. Are you scared? Because you fucking should be!"

I found the center of his eyes and locked into the darkest part of his pupils, felt his spirit tremble.

You know nothing of fear, Commander. Don't challenge me.

I'd wrecked his concentration. He refocused, readjusted, scrambled for control. Found it, my weak spot.

"Okay, well here are the facts, Foley." He put his palms on my shoulders and in one effortless push, seated me. He wanted me looking up. Instead, I stared straight ahead, into his belt buckle.

The USNS Mercy, I know that ship well. It rocked my aching empathy to sleep for five months. The sight of the belt was comforting, even if it was hugging his hips. His hips, how frustrated they must have been, to carry the weight of such an unkind spirit.

"Okay, bitch, I'll just talk to your forehead then. I know that you're fucking her. Every single fucking person in this OR knows you're fucking her. You are an HN, and she is your superior officer. Since you seem to care very little for your own well-being, I will speak a language you do understand. You are not the only one at risk here. She is a successful surgeon, and I assume she's worked hard to be where she is. I can take that all away from her. I can take everything away from her. Keep that in mind, every time you strut these halls like you own the place, every time you let her touch you during surgery."

Touching me during surgery was audacious, I'd give him that. She was wonderfully bold. She knew no bounds, only humanity. She was an extraordinary human.

Out, out, get out. Now.

My lungs were collapsing, my body trembling. He had me, he knew it, the knowledge radiating off the smirk stretching his lips to meet his right cheekbone.

Out!

I stood up and rushed out of the small office, stood in the hall, shutting off, and turning in, further, deeper.

"Foley, I am not done with you! Get the fuck back in here," he called after me. He followed, met me in the hall. All of my co-workers were locked into our display of his inhumane tendencies. Most of them couldn't see it, blinded by the gold eagle spreading its metallic wings over that man's collarbone. But he was just a man. A man with a fancy pin.

*

She didn't know. I never let her in. I never told her about him. Protecting her was my only priority.

I knocked on her office door softly, she brought out the meekness in me. I loved that about her.

"It's open," she announced from behind her desk, her throne. She was powerful.

I should've given her the chance to defend herself. It would've hurt her less. She looked up from her charting and smiled confidently. She understood happiness well. She taught me much of it. She taught me how to feel the ocean floor.

I met her smile, fell into her space. She caught me.

"Hey, Foley. Want to be fucked?"

No, no I can't have her. I can't hurt her. I can't. Tell her everything. Leave her safe. Leave her.

My lips were the only things that found motion. "Yes. Please fuck me." Tears were begging in my eyes, they wanted to drip onto her naked skin. She stood and moved toward me, pushed me into the wall when her motion found my stillness.

They want to hurt us, my conscience pleaded with her.

Her spirit wouldn't hear of it and her hands were on a mission, she must have me. She gripped the back of my neck and pulled me closer. Closer. My body begged her to take her blade and run it from my breast to my navel, stretch my ribs just enough for her to crawl inside. Closer. She pulled the drawstring of my scrubs and reached for me. Her spirit cradled mine and my tears had their way.

She pulled back, "Did I hurt you? Foley, what's wrong? Fuck, what did I do?"

I was past the hope of explanation. I had no words, only pain. I had decided I would not tell her. I'd be the silent hero. I knew everything. I knew nothing. I was no hero.

"Long day," I whimpered. I grabbed her waist and pushed her toward her desk, my attempt to reassure her desire through aggressive motions. I needed her. I didn't have a clue. I thought she needed me. Her perception of my worth had me conceited.

With one quick brush of my forearm and zero deliberation I managed to clear about a fourth of her desk. Papers scattered on the ground, of the important patient privacy kind.

"Foley," she caught my arm, "that's a terrible idea," she said with composure only she could carry, a full smile only she could muster in disapproval.

"I know," I choked on a disappointed giggle. "I saw it in a movie. Intensely misleading."

I got on my hands and knees and started collecting the results of my frantic goofy display of desire. She came behind me, took hold of my hips and pushed my face into the paper stained carpet. As I kissed a prescription for antibiotics, I heard her whisper, "Leave it."

I left it. I left it all.

That was the last time I snuck away to her office. The last time I rested my palm on the back of her gloved hand as she reached back blindly to grab an instrument off my table. The last bike ride through the clay playground of Guam's south end. The last dive, sharing her energy with the depths of the Pacific Ocean.

After that, when I caught her glance, it was only pain that I saw. Confusion and pain. But she was never cold and never cruel. She was kind. I had yet to learn the value of that magnificent human quality. She was a surgeon, a captain, and my superior something or another. But mostly and completely, she was kind.

And I was weak. Taken by the wrong hands, controlled by the wrong voices, stuck in a system that assigned power and with the same authority, took it away. A system that promoted dissociation from humanity.

The dissociation is acceptable if the humans wear uniforms.

It's not wrong if we're all doing it.

BACK IN AFGHANISTAN
Nick Willard

Bagram Airfield, 2014.

The ramp opens to a spring breeze and a view of snow-capped mountains. I ignore the engine noise and the dull ache for what I'd left back home, and take in the view. I step off the plane, catch that first groggy whiff of jet fuel and my body instantly registers where I am…back in Afghanistan.

We grab our gear, line up, and walk across the tarmac. Personnel specialists divide us up by service and unit, collect orders and identification cards, and lead us to a bare-walled room with airport seats. We watch a welcome video, like a corporate video for new hires but this one spoke of the mission, rules of war, and what to do during attacks.

From there, I become "my replacement." For the next couple days, that's how the guy I'm replacing introduces me. For the bosses, the conversation goes: "Hey sir, I'd like to introduce my replacement." "Alright, welcome, we're glad to have you. You been here before?" (Firm handshake, eye contact, smile.) "Yes sir." "Good, good, well, welcome to the fight. You have big shoes to fill.

We'll see you around." "You bet, sir. Good to meet you." (Firm handshake, eye contact, smile.)

I endure dozens of these conversations as the replaced takes me around. I spend hours shaking hands, completing paperwork, situating equipment, and orienting myself. Exhaustion from the 9-time-zone difference harasses me. They say it takes one day per time zone to fully adjust.

On Day Two, I'm ready for the replaced to go. The quarters and work areas are too small for both of us, and after he gives me the rundown I want to get started on my own. Midway through Day Three, I say, "Dude, you should cut out. Head over to the gym or BX or something...we're good to go here."

I'm pissed off the first few days. My body and mind reject everything about this place...the unclear future of the Afghan endeavor, the countless petty rules, the fact that my tour had just begun, the difficulty of even the most minor tasks, the inefficiencies, the fractured flow of information, and the vague yet ever-present threat.

I adapt, and my irritation turns into indifference, then strangely, acceptance. As the days wear on, the constant noise of aircraft, generators, and vehicles fades. I numb to the barrage of smells: citrus disinfectants, burning trash, sewage, sweat, and diesel. Typically, I'm half-nauseous for the first week and this time is no different. I drink 7-Up and eat just enough of the blandest food. My gut slowly adjusts to the dining hall offerings.

There's an overarching pressure to accept, or at least not publicly acknowledge, the weirdness of these deployed bases. Most people try to act cool, like nothing is awry, when nearly everything is tilted. Only here does a computer screensaver say "Got Bleeding? Use a junctional tourniquet!" or "Whole blood and platelet screening," or "Salsa Night Every Saturday," or "Controlled detonation in five minutes."

Troops dine with machine guns and pistols, amidst the civilian contractors and foreign nationals imported to cook and serve the food. World Wrestling or UFC streams on the TVs in the background. Civilian computer techs and other workers sport beards, ball caps, and tactical cargo pants mimicking the special operator look. A friend of mine calls this "deployment chic, the carefully cultivated look of the war-time contractor."

One night a group of surgeons sit behind me, and I catch a shred of their conversation: "You take the diaphragm out and the body opens like a book."

I've come to expect the most random and ironic experiences in these places. Odd convergences aren't surprises anymore. One day, I'm sharing a table with guys who could be Navy SEALs. Minutes later, I'm joking with a group of young motor pool soldiers. I've crossed paths with several people I hadn't seen since before the wars started. In conversations here, it usually doesn't take long to find common ground.

The T-walls, bunkers, sandbags, concertina wire, guard towers, floodlights, gates, and tactical vehicle parking fade into normalcy. I appreciate the rainbows of Conex containers punctuating the base's primary colors of concrete, tan, and olive drab. Coalition forces have occupied worn Russian hangars and office buildings for more than a decade now. Some display scars of past battles—bullet holes and shrapnel marks—and I wonder if the halls impart their lessons to those inside. In one, a display of rusted Soviet weapons, unearthed from around the base, recalls a war museum…a war museum within a war.

I'm amazed at how polite people are in warzones. I chalk this up to the fact that nearly everyone is armed. Or, maybe it's a sense that we're all locked down in this compound together. Despite technology, there's a tangible isolation within each base's walled perimeter. Events in other parts of this country, such as the recent assassination of three doctors or the British helicopter crash that killed five, might as well have occurred on the other side of the globe. Regardless, people make an extra effort to open doors and offer help. Drivers stop traffic to wave pedestrians across. Everyone smiles and says please, thank you, sir, and ma'am.

But, despite the appearances, this isn't the Afghanistan of ten, two, or even one year ago. The signs of a dying war are everywhere. Rows of MRAPs that recall *Star Wars* vehicles await their fate in fenced yards across the base. Forklifts shuffle weathered pallets of gear lining the airfield in a super-sized game of *Tetris*. Teams manage and sort the constant flow of surplus riding in on semis from closed bases. Temporary buildings from years ago lie bulldozed into two-story rubble piles within view of new construction rising from the dust, the products of half-decade-old contracts.

These days, there's more talk of standards, Article 15s, and stories of people getting sent home for minor infractions. A senior NCO barely introduces himself before telling me I'm wearing a patch with the wrong border color. I say it was the right color just last year, and he says things change. Later, another senior NCO chases me down to gripe about how my pants meet my boots. Another thinks I need to shave better. I'm corrected more in a week here than in my entire career. These beefs aren't worth the fight. It's better to smile and say OK, thanks.

When the mission becomes murky, and operations slow, bureaucracy creeps in to fill the gaps. The people I work with are motivated, positive, and doing amazing work in spite of all this. At a meeting, a chaplain says, "Morale seems to be up...at least for those headed home."

The key to mitigate this noise is to get into a routine, a battle rhythm as they say, and I'm nearly there. The days are beginning to blur, each one an echo of the last. I'm settling in for the duration and find a rhythm for the war's end.

BRINGING BUNNY BACK

Mariah Smith

L ong ago in Afghanistan, 2010 to be exact, a gray kitten was born on a small camp of US and NATO soldiers. She lived with her three brothers, eating out of trash cans, avoiding the wheels of military vehicles, and growing used to people. A soldier found her and fell in love with the spirited kitten and undertook a mission to get her to America safely. That soldier was me, and someday I will write this story as a children's book, with a gentle narrative and simple, happily-ever-after that ends with the arrival of us both back home in the US.

Here's how it really happened.

The Alamo was a housing compound in Kabul, Afghanistan. It sat slightly apart from the larger base complexes of Camp Eggers and ISAF HQ. About 60 soldiers lived apart on this compound, walking to work down a muddy road each day, past hired guards from many nations. The name came from the fact that the trailers were somewhat isolated and enclosed by a traditional mud wall, a lonely fortress, not far from one of the most frequently bombed traffic circles in Kabul. The accommodations were comfortable. Pine trees shaded a small courtyard, there was hot water most of the time, and the units had bunk beds, heat, and air conditioning.

A far cry from the desert I experienced in 2003 as a military police platoon leader where we lived out of our trucks, ate MREs for months, slept on the ground, and went 36 days without a shower at the start of the Iraq War.

That tour in the capital of Afghanistan was a surprisingly happy time for me. I had already deployed for four previous tours to Djibouti, Iraq, Kuwait, and Khost Province, Afghanistan as a military police officer. I had just been promoted to major and was married the month before I deployed for this fifth tour. I loved my job working as a liaison between NATO Training Mission Afghanistan and Congress. It was an optimistic time in Afghanistan, perhaps hard to believe now, when massive amounts of energy and resources were directed towards training the Afghan National Army and Police. My dad was serving in Kabul as well, a retired Navy officer working as an army civilian with US Forces Afghanistan on a country-wide project to vet the local and foreign contractors we hired.

At NTM-A I worked late hours, and often returned to the Alamo well after dark. I spotted the kitten in the spring of 2010, a few months into my yearlong tour. The litter consisted of her and three brothers—two tuxedo kittens and a long-haired gray tabby like her. At best guess her father was a well-known large tuxedo cat, who always had a smudge of dirt on his white nose and could often be found gregariously mooching food from the guards. Her mother was a small short-haired female gray tabby with permanently crossed pumpkin colored eyes. While the adult cats were socialized to humans, the kittens were feral, all except this one. She seemed to have been born with an affinity for people.

I have always been an animal lover. Over the years my household has consisted of Sam—a chubby, cowardly cat adopted during my first tour in Korea; Sadie—a fierce little mouser adopted from an elderly lady in Fort Campbell, KY; Annie—a beautiful Gordon Setter who had been abandoned at a shelter for ten months in Fort Leonard Wood when I found her; Bud—a magnificent and tragically short-lived Rottweiler mix found running free at about six months old; and Daisy—a street urchin disguised as a cartoonish Basset Hound from a pound outside of Fort Bragg. In every military move I've toted around a little metal sign that says, "All strays welcome" and hung it up in each new house, and the strays always seem to find me.

I looked forward to my nightly walks home and often brought the kitten a chicken breast or some tuna fish from the chow hall. Once, when she couldn't have been more than ten weeks old and still small enough to sit in the palm of one hand, she ravenously consumed an entire grilled chicken breast the size of her torso, and all night I lay awake in agony, certain that I killed her, because it was unfathomable how she could eat something almost the same size as her and not rupture her stomach. Like many soldiers and veterans, I had an uneasy relationship with sleep. First and foremost, the Army never let us get enough of it. And when I did get to sleep, I had vivid nightmares and sleep paralysis that I had since I was a child. Since Iraq in 2003, I have been periodically plagued with a recurring nightmare where my weapon jams or falls apart in my hand at the moment when I encounter the enemy. I am powerless to stop them and if my pistol does fire—it's almost always a pistol in the dream for some reason—the bullets bounce impotently off their chest. I wake up gasping the instant they are upon me and I am about to be killed.

The kitten needed a name. We kicked around "Nermal," the world's cutest kitten from the Garfield cartoons, and the inelegant Dari word for "cat" which sounded something like "pee-shak." Eventually I fell back on "Bunny," given her resemblance to a wild baby bunny with large ears, a thick wild gray-brown coat, big, Thumper-like back feet colored black on the bottoms, and a short upright kitten tail.

Summer moved into fall, my favorite season and the time of year when I missed my home country the most. I began working longer hours and Bunny almost always waited for me at night in the courtyard of the Alamo. I would sit outside with her on my lap until I was so chilled from the cold ground that I was driven into our room. One night when she wasn't outside waiting for me, the on-duty guard motioned me towards their shack and pointed to Bunny sleeping blissfully on the seat of a chair. The guards were contracted private security officers, mostly from Afghanistan and the Philippines. Another time they created a toy for her, tying a cigarette butt to a long piece of string and dangling it for her to pounce and chase. Everyone collectively cared for her, but the more I grew to love her, the more I worried about something happening to her. While base cats are generally better tolerated than stray dogs in the CENTCOM area of responsibility, every so often some bastard garrison commander would decide that there were a few too many and round up whichever ones could be caught and have them destroyed.

On an earlier tour in Babylon, Iraq, a decree was issued by our higher headquarters that all stray dogs on camp must die. I don't know how or when it became an accepted and encouraged military pastime to kill dogs, but it did. Senior leaders in our battalion, sergeants, and officers would go on nightly "raids" with the sole purpose of killing as many feral and local dogs as they could. They clustered around the operations tent in the morning, chortling to each other like assholes, displaying the nightly body count and retelling about which dog had run particularly hard from them or hid especially well before being shot.

One night I sat on a small patch of high ground, overlooking Saddam's labyrinth and the ancient ruins of Babylon. I leaned against the statue of the Goddess Ishtar in her incarnation as a lion devouring a man, a place I often went to be alone and out of the operations center tent for a few minutes, never ceasing to marvel that I was free to roam the historical site. It was well into twilight, and as I sat a shadow of a dog ran for its life, crossing the small ridge in front of me. A moment later, a member of my unit silently followed, shotgun held at the high ready.

But back to Afghanistan, seven years later: sometimes bore-dom is the most dangerous enemy on deployments, along with loneliness and the feeling that I have no control over my life. Once it routinely dipped below freezing, I began to worry about my Bunny cat in earnest. One November night when it finally became bitterly cold, I had lain awake half the night concerned for the kitten when I heard a plaintive and quiet "Mew" at my door. I don't know how she picked our second story metal door out from the long line of trailers in the Alamo. But I sprang out of my cot and threw open the door. There she sat, as prim as can be, gazing up at me, cold wind ruffling her fur. It's against General Order Number One to have animals in your living area. Or members of the opposite sex, or alcohol, or basically anything fun or cozy. So I'll leave it up to your imagination to fill in what happened next. Suffice it to say Bunny didn't freeze to death that night.

On deployments I miss my pets terribly. I feel like I am better able to comfort myself, stabilize, and clear my mind when a cat is purring on my lap or a dog is snoring on the couch next to me. When I wake from a nightmare or am unlocked from a bad bout of sleep paralysis, putting my hand on the warm fur of a pet sharing my bed brings me near-instant peace. I began riding horses when I was four, and spent many happy years in 4-H and Pony Club. Growing up in Maryland, outside of Annapolis, I was given free run of an area just rural enough where I could ride through the farm fields and woods almost every afternoon after school and all weekend, every weekend. At the farm of my 4-H club and where I kept my pony, the other kids and I climbed through the hay lofts of the old tobacco barns and cuddled the litters of barn cats. We slept in the barns with our horses when they were sick, and during Halloween we transformed the barns into massive haunted houses. We raced our ponies against each other in the long paths cut through the corn fields. Until I went away to college, that was how I spent the majority of my time—outside, with animals, as much as possible.

With every day that went by, I was worried that something would happen to Bunny, that she would be killed or injured. All of us know the terror at the thought of losing a loved one—it's something always with us in a war zone. I can't imagine what parents and spouses and children go through on the other side. My mom was at home by herself looking after my pets with one kid and her husband deployed, and the other kid, my younger brother, away at sea for weeks or months at a time on an equally hazardous underwater exploration job.

Somehow—probably Google—I found Pam that winter, an American living and working in Kabul who had founded the Afghan Stray Animal League and Tigger House—the physical shelter for the League and one of the only animal shelters in Afghanistan. Pam and I made a plan to save Bunny. The kittens were beginning to mature and if nature took its course, Bunny would most likely be a teenage mom herself by the spring, if she survived the winter. Her survival was questionable, being vulnerable to feline leukemia and rabies, the wheels of heavy military vehicles that rumbled by our walls, and animal-killing heartless bastards.

Christmas Day dawned chilly and bright with a dusting of snow. My dad made the trip from Camp Phoenix to Camp Eggers on the Rhino Bus, an armored transport vehicle that regularly made the rounds between the small camps in the city. Later in our tour there, that same Rhino was hit by a suicide truck bomb, killing everyone inside.

The Tigger House veterinarian arrived by taxi in the afternoon, a handsome Afghan man toting an empty cat carrier who called me on my cell phone to meet him at the entrance to the Alamo. I didn't know how long it would take to locate Bunny, so I took the carrier from him and went off in search of her, one of my worn tan t-shirts folded into the bottom of the carrier. Dad and the vet stayed near the entrance of the compound talking to the guard, a friendly Afghan security officer with a magnificent Sam Elliott mustache.

As luck would have it, I found Bunny within minutes, rummaging for food in a trashcan. She turned at the sound of my approach with a chirp of greeting. I didn't know how much of a struggle she was going to put up, having never been crated before, so I knelt down and opened the door while petting her. Bunny strode into the carrier completely at ease. I returned to the front gate where the vet had filled the guard in on our plan.

Dad produced $120 for the vet, our donation to the Tigger House for Bunny's spaying and shots and to cover his cab fare, and off he went. The Afghan guard exchanged some rapid-fire Pashtu with the vet, gave me a warm grin and poked a finger into the carrier to say goodbye to Bunny. We had a connection for the remainder of my tour. He knew one English word and I am embarrassed to say I didn't know any Pashtu. But every time I walked home and he was on shift we would greet each other happily.

"Cat?" he would ask, smiling.

"Yes, the cat, she's good, she's coming home with me!" I would answer. Then we would exchange thumbs up.

I might not have been able to ensure anyone else I cared about in the country was safe, but knowing the kitten would live made me happy. I kept in touch with Pam and she told me that this wasn't really a country where people adopted cats from a shelter on a regular basis, but if I wanted to, she informed me, there was a way to bring her home. Pam told me about Puppy Rescue Mission, an awesome organization still hard at work today, helping service members rescue and legally bring home the stray animals they bond with on deployments. It would be expensive—over $2,500 to legally bring Bunny back to America. Puppy Rescue Mission was very willing to help fundraise and has successfully helped many service members bring their companions home, but as a major with deployment pay, I felt like I needed to pay for Bunny's journey myself.

Bunny began her round-the-world journey as I prepared to leave Afghanistan myself. Once more the vet came out by taxi, this time bringing Bunny in her little kitty carrier to confirm her identity. Right there on the busy street in front of the Alamo, he plucked her out of her kennel by the scruff, flipped her over to show me her plump shaved belly where she had been spayed, had me sign her vaccination record and then plopped her into my arms. I still have the photo my roommate Tami snapped at that moment: Bunny is clinging to me and I to her, and she is hiding her face against my neck and under my hair. I gave her one last hug and handed her back to the vet to start her journey. She flew from Pakistan to Germany, and by a stroke of good luck arrived at Dulles Airport the same day I did. My mom and my friend Erika picked us both up within an hour of each other. A now-defunct magazine called *All You* came out to the house a few days later to snap some pictures for a story about Bunny and I and two other military women who had adopted dogs through Puppy Rescue Mission. All was well, for a little while.

Earlier that year, while I was several months into my Afghanistan tour, my husband and his National Guard unit had deployed to the Southern portion of Afghanistan. My husband's tour ended about six weeks after mine. We had spent almost all of the first 16 months of our marriage apart. We had met about a year and half before the deployment, the week I returned from my first Afghanistan tour, where I had been deployed for 15 months as a company commander with the 82nd Airborne. I came home realizing that I was completely devoid of anything resembling a personal life, met my future husband out with friends at a bar one night, and jumped in with both feet and a blindfold on.

Shortly after we met, I was transferred to another post, and much of our courtship happened over long distance. We moved in together only a few months before we married. I felt anxiety at the homecoming—we'd been apart for as long as we had been together, and I realized I didn't know that much about him and vice versa. Once he was home, he permanently evicted Bunny from the bedroom and developed an active dislike of her. The excuse he gave me at the time was because she disturbed his sleep, and cats were "dirty," but looking back, I think he hated anything that diverted my attention from him. He frequently told me he'd let me have this one cat, but she was the only cat I was ever going to have, after this we were done with indoor cats. I've learned there are two types of people in this world: the type who think that animals don't belong in the house and the good type. Recounting the relationship red flags—and there were many looking back—I now know this is a deal breaker for me. But back then, wanting my marriage to work, I thought it was up to me to make sacrifices.

Granted, there might have been a smidge of justification to the bedroom banishment, as Bunny was apt to walk across him in her efforts to get to me on the far side of the bed. It was a challenge to confine her and get her to comply with his sleeping arrangement demands. A closed bedroom door wasn't sufficient. Bunny would sit outside and yowl in frustration while digging at the carpet around the door jamb, resulting in a small hole dug down to the plywood. Next, I tried to close her up in the kitchen. Our house was built in 1963, and the kitchen was accessed by a door at either end of the room that could be shut. I quickly learned how clever my kitten was and how good she was at opening doors, even latched ones. In the end the only thing that worked was to tie the doors shut with rope, a ritual I followed every night as my heart broke. Once barricaded into the kitchen for the night, Bunny would cry herself to sleep and I would cry, too.

I hate to think of the wasted three years that followed. A relationship can either be the environment in which a person grows into the best version of themselves, or it can confine and diminish. My three years of marriage conditioned me to hate myself more than I ever had in the 30 years that preceded it. His criticisms came more frequently as time went on. My hair was wrong, my clothes were wrong, I spent too much time at work. I was inefficient, messy, unfunny. My job was both unimportant and too time-consuming. I didn't care about pleasing him with the things I knew he liked because I was selfish. I put off so many things I wanted to do and try because he'd make me feel guilty about showing interest in anything that would take time away from him. He drank more and more, and I drank with him.

We started going to marriage counseling because that's what I thought might fix my misery, but later I realized I was just looking for some authority figure who would tell me I was allowed to leave him. Once I attempted the divorce was when it truly got scary. At first he forbid me to talk about separation, and took to cornering me in our bedroom or in the living room, forcing me to spend hours detailing my shortcomings ad nauseum and describing to him how I was going to be a better, less selfish wife. He applied intense guilt and anger towards me if I asked to go out with friends, a sign to him that I was unfocused on improving the marriage and uncommitted to putting in time to fix it. He even wrote out 3 × 5 cards of what I was supposed to say to him: they were a script for me to follow to ensure he heard exactly what he wanted to hear from me. I became scared for Bunny's safety and my parents and friends became scared for mine.

By this time Bunny was a rambunctious and large four-year-old cat who could jump from the floor to the top of a door frame and perch there like a fluffy gargoyle. He had never liked her, and in the days that followed some of our fights, my mind would race, wondering if he had taken her somewhere and dumped her, or shoved her out of a car door and told me she had "run away" just to hurt me. The thought of losing her was immensely more painful than the thought of losing him. When I was on the verge of escaping, I created a ruse to take Bunny to my mother's house under the guise of a series of vet visits my mother would take her to while I was at my military school. My husband saw through my ruse and before he would let me leave on my trip, after an hour of berating me, he made me drive the 40 miles to my mother's house—me sobbing all the way while he lectured me from the passenger seat about how selfish I was—to pick Bunny up and return her to our apartment, to "ensure" that I would come home from my military school that weekend.

His instincts were right. I had intended to leave him while I was safely away at the military school surrounded by people I trusted, and Bunny safely with my parents. There was no way I was leaving her vulnerable as an outlet to his anger. By this time I had learned he was vengeful by nature, and believed in hurting people in an equal or larger measure than how he perceived they had hurt him. In marriage counseling, he had told an awful story with pride about extorting $6,000 from a young girlfriend years prior, when she had decided to leave him and return to her home-town. He held her possessions hostage in their shared apartment until she paid him as much as she could scrape together. He did it because he perceived that since she was ending the relationship, she should pay him back for meals and other gifts and sundries he had treated her to while they were a couple. I realized I would have to appease him for a little longer until I could get my Bunny cat, and myself, to safety.

It took too long and I lost much, but with the help of my parents and some very beloved friends, I broke free and immedi-ately transferred to Fort Bragg, North Carolina, a place I adored. I bought a small ranch house on two acres in fox and longleaf country in Moore County, as far away from Fayetteville as I could get. North Carolina has an infuriating law where you have to get your spouse's written permission to buy real estate, even if you are estranged and you use only your own money and only have yourself on the title and mortgage. It took all of my diplomatic and negotiation powers to swallow my contempt and fear of him long enough to get him to sign the papers to "allow" me to buy my own house in my own name. I was far past being done with him "allowing" or "forbidding" me to do anything.

My relief in my freedom was short lived. The next two years were the most exhausting and stressful years of my life. He began a sustained campaign of online and physical harassment, humiliation, and continued emotional abuse. He contacted my commanders relentlessly with false allegations and demands until they, too, became deeply afraid for my safety. He demanded four years of alimony in exchange for ceasing this behavior. He broke into my house and placed hidden cameras, and once the police learned we weren't divorced yet, that it was a "domestic situation without children involved," they did nothing. I hemorrhaged money, all my savings, on legal fees. He justified his behavior by informing me in long rambling emails that since I had hurt him by taking away the marriage, he would hurt me by taking away what he perceived I valued most: my career, my reputation, and money. I showed my commander and my divorce attorney the multiple texts I had from him that read: "I am going to get what I want out of this, or else." On our first meeting after I left him, he had solemnly slid a piece of lined paper across the table, like we were in salary negotiations. I've kept it to this day. It had a list of the ways he wanted to humiliate me in bullet points at the top and then the number $225,000 circled in the center. "That's what I want," he said. "To not do those things listed." I made the terrible mistake of laughing in nervous disbelief. Since I didn't have the $225,000 and wouldn't have given it to him if I did, he spent those two years working his way through everything on the list with some extra things thrown in for good measure.

Every night for two years I had the same dream—a variant of a dream I first began having in 2003 in Iraq, about the enemy: Even though I was securely bolted into my own house in North Carolina, the dream would start with heavy footsteps on the porch, and noises at the window. Somehow he makes it into the house, despite the locks and the alarm system. I have always slept with the .45 my parents gave me at commissioning on my nightstand. This is where it became like the old Iraq nightmare. The enemy is in front of me. This time the enemy is my husband, here to kill me. Once, blind drunk, he'd told me he fantasized about commiting a murder/suicide if I ever left him. Later, he said he was too drunk to remember it, but I took him seriously.

In the dream I have my weapon in my hand but it disintegrates into a mass of parts, the slide falling off, the barrel unseating, the magazine falling out. Or, I would pull the trigger as the enemy advanced but bullets bounced harmlessly off him like it was a staple gun, or the trigger malfunctioned, or I lost all strength in my hand. For two years, I woke from this dream every night around 3:00 A.M., disoriented and panicked in the house in the woods. But always Bunny was there, no longer tied into the kitchen away from me. She'd be draped across my legs, her body like a weighted blanket, her long belly fur like a dirty mop, purring and blinking at me with hooded eyes, her paws kneading the blanket over my legs. "It is OK," she'd rumble at me, "I am here, and we are safe."

I had moved in next to a wonderful and generous semi-retired couple who lived on 15 acres. Horses entered my life again when I needed them the most. Every weekend the wife, Linda, and I would saddle up and ride her two horses to the 4,000-acre Walthour Moss Land Foundation. We'd jump log fences between trees, galloping alongside each other the way I had as a child, racing ponies through the corn fields. Back at her place, escorted by a pair of farm dogs, we'd stomp up to their house, dirty and happy, where her husband Sam had pancakes waiting for us. After every ride I felt a little more whole.

Bunny had to re-teach me what my marriage had destroyed in me. That you can be who you are and still be loved. That you don't always have to be nice or be perfect and yet you are still worthy of being loved. My parents and my best friends have lived this most fiercely these past few years, supporting me with time and presence and acceptance when I was at my very worst. But in saving Bunny, first from Afghanistan and then from my ex-husband, I eventually saved myself. And having her in my life helped me get better day by day.

Every time I walked through the door of my home, Bunny was there to greet me, demanding to be picked up in what we call the "Bunny carry." Paws over my right shoulder, cheek against my temple, purring until she has had her fill after a few minutes and jumps down. I call her Monster or the Scottish Wildcat, Bunnopolis, Bunnicula, or the Afghan Princess. I, and those closest to me, adore her even though she is at times moody and aloof and can just as soon sink her teeth into your palm as she can curl up purring on your lap. She has tiny stuffed animals the size of silver dollars that she carries around the house in her teeth. She tosses them in the air to entertain herself or bounds onto the bed at night and drops them on my chest to play fetch. Time and time again, I'd throw them for her, midnight tears forgotten, her bounding off the bed to retrieve them and leaping onto me again to repeat the cycle. She has a bigger vocabulary than any cat I have ever encountered, a language of trills, happy chirps, inquisitive beeps, growls, and plaintive "meows."

In late 2015 I moved back to D.C. with the Army. The nightmares finally stopped. The endless divorce mercifully came to close when he ran out of the money necessary to fuck with me. He had hired a truly awful divorce lawyer, combative, condescending, and expensive, just like him, and we each spent $90,000 in legal fees arguing about how much money I was going to give him, just to come right back to what I had proposed in the very beginning, before either of us spent a dollar—that we divide our joint bank accounts evenly and go our separate ways. I did agree to his demands that I return every gift he ever bought me, and he left the courtroom the day of our divorce with a bunch of ladies purses, a ladies watch, and the engagement ring. I've never missed those gifts or him for even a moment.

I bought a small 100-year-old horse farm in the Shenandoah Valley with my parents and my brother, and we are slowly fixing it up, one Saturday at a time. I ride every weekend and grow stronger each time, inching closer back to the authentic person I once was before the terrible marriage, before the Army, and before the wars. As I type this, Bunny prowls my apartment that overlooks the Washington monument and the Pentagon, pausing often to stand on hind legs and put a paw on my thigh and gaze at me, accepting some head scratches before moving on. She leaps onto the curio cabinet by the massive window. The cabinet that has the collection of lion statues on top of it, gathered from all over the world. She waits until she has my full attention and then she slowly and gently pushes the smallest statue, a tiny brass lion from the bazaar in Gardez, Afghanistan, off the ledge and onto the floor.

WOOD FIGHTING WITH STEEL

As told by Steven Neichin to Sindre Leganger

STEVEN NEICHIN:

I once jumped out of a helicopter with a parachute, and I was approaching the ground and I came under fire from the Viet Cong. You know you're under fire—you can't see a bullet, but you can see a tracer, and every ten bullets there's a tracer. It's white. I saw these tracers coming at me, between my legs, to the left of me, to the right of me.

I started bargaining with God, I said, "OK, take my left foot, but don't take my balls or my penis, and don't take my right hand, and don't take my eyes. Don't let anything happen to my face, but you can have my left foot."

Then I hit the ground, and it was over. I survived. I have to tell you the truth…I went through such fear and horror during that experience, that I—don't feel fear anymore. Since that couple of minutes that it took, I have not felt fear in the same way again.

*

STEVEN NEICHIN:

It's wood fighting with steel, right? When I first moved here *[the woods of Norway]*, I used to spend seven months chopping wood, because the place wasn't insulated and I had to burn wood constantly in order to keep it warm…So that's what I'm doing.

SINDRE LEGANGER:

When you're out here, do you ever stop to wonder how you ended up here?

STEVEN NEICHIN:

To be honest, my life has a miraculous quality. I began to feel that in Vietnam.

My codename was 32 November—the N of November after my name Neichin. One of the glories of war is the love and trust that develops between the men in your platoon. There's no love like that.

This wood has been drying all year. It takes a beautiful flame, see? The winter is very lovely here. I sit and relax by the fire, and I have no thoughts in my head. It's so peaceful, you know?

It was in 1991. It was at Tai's Bar in Brooklyn. It was a gay bar and everyone was dressed in black, except one man. He's wearing a white shirt. We started talking. I looked at him and I said, "You are Norwegian."

He laughs and he said, "I don't know how you know that, but I was adopted by a Norwegian family. Yes, I am Norwegian, and live in Norway." Imagine…

So we walked home together and he stayed with me for three days while I sang to him. We fell in love.

[sings]
I see him,
As he wakens in the morning.
He reaches out his hands and without a word,
Has his fingers softly fall upon my face.
He lights the flames of desire and makes me want him.

He was absolutely the best, and it's a thousand pities we couldn't manage to build a relationship together. We were married for eight years.

*

STEVEN NEICHIN:

This is the thing about Vietnam veterans—we like to be alone. We need to be alone. We need our own space. But the reason that we don't like to talk about Vietnam is because ordinary people do not understand this, and you don't wanna see ordinary people's reactions, because the reactions are on such a low level that it's horrifying to talk about Vietnam.

They wanna know how many people you killed, like it's table talk…Like I wanna tell a stranger how many people I killed. That's the only thing that they have on their minds. Did you kill someone? How many? That's one of the reasons we don't talk about it. We pretend that it's all so horrible and awful. We just don't wanna talk about it to ordinary people, because it was an extraordinary experience to be in combat, to help people, to be close to people, to be in a trench in a three-day bombardment. Imagine how close you become to the person next to you.

Vietnam was like an extension of my childhood, because it had the same quality of terror and horror, with violence and the possibility of death every day. My mother was schizophrenic and my father was an alcoholic, very violent. He himself had been in World War II. He was a doctor in the South Pacific, and I think it was hard for him to come back and find a one-year-old baby boy that was the center of attention.

One summer my father locked me in the house for the summer. I wasn't allowed to go out. Other times I had to sit in a chair all day, and he would fly into a rage and kick me in the shins with his shoes. Unbelievable pain…It was obvious to me, even as a little child, that he was insane, that something was terribly wrong.

I remember once I did buy a hamster, and I put it in a box. My father took it and stamped it to death against the curbstone. What do you make of that? I'm not a psychiatrist, I was just a kid. I needed my mother, I needed my father, and that's what I had.

I once had a friend named Arlene, who used to have these horrifying conversations. What we would have to do to be loved—we talked about that. She would have to get braces on her teeth, and I thought that I would have to give my life on the battlefield to be loved, to be respected, to be worthy of something. Vietnam was perfect for me, because I had a death wish, so I was psychologically prepared for Vietnam.

*

STEVEN NEICHIN:

Barry Sadler had been a Green Beret, and he wrote "The Ballad Of The Green Berets."

> *[sings]*
> *Fighting soldiers from the skies,*
> *Fearless men who jump and dive.*
> *A hundred men will test today,*
> *But only three wear the Green Beret.*

I thought, "OK, I'm gonna be one of the three."

I was in sort of a subculture which was anti-war. People I knew would claim to be gay whether they were or not, and they wouldn't take you if you were a homosexual. And they were really shocked, horrified that I volunteered.

I was not sexual in any way. No wet dreams, no masturbation, no sex until I was 15. Then I read a book called *The Chapman Report*. It was a book about sexuality, and I started thinking about sex.

There was this boy in my Sunday School that I thought was sexy and handsome. Thinking about sex, I thought to myself "I wonder what it would be like to masturbate," because I had never...So I did. My, my, my...What an extraordinary experience that was.

My first thought was, "Here in your wretched life there is this magnificence," because the pleasure was almost unbearable. So I became a great fan of masturbation, and always thinking of men, and not women. I never thought, "One day I'm gonna grow up to be a homosexual." Gay people were like the cartoon characters, at best, that people laughed at. Or they were perverts and degenerates that people felt free to hurt and kill. I certainly didn't wanna be like that. I certainly did not.

To be honest, I really didn't wanna go on living, but somehow I wanted my life to have a meaning, like "Get it over with in a meaningful way." So I wanted to be a medic in the special forces.

You get on a plane, and it's a little strange, because there's no one on the plane but soldiers. I forget exactly how long we were in the air...I think it was 15 hours. Basically, it was all about wanting to just get off the plane and get started with it. The strange thing was when we reached Vietnam, the plane came under fire. I didn't have to wait for my Vietnam experience to begin after a while; it began immediately, while I was still in the air.

So there I was, in Vietnam, 1968, during the Tet Offensive. The Americans were in retreat, the Viet Cong were winning, bombing our bases, so eventually I did get out into the field into a top-secret mission in Southern Vietnam on the Cambodian border, in a camp that overlooked the sea, and there were the Seven Mountains standing up there. Mountains were named Núi Dài, Núi Cô Tô, Núi Cấm, Núi Tượng. I learned that there were 20,000 villages all around us, and 23 Americans on the A-team. I was their doctor, I was the only medic down there, so you can imagine the impact of that situation on a 22-year-old man.

[My commander] was 26 years old, he was tall, dark and handsome, a very brave soldier, captain. I got an intense feeling of attraction to him, a sensation I did not know what it was. I had never had it before.

I used to see 200 people a day on the average. I delivered their babies, pulled their teeth, inoculated them for diseases…It was extremely fulfilling for me. Of course, it burns you out though. I couldn't find time to go to sleep, I was working all the time, so I used morphine, I used Demerol, I used amphetamines to stay awake, I used Seconal to go to sleep…I became a polydrug junkie. Towards the end of it, I confess that I lost my mind.

I remember the American Forces took a mountain top, it was called Núi Cô Tô. 950 casualties, Americans and Vietnamese, and I was the one who received these bodies from helicopters. It took me almost four days to get them off the landing strip. They were beginning to stink.

One of them was a good friend of mine, and he looked like a little angel sleeping. I remember thinking, "You should feel something. This should bother you." But I felt nothing.

SINDRE LEGANGER:

Can you try to describe how your relationship with your commander developed from just meeting each other into becoming lovers?

STEVEN NEICHIN:

It's not that it developed, it was just there. Suddenly, it was there. Every night when we were in the team house, he'd come up to me and say, "Doc, come on and take a ride."

I'd say, "Sure." We'd go out, get on his motorcycle and take a ride, with my arms around his waist. Like a girl. Like a woman.

My commander and I were very close, and anytime he went on these operations, he would take me with him. One day we were on an operation to remove a nest of snipers from the top of the mountain. The way we did this was to walk down the valley in their range, and to try to draw fire so we could locate them, call in the gunships and blast them out, and kill them.

We marched across the rice paddies, we came under fire, we took cover behind this mud dike that was about six inches high. You hear the rounds going off, you see the fire from the rifles up on the hill, the spark, and you see the rounds hitting at your feet. You hear them through the vegetation. My commander had the radio. He said to me, "OK Doc, I want you to run across the paddy and draw rounds while I call in the gunships."

I didn't think. You see, that's the thing about combat—you don't think. You don't reflect, you don't wonder. You just do, you move. I gave him a dirty look, I got up and I ran.

I started running across the padding, sort of weaving from side to side, and I thought "This is the end." I ran so hard that my belt flew open and my pants fell down. I dive behind a bush, and there was a red ant hill. I'm talking about Cambodian red ants. I thought, "Oh my God…What on earth have I gotten myself into now?" I stood up and brushed them off, pulled up my pants, tightened the belt and started running again. They were so close to me they were hitting my boots, if you could imagine.

The gunships came and blasted them out. There were five of them. So he and I killed five people. I mean, if you can call that killing. I took part in killing five people.

We never talked about it. We never discussed it. You don't talk about these things, you just do them. Say a few words, that's all.

We loved each other. We did not know—neither he nor I—that we had a homophile tendency. What you see is normal for all men, and comes out in all-male company when you're together and you have to rely on one another. It's a very normal and a very beautiful form of love, I have to say that. It's not a perversion, there's nothing dark about it, nothing evil about it, nothing wrong…It comes out and it's there. Some of us are more courageous about admitting it than others.

A couple of months later I got evacuated and that's the end of it. I was sent home.

SINDRE LEGANGER:

Did you ever see any of them again?

STEVEN NEICHIN:

No, I never did.

*

STEVEN NEICHIN:

This wood is wet, so it's not so easy to chop. But you know, after a while it gives in.

SINDRE LEGANGER:

Looking back on your life, can you reflect a little bit about what love has meant and what love has been in your life?

STEVEN NEICHIN:

You know, it's like a line from one of Loretta Lynn's songs. She sings, "His love is all he's got to give, but he gives it all to me." It's been my salvation to love. I couldn't have managed without.

That's what got me through Vietnam, to tell you the truth.

> [sings]
> Love is what kept me going, keeps me going.
> And love is the foundation we lean on,
> All you need is love to ease your mind,
> And does it have to be right,
> To be called love,
> When he gives me more lovin'
> Than a lifetime of lookin'
> Could ever find.

It's one of my favorite songs.

EASY LAY
Derrick Woodford

I t had only been a couple months, but I was getting settled into life on Eielson Air Force Base. I shared a room with Matt, an Italian New York native. He cracked opened a couple of beers daily after work, and went through a case on the weekends. Barely 21, drinking wasn't new to him. He had previously been busted for underaged drinking on base. What else did you do on base in the middle of Alaska while serving in the military? Sure, some of the married guys hunted and fished, but what do you do with five hundred pounds of moose meat when you're single and share a dorm room?

Matt despised authority and the military, but I thought maybe it was moreso people who told him he couldn't drink, or drank too much. He still felt the sting from all the work details he performed to atone for having been caught. We both worked in the communication squadron and it was the first duty station for us both. Matt had been on base over a year now. I secretly depended on him to introduce me to people and invite me to the small dormitory parties I pretended to be indifferent about. Even in the military, meeting people could be challenging.

I remember my first time navigating the dining hall alone, tray in hand. I spotted a table of three other young black men like myself—there weren't many of us on base—and the tallest of the group gave me a nod. It was probably obvious to everyone that I was a FNG, a Fucking New Guy, but I walked over and pulled up a chair.

"What's up, yo?" the tall one said.

Barely audible, I muttered, "What's up?"

I eyed the one with a large friendly smile and buck teeth. The Bible near his food tray is what caught my attention.

"Where dey got ya working?" he asked.

"I'm in the communications squadron."

"Me and Jones in supply," the third guy stated. He had smooth dark skin, reminding me of an island native. He eyed me up and down.

"What dorm they got you in?" he continued.

I swallowed my first bite of meatloaf. "2206."

"So, Woolford," the one with the Bible started. "Where you from?"

I didn't correct him, telling him my name was Woodford, but most said it similarly, somehow pronouncing the "D" like an "L". We never exchanged names out loud, but most circles even in private settings referred to each other by last names. I assumed they didn't deem introductions necessary. We wore our names on our uniforms. Bible guy's name tag said Jackson.

"I'm from Cleveland."

The tall one spoke up again. "You grew up in Cleveland?"

"Well technically Warrensville," I said. "It's a suburb of Cleveland."

They all looked at one another and presented wide grins. I clearly wasn't in on the joke.

"That makes more sense," he said.

I never ate with them again and somehow I think we were all OK with that. My biggest worry while serving under Don't Ask,

Don't Tell (DADT) was being found out. The subtle implication that I wasn't black enough was a whole new set of worries that would taunt me, but at least one that didn't threaten my livelihood.

One evening I returned to my room to find Matt having his usual after-dinner Budweiser with Mike, one of our suitemates from next door. We all shared a bathroom between our two rooms, which made getting ready for work in the morning often challenging. Luckily, Mike worked nights at the dining hall, leaving only three of us battling for the bathroom in the early wee hours. The third being Mike's roommate.

I settled on my bed as they talked and watched syndicated reruns of Seinfeld. An hour or so had gone by when there was a knock at the door.

"It's open." Matt yelled with his New York Italian accent.

Jenny, a pleasantly stout girl with a bob cut entered. Jenny lived down the hall. With so few women, most had rooms to themselves. A petite redhead with shoulder length hair I had never seen followed in behind her. Red was somewhat an understatement, especially in contrast to her white porcelain skin.

"Hey guys, this is Mandy," Jenny explained. "She just arrived a couple hours ago."

Once you learned of your new duty station you would be assigned a sponsor to help with your transition. Some of the responsibilities included making contact with the FNG—or gal in this case—and helping with room assignments, and showing them around. Jenny appeared to be Mandy's sponsor.

"So this is Mike, Matt, and Derrick," Jenny said pointing to each of us.

Mandy grinned nervously revealing perfectly chemically-whitened teeth.

"Hey y'all."

She was definitely from the South. Her gaze swept the room, then landed on me. Her smile grew bigger. I returned a friendly forced smile. In my peripheral vision, I could see Matt and Mike taking her in and Jenny being disgusted by it all. Mandy was new prey, and also quite pretty. Matt once told me a five was elevated to eight here.

"Even ugly bitches are living the life,"—his words.

I guess you could say Mandy was naturally an eight, so I didn't know what that made her on Matt's Alaska scale. I suspected out of his league.

Matt asked, "Where do you work?" He too was grinning ear-to-ear.

"Dining services," she said. "I'm a cook." She hadn't stopped looking at me as she answered Matt's question.

Mike chimed in, "That's where I work."

I plainly saw the dirty thoughts cooking in his eyes.

"I'm just showing her around," Jenny interrupted.

Mandy occasionally glanced away to finally acknowledge the other people in the room, but her eyes always returned to me. I attempted to conceal my awkwardness with a question.

"Where are you from?" I asked.

"Kentucky," she giggled. "I know. I have an accent."

"No shit," Matt said.

By now the others had noticed the attention I was being subjected to. "Well, OK. Let's get going," Jenny said. "I still have to get her settled and fed…Later guys."

A mere second after the door closed Mike shouted, "You dog!" His exclamation was directed at me.

"What?" I said.

"She was eye-fucking you," he said. "She walked right into the room and started eye-fucking you. She's hot dude. That's an easy lay."

I played dumb. "What are you talking about?"

"Dude he's right," Matt said. "She wants you."

The fact that they were aware of this posed two potential problems for me: First, I was serving in the military under DADT, which led me to logically conclude that I needed to fuck Mandy. If I didn't, I ran the risk of being discovered. She made it quite clear that she was attracted to me. If I passed on her, people would be suspicious. Second potential problem: I didn't want to fuck Mandy. I was already quite familiar and far along with the male anatomy, and quite happy with my decision. No, scratch that; it was never a decision.

Suddenly, I was reminded of the conversation I had with my mom when I came out to her.

"Have you slept with a real woman?"

"Yes, of course." A lie.

Straight people weren't expected to experiment with the same sex and make a life-long decision based on the experience, so why would a gay person with the opposite sex, except: had I said no, I would have been expected to do that very thing.

Three days after meeting Mandy she was already cooking me breakfast. Not that we had hung out or even done the deed, but because she worked at the dining hall and she cooked me omelets nearly daily. Sure, we all received omelets made to order, but I suspected mine were made with a little extra love, always served with a big smile.

There was never what I would call "courtship" between couples on Eielson. We were far from town and often dealt with inclement weather. For the most part, airmen drank. That was usually at the enlisted club, or dormitories. With each mini dorm party, the space between Mandy and I closed, so to speak. With not many places to hide in a dorm room, she often cornered me with idle conversation.

Soon that progressed to dancing together, awkwardly, among our peers to whatever rap song she just couldn't sit still for. I remained neutral and conflicted, but Mandy persisted. After one particular late Saturday night, we ended up alone in her room on her bed facing each other, lamenting on how drunk we were. I remained aware that several people saw us leave together.

I planted a kiss on her thin pink lips. It revealed that Mandy was a closet smoker, but that didn't bother me. For some reason, the taste of cigarettes countered her undeniable femininity, making the kiss more bearable for me. Thoughts of the Marlboro Man crossed my mind. I placed my hand on her hip, kissing her again, but this time deeper. Secretly I wished she were Casey, who was married but showed up to the dorm party that night. I guessed he was about 6'3", muscular build, "corn-fed" as they say. He too had a Southern drawl that tickled my ears.

"You have to pretend this here cigar is a blunt," he said. "Now open your mouth."

He'd taken a long drag from the cigar while I sat there dumbfounded, with my mouth agape. He brought his lips a half inch from mine and then proceeded to blow a puff of cigar smoke into my mouth. This happened in the middle of the party, with everyone watching, seemingly completely normal to everyone in the room but me.

"But it's supposed to be weed smoke," he chuckled.

But in that moment, I did feel high. High on my own adrenaline. What the hell was he doing? Teasing me? But it was his lips I imagined as I continued to kiss Mandy. I ran my hand up her over-sized Biggie Smalls t-shirt, feeling her small fleshy breast and erect nipple. She moaned.

When I felt brave enough, I pulled her shirt up over her head revealing a black lacy bra. She looked away nervously. I kissed her more. Kissing was safe enough.

I didn't want to be there, but I had to be there, because any guy at that party would have wanted to take Mandy back to her room. Saying no was not an option. What red-blooded American male says no to pussy? Clearly me, but I had to play the part.

I undressed her down to her matching panties. I undressed down to my boxers. My dick hadn't exactly jumped on board with my plan yet, and I was ready to blame the alcohol if things didn't go well. I got between her legs and removed her underwear. She didn't resist. Her expression was unreadable.

I looked at…IT. I hadn't seen one in person before and here it was right in front of me. There IT was, with all its complicated tucks and folds like a gift needing to be unwrapped.

Where was a Mandy in my life a few years ago before my declaration of dick? Would it have made a difference? Would she have been more desirable then?

I still wasn't ready for penetration. I attempted to buy myself time. I closed my eyes and dove into her head first, an unexpectedly brave attempt on my part. My tongue darted around. For whatever reason, it initially reminded me of being a child and sucking on a penny. I reverted to my high school sex education classes. The clitoris was outside towards the top of the vagina…I think…I noticed I was thinking in very clinical terms. Vagina. Clitoris. Intercourse. Very professional and respectful, like a doctor.

I thought maybe I hit the spot, because she began moaning louder. Her hips began to arch. I wondered if she was faking it. Then I imagined her telling all the other women how good I was at cunnilingus…Did I really want her telling that to the other girls on base? That I was good at cunnilingus? I pictured them lining up at my dorm room demanding it.

Maybe it was her moaning and my need to please, but I finally rose to the occasion. An alter ego took over. *I can do this. This is mine. My sexuality is fluid.* I pulled her hips close to mine. Our genitals touched. I made my move.

She quickly placed her hand on my chest. "No, stop," she said. "What?"

"I want you to stop," she said. "You need to put on a condom."

"Well, do you have any?" I asked.

"No."

I sighed deeply, "You sure you want me to stop?"

She rolled to her side. "Yes, I'm sure."

I collapsed beside her in feigned defeat. We lay in silence for a few moments. She turned towards me.

"The last time I had unprotected sex it ended with me having an abortion."

I had no response; I simply took her in my arms. She drifted off to sleep.

Mandy and I would have a couple more similar nights, one of which actually ended in intercourse. It wasn't a life changing experience. It didn't make my life in the military any less difficult. There were no high fives, because I told no one. There was, however, a tinge of guilt. I was using Mandy to fit in, look the part. And part of me did want to have sex with her to satisfy that ridiculous notion of whether or not I needed to try it first—like comparison shopping. An idea put in my head by my mother, and maybe even society. After all, the military was deeming my "lifestyle" not even appropriate to talk about. Don't Tell. Don't Ask, Don't Tell. It's that attitude that keeps men and women in the closet even today. Sacrificing our own happiness simply to fit in, maybe even struggling in relationships we have no business being in.

To some degree, I had no choice but to play the game to make it under DADT, but stringing Mandy along was my own personal regression and that was unfair to her. I believe she sensed my disconnect, because after we did the deed, we drifted apart. We spent less and less time together. Honestly, it would be much later in life that I saw my own fault in how I treated Mandy. Then, I saw myself as sort of a silent victim of the military system and the culture of that time. And that's a possibility. But the truth is, I wasn't allowed to be myself and if I were, I probably wasn't brave enough to be myself just yet. So until then, I merely survived under the shadows of Don't Ask, Don't Tell, compromising my convictions, not for actual acceptance, but for the sole purpose of blending in.

RAPE JOKES
Allison Gill

I ran out of the college money my dad had willed me after only four semesters, so in 1994, at the age of 20, I dropped out and moved to Los Angeles to be a *musician* and an *actress*. I had grown up on stage, playing piano and guitar, singing, acting, dancing; so I thought I'd have a go at it for serious since I couldn't finish school.

In hindsight, I was killin' the game; acting in big films like *Father's Day* and *Army of Darkness*, playing in bars and coffee houses, hanging out at the Emmys; but I was totally without experience and completely unaware of the long and arduous path most actors face, so I convinced myself I must have been a failure. I ended up joining the Navy, which had been romanticized in my family. My parents fell in love when my dad was in the military. I thought I'd travel the world and find a man, or at least finish college.

I was one of the first women accepted into the nuclear program. I went to boot camp with 84 other women, but when I got to nuke school, the balance shifted. There were four of us. And 600 men. That's 150 men for every woman. I was literally and figuratively isolated from the start. My living quarters were on the opposite side of the base, in the old staff housing, because the barracks didn't have female facilities. All the men had to take sensitivity training because I was there. They even sent a dentist to give me my pap smear because there was no GYN on base.

So when I was actually invited to a barracks party, I jumped at that chance. Having just finished boot camp, my wardrobe was limited to the standard issue dungarees: a super-sexy and now obsolete uniform consisting of a long sleeve button up denim shirt and high-waisted bell bottom jeans. I walked into a room full of men playing spades, dominos, and drinking games, and made my way around the room until I found a group to settle in with.

This was a group of people who had promised to literally take a bullet for me, so I didn't think twice about being the only woman there. This was family. These were my shipmates. I ended up talking to a cute guy and was having such a good time, I didn't notice the hour until we were the only two people left in the room. I would tell you what happened next, but I don't know.

What I do remember is stumbling into the police station at 4:00 A.M. wearing only a blanket and bleeding. I told the Master at Arms that I thought I had been raped, and he led me to a cold room with a slick waxed floor and sat me down on one side of a metal desk under a single industrial pendant lamp. I was too young to know how cliché a scene it was. I sat there, terrified, 19, fresh out of boot camp; compliant, obedient, broken down and without a sense of self; a blank slate with no esteem. That's when the interrogation began.

Why had I been there? What was I wearing? Was I drinking? Was I flirting? Do I have a boyfriend, and were we fighting?

What happened in the police station that night was the real trauma, because I can recall every second of it. A second man came in and briefed me on the consequences of filing a false rape report. He said I would be court-martialed, that I would lose my place in the most prestigious school in the Navy, and my rank. He said I would lose all my benefits including my G.I. Bill and probably be dishonorably discharged, and I could even be charged with adultery because my rapist was married. I'll never forget his parting words as he ushered me out of the police station wearing only a blanket: "Why don't we chalk this up to what it really is; a series of bad decisions on your part."

I was terrified. They'd convinced me it was my fault. I was ashamed, and I definitely didn't file a report. That self-blame was so deep in me, that years later I would repeat the bullshit they fed me to my best friend after *she* was raped.

"You shouldn't have flirted. You're smarter than that. You shouldn't have put yourself in that situation." *Their* words coming out of *my* mouth; the biggest regret of my life.

After the assault, I reached into my limited bag of coping tools and the first thing I found was booze. My relationship with liquor went from light and fun to utilitarian and medicinal before I was even old enough to legally drink.

Drinking was the best way to keep up the charade of self-blame and ignore the truth. I found myself drinking with classmates during any free time we had. I would drink every night after mandatory study hours, drink so much I could barely keep it down during the mandatory two-mile run every morning at 0430, but so many other people were puking that it seemed completely normal.

I learned a lot about booze over the next decade, specifically that it's a super-temporary solution that does more harm than good. Brains are amazing things in that they never stop working on our behalf, but we can only keep them quiet for so long, and when alcohol was no longer doing the job, I launched the "more sex initiative."

Using sex to cope employs the same mechanism as an eating disorder: it's about regaining control over your body. Having all sorts of sex at my own discretion and on my own terms was how I achieved that. It was a pre-emptive strike—shock and awe—like my brain was initiating sex with people before they could rape us. I even traded sexual favors for the test questions ahead of time with one of the teachers. Boy, I sure showed him who was boss! Ironically, he was my Heat Transfer and Fluid Flow instructor.

But sex eventually became a chore, killing any kind of meaningful relationship during the 15 years that followed. The loneliness compounded with the trauma worsened my depression and compounded the need for more adaptation strategies.

That's when I began overachieving, and it's the only coping mechanism that I've never quit using. After the rape, I dove into my school work. I studied until midnight every night of the week and raised my grades from a 2.8 to a 4.0. I graduated Nuke School with a perfect score despite drinking, depression, and crippling anxiety, armed only with booze, a stack of books, *and the heat transfer and fluid flow test questions*. It would turn out though that even overachieving can backfire: When I filed my claim for PTSD with the Department of Veterans Affairs, it was denied three times over five years, and not only because I had no proof. The VA said that I couldn't have been raped because my grades got *better*. They reasoned that no one's grades get *better* after a traumatic event.

After many years of failed attempts to cope using booze, sex, and achievements, I turned to yoga, which I won't talk about too much because people want to hear about yoga like they want to hear about doing CrossFit and being vegan. The word "yoga" comes from the Sanskrit "to join" or "to yoke". Knowing that traumatic events drive a wedge between the mind and the body, mitigating that duality with yoga was a very powerful way to heal myself. I remember my first yoga classes, feeling very uncomfortable during hip openers and heart openers and other vulnerable positions. I would break down sobbing sometimes because I was processing events instead of ignoring them, which led me to believe yoga is the best non-medical treatment for PTS, and I'm still trying to get the VA to cover my classes instead of the mountains of antipsychotics, SSRIs, MAOIs, benzodiazepines, and antidepressants they often push with pain medications that could render me flatly affected, comatose, or dead. I'll take yoga, thank you.

Many years later I would stumble upon my favorite coping mechanism, or rediscover it, rather, almost completely by accident.

I had been a musician by trade before joining the Navy. A serious musician. A classically trained, coffee-house, feminist, angry, Lilith Fair, minor-chord musician! But one fateful night in 2004 I went to a Flaming Lips show and Liz Phair was opening. If you know those bands you know that's a weird combo, and when Liz Phair was on stage, most of the Flaming Lips fans were ignoring her, until she started singing a song called *Hot White Cum*. The whole place stopped and turned to look to the stage like a needle had come off a record. You could see the furrowed brows and confused looks: "Is she singing about *cum?*" Until the chorus came again and yes, she was indeed singing about cum, and I realized what I had to do. I had to write songs about cum. I wanted to write about sex stuff because that's what people paid attention to.

I started an imaginary band called The Crooked Bush with our first album titled, "Giraffe Deep Throat." So many of my songs were about rape, and I didn't even know it. As a musician and a comic, I wasn't aware of why I wrote what I wrote until much, much later. Because of the discovery, I recommend to creative types that they go back and revisit their old work; there are clues in there about who they are and what they've gone through that they may have never realized. I don't play the songs anymore for several reasons. I've moved on and comedy evolves. Those songs served their purpose, but if they are ingested without irony, I decided they would actually perpetuate the rape culture.

I was writing songs about rape that I could laugh at years before I *realized* I had been raped. Maybe I was prepping myself with humor for the big reveal.

But even though the songs are retired, my jokes are still largely about sex, drinking, and rape, because that's how comedy works; we take our trauma and spin it into gold to make people laugh. We're like twisted alchemists. We laugh at our own sadness to vanquish it. Getting it out of our heads and into the world, then repeating it over and over like exposure therapy. Laughter kept me alive during the years before I even recognized what I was up against, and making other people laugh with reworked trauma felt cathartic.

In fact, a guy I was dating a few years back asked me once if I wanted to try rape fantasies. I said, "No!" And he said, "That's the spirit."

MONSOON SEASON IN PURGATORY

Nikketa Burges

I am moving to the desert, specifically El Paso, Texas, because I joined the Army and was to be stationed at Fort Bliss (named after a dude, not the feeling you get while you're there). A pothead/punk rocker/pacifist who hasn't even grown up at age twenty-eight did the one thing she'd vowed in her adult life to never do: work for the military industrial complex. Let the record show that as a girl she was groomed to be a G.I. Joe/assassin/apocalypse survivor by her mentally unstable/addict/Vietnam vet father. The majority of said grooming was done in the dog shit-laden backyard of the Burges home on the outskirts of downtown San Antonio. This elite training consisted of briefings on how the revolution was imminent and donning her father's Vietnam-era Army gear to low crawl through the dog shit yard now staged with Black Cat fireworks for a more authentic feel, whilst her father slugged Lone Star tall boys. Nevermind the borderline reckless endangerment of small children; it was the late 1980s and we were well armed.

I thought of my childhood training the day we threw hand grenades in boot camp, before waddling down the bunker corridor all decked out in Michelin Man battle rattle to our designated lane that resembled some sort of Chernobyl-esque zoo exhibit, its large-pane blast-proof glass separating us from the nonexistent resident of its enclosure. The drill sergeants made us line up, backs to the wall of the narrow hallway, as they berated and pushed us, smacking our helmets and tugging on our flak vests—affection in true army fashion.

The first grenade I threw turned out to be a dud, and after waiting a couple seconds for the explosion, the cadre pushed me to the ground and positioned himself on top of me stirring within me an uncontrollable arousal, and I let out an audible moan. It was awkward. For all parties. But what I realized at that moment was that I hadn't so much as touched myself outside of an expedient and very public lukewarm shower in almost ten weeks.

What became clear to me on that humid and uncomfortable day on the hand grenade course was that more than my family and friends, cigarettes, Starbucks iced quad venti soy lattes, my dogs, Whole Foods and French cheese, good beer, red wine, Jameson whiskey, shitting and showering in solitude, I missed sex. Sex with a partner or with myself, reckless, angry, dirty, sloppy drunk, break up, make up, shameful hot sex, and not with any particular person. Just any old penis, vibrator, or two minutes alone with a retractable shower head would do.

When I finally made it to the medic schoolhouse and the head instructor, Sergeant Bradley, took an interest in me, I was over the moon. He was an E-7 who was probably around the same age as me. I drank his attention in, the kind of self-indulgent drinking reserved for 21st birthdays, Irish wakes, or Sodom and Gomorrah. This rockstar instructor, who was the cat's meow of whiskey (medic) school, was interested in me above all the spritely and taut 18-year-old students. And for a fleeting moment I was somewhat of a rockstar too. I stood firmly planted, walked with a sway in my hips I had reserved only for approaching a pole I was about to dance on at a time when my tits were set geographically closer to those of my female army counterparts, I mirrored his nasty little smirk at all times and recklessly abandoned all my inhibitions. It was a freedom I'd only felt when on ecstasy, when good ecstasy was still around.

I failed my first attempt at the required EMT exam; I was battling a cold, and that morning awoke in a puddle of drool atop my incomplete homework assignment. As I was held after class to accept my punishment along with several others, I could hardly conceal my contempt when Bradley asked me why I had neglected my work. The essay was 500 words on attention to detail and the punishment was another, corrective essay. I'd eventually write two more over the span of my time in the service. The remainder of that first week flew by. I scored an eighty-eight on my first whiskey exam, offering little academic comfort.

The following week would be the start of "going down the hill" class in the field, which in reality was a neglected playground and a couple pavilions settled among the live oaks behind the schoolhouse. Our first class was on drags and carries, a source of great relief since I felt it was an area I could easily excel in and perhaps even enjoy myself. Additionally, Sergeant Bradley would be back from leave.

That first day down the hill was everything I loved about the Army: dirty, challenging, painfully fun. It was a perfect day. Bradley spoke to me like a human, even cracked a few jokes. The slate grey sky cluttered with clouds fluffed and low-hanging like Macy's Thanksgiving Day Parade balloons, humidity and electricity thick in the air. While I was in the middle of dragging a male soldier who was probably about two hundred pounds with all his gear, Bradley stepped right in front of me and pantomimed tying his boot just as I had started to build up my momentum. My initial reaction was anger until my brain identified this as his playful way of flirting. "Excuse me Sergeant!" I squeaked in my best cheerleader voice, and changed my course. He shot me a grin as I passed him, and I couldn't help but smile to myself.

Bradley later began asking me about me; where I was from and why I had joined. I pointed west and said, "that way." He looked at me confused, and I said, "No, literally, I am from that way, I live five minutes from post. I joined to see the world."

He chuckled and kept up the small talk, inquiring about my test scores. I shifted my eyes down, admitting to an eighty-eight. He made a snide comment about my score sucking, and almost out of reflex I shot back, "With all due respect, Sergeant, you weren't here to teach the material. So in truth, it is your fault that my score was so low."

A look of pure shock gripped him, and the other NCO standing benignly with us roared with laughter. I was sure he was going to front lean and rest (push-ups) my ass. Instead he gave me a look that said "fair enough" and laughed along with his colleague at what I thought at the time was my ballsy attitude.

At the end of the school day formation, I was feeling pretty confident of my standing with Bradley, so I asked him if he had read my corrective training essay.

"Yeah Burges, I came back from leave just to read your fucking essay!"

"I don't know Sergeant, just thought you might pour yourself a nice scotch on the rocks and have a good read at the end of the day," I replied.

"How did you know I drink scotch?"

"I was a bartender for many years, Sergeant. I can read people."

And with that he smiled, shaking his head as he walked away. Some minutes later he emerged from the stairwell and as he walked by me said, "I read your essay Burges; it was very good."

I just about came in my ACUs. I was bouncing off clouds the entire march back to the company, but as the evening progressed, I began to doubt that he had indeed read my extremely inflammatory little rant. His very nonchalant attitude about it was a dead giveaway. I had written a piece that was, in its nature and in those circumstances, completely disrespectful, sarcastic, and, well, funny. Not the essay of a serious service member by any means. In no way was his reaction that of an NCO who had read my impolite little diatribe.

We began making regular trips down the hill for class. Fully in my element, I let loose and enjoyed myself immensely, especially because—oddly enough—my battle buddy Allison and I were always in Bradley's group. At one point he accused me of being a troublemaker; I looked at him, mouth agape. "Me? No, Sergeant…Never!"

I had been a veterinary technician for three years, I could hit a healthy human vein blindfolded and shitfaced drunk, I was restless, and like any restless child, I liked to push buttons. I felt this sense of safety, like the instructors couldn't touch me, and I started to believe I was something special. All the while, the back of my mind was occupied by two nagging thoughts: had he really read my essay, and was this attraction mutual?

The following day we were scheduled to be in the classroom. As I reached the threshold, I saw Bradley against the front desk, the slow lines of his muscular back outlined flawlessly through his tan t-shirt, monochromatic tattoo peeking out the sleeve. In my periphery I could sense him looking at me—a familiar hot rush, the feeling of wanting him in my bones. It always overcame me whenever I was in close proximity. I echoed basic instructions in my head: control breathing, don't stumble, eyes forward.

"Stop," he said in a low stern tone.

I pivoted and came to parade rest in one fluid motion, as if almost expecting the command. His dark eyes narrowed as a sly smirk grew on his face, displaying a row of charmingly off-set teeth.

"Yes, Sergeant?" My eyes lowered to the papers in his hands.

The fucking essay! My heart was in my throat, my eyelids peeled back, and my breath quickened.

"Sergeant…I…Shit," I stumbled.

"So…I read your essay Burges, and I'm not sure if I'm really amused or really angry, so I'll let you know by the end of the day. Now go sit down," he growled.

The entire class witnessed this exchange. I shuffled to my seat. I looked to Allison for comfort, but her big blue eyes showed more white than amnesty. I sank into my chair and rested my head down-turned on my hands. I could feel everyone scrutinizing me. My ears began to burn, my face suffused deep red.

I spent the rest of class tortured and quietly distracted. Toward the end of the day Bradley called me, along with three others, out into the hall. The men's room was situated directly across from our door, filling the space with the acrid smell of urine. Fear sharpening my senses and the overpowering odor made me queasy and lightheaded. The good sergeant called us out to ask for our assistance in controlling the class, being that we were the elders. I was utterly perplexed, only the day before I had been labeled a troublemaker.

"You may go," he said.

I quickly turned to retreat back into classroom, safety in numbers.

"Not you, Burges," he paused, watching the others leave us. "Look, I get it, Burges. You're funny, and the essay was good; however, if someone else were to read it, someone not so cool, you would be in a lot of trouble. That's it, consider this your verbal spanking."

I blushed, not because of the scolding. It was the visual of receiving corporal punishment in the empty whiskey classroom, the low light of the late afternoon bouncing off the whiteboard, ACUs around my ankles, red handprints welting up on my ass and bent over that very same front desk he so coolly leaned against earlier that day. Humiliating and raw, the image slammed into my already swimming head. Steadying myself against the wall, I attempted to rebut and plead sincerity to no avail. I was transparent.

There was a clear and fundamental shift in the way we interacted from that day forward. It was as if we shared a secret;

something transpired between us in that piss-stink hallway that transformed our relationship, the paint-shellacked cinder block walls no longer surrounding us, nor Fort Sam Houston Texas holding us. Every chance he had thereafter, Allison and I were held after class, mostly to laugh at our fellow students. He eavesdropped on my conversations and created inside jokes out of them, subtle eye contact became less subtle. I could feel my classmates leering at me more and more every day, jealousy or suspicion hanging in the air. And I relished it.

The Saturday night before the EMT retake I was all nerves. I sat out on the company training area with Allison and tried to quell the nervous pangs, one earbud plugged into my skull blaring Tom Waits. With my one free ear I heard "At ease!" called, which signified an NCO walking out onto the training area. Assuming it was the change of quarters NCO, I ripped the bud from my head and jumped from my seat to fall into parade rest, turning to find Bradley sauntering out.

"Carry on."

"SOLDIER MEDIC, Sergeant!" We shouted in unison.

"Warrior spirit," he muttered.

I took care to scream the response in my signature cheerleader voice, so he was aware of my presence, unaware at the time he had come there looking for me. I stood there watching as he stalked along the perimeter of the company. He had the look of a wolf, something predatory in his movement, this smooth measured gate, shoulders square and chest out. I followed him with my eyeballs without the slightest care as to whether or not he felt my gaze locked on him, even as I continued my conversation with Allison. He changed his course, parted the crowd and cut toward me, our eyes meeting and holding there for an uncomfortably long time.

Immediately I went to parade rest, "Good evening, Sergeant!"

"I wanted to make sure all of the re-testers were doing OK, but particularly you." He furrowed his brow at me, softening his features and speaking in a sweetly sadistic tone.

I was a puddle on the cement. "I'm still nervous Sergeant, but thank you."

"You're going to do great Burges, you've got this."

The crowd blurred out of focus, blending into the cold colored concrete barracks, the noise dialed down to a muffled hum.

"I have a friend coming to teach yoga in the morning; it should calm my nerves," I said.

"What time? That would be worth getting up to watch."

"Zero nine, Sergeant, you should join us."

"Relax, Burges."

"I'm trying, Sergeant." As I said this I realized he was instructing me to stand at rest. I blushed again and shook it off, sincerely thanked him for his concern, and assured him I had been studying. I hadn't. And with that he wished me a good night.

I made eye contact with Allison, who had been there the whole time, although I had forgotten this. I motioned for her to follow and stumbled into the stairwell like my blood sugar was dangerously low. We just stared at one another for a few moments. In a whisper, I asked, "Did you-? Was that-? Fuck!"

"Uh...Yeah!" She said with eyes still wide, and her face awash in confusion. I did a couple of 360s, compulsively pacing like an animal held far too long in a turn-of-the-century circus enclosure, muttering profanities, searching, unsure of to what to do with myself.

"I have to go," I panted.

Floating back to my room, shit-eating grin spread painfully across my face, spastically I fumbled for my key, adrenaline surging through me. They told us about this affliction in whiskey, fine motor function being disabled due to norepinephrine-induced strength. I fell into my room and back against the door as it slammed shut. It felt as if all the air had been sucked out of my neatly packaged room like a vacuum seal on Tupperware. A sigh of "FUCK!" pulled from deep within me.

I passed my EMT exam the following afternoon and was first into the classroom that Monday morning. As the other soldier medics began to trickle in, Bradley looked directly at me and asked if we retesters had all passed. Wide-eyed and with a poorly restrained smile, I nodded my head like a six year old agreeing to sprinkles on her sundae. He pretended to look at the roster as his smile grew. And just like that, the moment passed. He stepped into his Instructor Bradley character, and with his usual contrived tone of impatience, ordered everyone to their seats.

It was around that time I fell in love with him. Our brief interactions lingered longer, glances turned into magnetic staring contests to see who would blush and deviate first. One day in the swirl and blur of that time, Bradley caught me singing Dolly Parton (I always sing to myself when I'm in love), and he sidled up behind me and in a low smooth tone, not quite a whisper but with words intended only for me.

"Are you singing '9 to 5' Burges?"

My voice cracked, "Yes, Sergeant!"

I broke out into a full bodied laugh, for two reasons; first he had caught me singing, and secondly he knew the song. He prodded everyone into break time formation, "Hurry up, soldier medics, some of us have to work nine to five!" I turned crimson and hung my head, painful grin plastered on my face, as I stood there at attention.

The next morning as I walked into the classroom, Dolly came over the speaker. Her ballad to the overworked and underpaid had become "our song." And there he stood grinning at me like a smitten idiot.

One day right before heading back from morning break, Byrd, a soldier medic with a face suggesting botched plastic surgery, but a hot ass on the other side, pulled me aside to inform me that everyone knew I was fucking Bradley. It was one of those conversations where she was pretending to be concerned for me, and the potential uniform code of military justice action that could be taken, but what she was really saying was, "Bitch, I got your number, I know what you're up to."

The problem was: I hadn't fucked him. Though the previous afternoon he had asked me if I was single and then propositioned me to meet him in the empty classroom, it felt as if the guilt was seeping from my pores as I played dumb. It was like a game to me, and I enjoyed it, teasing him.

I am bad at love, men, and relationships. I fall in love fast and hard, with men who often times I don't really even like. I love them, but I tend to choose bad men, men who are less than intelligent, attractive, strong, or kind. Liars, men with substance abuse problems or mommy issues, who put their shirt on before their underwear. Men with small hands, giant egos, and poor hygiene. More than likely I stay with them because I hate myself, or maybe because I feel like all they need is my love to help them become who they will never be. It's possible I stick to the safer, low-hanging fruit because I am a coward. Whatever the case may be, I lose myself in it, and I was lost.

The worst part of this "love story" is when I heard a piece on NPR about military instructors at Lackland fucking their trainees. I felt disgusted. Somehow I had deluded myself into believing we were apart from that, that I was special and this was some sort of romcom. But it was a shitshow. Maybe a part of me knew that as soon as we fucked, this pseudo-innocent romance would be over.

The day we finally met outside of the post fences, uniforms, customs, and courtesies that encapsulated this relationship, I spent all morning getting dressed and doing my hair. I wore my vintage high waisted ankle length green and white flowing skirt and a tight white tank top with my cognac colored leather gladiator sandals. I arrived to the bar early and had one too many beers by the time he arrived late, wearing his Army issued tan boots with a white t-shirt and jeans. I think the back pockets had some fucking bedazzled embroidery on them, which should have been a red flag, but I was in love.

We talked for hours about our lives, the Army, and what had brought us to joining. It was like a typical date but I had too much to drink, and after the hours of talking, flirting, and laughing, I found myself at his dingy studio apartment feverishly making out with him on the stained and dirty carpeting, rough like steel wool grating the skin from my knees as I straddled him, the friction of the carpet against my knees, my body against his, the heat from all of these things mixing together producing this sickly sweet smell of wet dirt and AXE body spray.

His mouth tasted like orange kiwi gum and Dos Equis beer, his neck like sweat and chemicals. Grinding into the pulsating heat through those stupid embroidered jeans, paired with the lack of any sexual contact in a very long while, had me on the precipice of coming. And I stopped and did the thing that you don't do, but the kind of thing that I do. I asked him a simple question, a stupid question, because I was indeed a stupid girl.

"Do you like me?"

DARK ACID HEARTS
Colleen Campbell

I was tired of all of it. From the back-to-back deployments, the endless hours at the duty desk, to the requirement that my hair be tied up in knots nonstop, and the need to work twice as hard as male soldiers. If I hadn't been in so much distress with the operational tempo, I would have passed the paper with the microdots to the comrade sitting next to me in the smoky barracks room. I forget whose room we were in. But it was one of the rooms where most of the barracks-wide parties started.

I didn't pass. I didn't even think about it. I didn't think about the rules, regulations, or consequences. Just the animal brain's need for flight. Yet I couldn't go, run, or fly anywhere. No, I didn't think; I didn't pass. I pressed the little square of paper to my tongue, closed my lips back around my teeth and smiled at everyone in the room—my brothers and only one other sister in arms. All of us sitting in the single-soldier housing on a long weekend, I forget which holiday it was—Memorial Day? Labor Day? Didn't Really Matter Day? What mattered was we were bored out of our skulls after dodging bullets, bombs, and communicable diseases in Somalia, then Sarajevo, and our latest "peacekeeping" gig, Haiti, meanwhile trying to "celebrate" the 50th anniversary of World

War II battle sites. Like Joker in *Apocalypse Now*, I photographed and wrote my way through forward deployments, as well as the public affairs battles, and the rear-echelon skirmishes. It was all a fight, no matter where I stood.

Not too long after the sheet of acid had been tucked away by the German dealer, Jürgen, some smart-ass punk from Connecticut who was in 1st Platoon pulled Pink Floyd's *The Wall* out of a locker and shoved it into an aging hand-me-down TV/VCR combo. It wheezed to life and in no time images of screaming madness became 3D without the need for funky glasses. The microdot was working fast. I'd experienced enough LSD trips in college, before I ran out of money and had to join the Army, but never microdot. It was a different trip right from the get-go—stronger, faster, more powerful. The intro to *The Six Million Dollar Man* ran through my head.

Everyone was laughing and being silly. Trying to make someone freak out. I stood up and announced that I'd forgotten something in my own room and I'd be back to share with everyone. Miller followed me out.

"Are you sure you're coming back, Chica?" This white dude had been spending too much time with the Latino-heavy S1 (personnel staff crew) and Miller thought it was cool to use their lingo.

"You betcha," I snorted in my best Midwestern sweetness. Despite my earlier declaration that I would return, I had no intention to go back in that room—even if Miller was oozing with sexual energy and I was, well, I was his capacitor. I had been taking in his sexual energy for months via nonstop flirting, insulated from him by duty, by rank, by my former civilian life, and past failed relationships. Like a capacitor, I was saving that energy up for the right moment. But stoned out of my mind on microdot was not the right moment. I turned my back on him and turned the corner to the stairway. He didn't follow, likely called by the eruption of laughter from the room I'd just left.

As I climbed the stairs, I smelled the fifty years of G.I. dust up and down the hallways and in the stairwell. The dust infiltrated my nose and brain and spoke to me of how America was so great, yet so wrong in so many ways. I felt tears begin to well in my eyes. So I quickened my pace; a freshly minted corporal crying in the barracks hallway would raise too many eyebrows and questions. I needed neither.

In my room, I bolted the door, leaning against it for just a moment to catch my breath. I really needed to quit smoking. The room was gratefully quiet and empty. My bunkmate was down the hall in her boyfriend's room, or on duty. I couldn't remember at that moment. It didn't matter. I could be alone and be silent. That was all that mattered. My tears departed with as much haste as they had gathered.

I ripped off my boots. At that moment it felt like those boots had been on my feet for more than a year. Then I stripped off my Battle Dress Uniform and tossed it in the direction of my laundry bag. I had to move my boots to a boot tray near the door. The boots were muddy from being at the range all day. That was the one thing my bunkmate and I agreed on. The boots didn't touch the big area rug. We had huffed that rug by foot the six blocks from the post exchange to our barracks room and then climbed the four flights of stairs up to our floor with the rug on our shoulders.

Roomie had a brief affair with Miller. It didn't last long. During it, I wasn't jealous, just confused. Neither were each other's type. But I wasn't convinced Miller was my type either. The whole feeling of an "As The Barracks Turn" environment empowered me to keep him at dress-right-dress' length away.

Standing on that area rug, a pain signal from my feet flashed like Las Vegas neon. Daily my feet ached from my combat boots. I tried all kinds of sizes, tricks, to correct it. Nothing worked. They just always hurt. I learned to ignore the pain. That was the number one thing I'd absorbed so far in my years in the Army. *Ignore the pain.* It will go away. If it didn't, no one cared anyway.

But that night, the aches and pains had a voice all their own, it wasn't just my feet. It was the loneliness of being one of the few women in this small barracks, of not being sure that I was cut out to continue in this army life. I felt that wild recklessness that always lived deep in me, which I struggled to channel into anything positive. For a while the military had focused that energy, but now it was playing with the LSD and incubating a rash of foolishness. In response, I shoved myself towards the shower. I regretted taking the microdot and wanted to wash it away.

The water was warm and felt like little tiny feet marching up and down my back. I scrubbed the day of marksmanship practice off and began to observe a strange light that undulated under the water as my body parts moved in and out of it. The acid was playing games with my eyes and brain. I knew it and worked hard to keep a hold of a corner of reality—like walking away from Miller initially—while letting the trip settle me down from my agitation with everything that had been going on.

I just stood there, going back and forth between utter calmness and hysterical crying, consenting to the water slapping me between the highs and lows. Thoughts of *why did I choose this life*, and *what is wrong with me* fueled my weeping. There was no answer at that moment. I would not see an answer any time soon.

I decided to leave my watery roller coaster and shut off the shower, when I heard a banging at my room's door. I wrapped one of the huge towels I'd bought when I first arrived in Germany around me. It was more like a terry-cloth sheet that they sold at the local German market. You couldn't buy towels like this in the States. I loved it and planned that, before I rotated out of Frankfurt, I was going to stock up and make sure I had a whole linen closet worth of these towels to take back home with me. Wherever home ended up being.

"Coming," I said.

"I hope not without me," it was Miller's voice on the other side.

I looked through the peephole. I could see someone else's shadow staying out of range from my view.

"Who's there?"

"Miller."

"And?"

"Just me."

"Liar," I said as fiercely as I could muster after my emotional watery journey.

"It's just me." Then I heard a giggle.

"Go away."

"Ah, come on, Campbell; you said you were gonna come back."

"I needed a shower. I'll come back when I'm damn good and ready." I kept staring out the peephole.

Someone was jiggling the room's door. But it wasn't Miller, because I could see him standing a good four feet back from the door.

"Go away. I'll come back down when I'm good and ready and if you keep pestering me, I'll call the MPs."

Just then someone in a huge afro wig and sunglasses jumped up into the view of the peephole, and I went stumbling back from the surprise and landed on the boot tray. Gross range mud was all over my nice bath sheet.

"Fuck. Now I have to take another shower." I whipped the bath sheet off and threw it towards my OD green laundry bag hanging at the end of my bunk.

"Sorry, Campbell." It wasn't Miller's voice. But I couldn't place who it was. Likely the afro wig-wearing accomplice. "We'll leave you alone, party pooper."

I could hear boots clomping down stairs. I checked the peephole again and couldn't see anyone or any shadows.

Back in the shower, I imagined myself doing miserable prank-type things to all the guys that had been in the room earlier and had dropped acid with me. I giggled to myself and allowed the acid to work its magic to get me feeling lighthearted and into the perma-grin stage. Out of the shower I thought I'd wrap a new clean towel around me and just read some more of *Heart of Darkness*. It was the book I kept by my bunk. It either enthralled me or put me to sleep. But, I never seemed to finish it. I turned on just the reading lamp and crawled into my bed.

I had a paragraph read when a knock came at the door again. This time I didn't answer. I just looked out the peephole.

"Hey, Campbell; it's Miller. Sorry about earlier. Everyone else left to go drinking down in Sachsenhausen. It's just me."

I cracked the door open before I realized I was still only in my towel.

"Hey, look at you," he said, releasing more sexual energy. "You're queen of towel world."

I went to slam the door and he put his size 11 boot in the door.

"I won't hurt you," he said. "Just give me a chance; you've been ignoring me for three months. Give me a chance already, would ya?"

"Fine, you can come in; but, you know I can kick your ass."

"And a fine ass kicking it would be," he snickered.

"Flattery will get you locked out," I said and went to close the door again.

"But don't you want a king of towel world?"

"Why can't you just be the queen's servant?" Two can play this game, I thought. I let him in and locked the door. One intruder was enough. I knew I could handle Miller. "Sit down," I motioned to the chairs in the common area between the two bunks in the room. I went into the bathroom and closed the door. I needed to pee. But I sat there unable to do so. After about five minutes, Miller tapped on the door.

"Campbell, you passed out in there? I thought acid was supposed to keep you up all night?" He didn't seem to be tripping much at all. His voice was calm, low and thrumming into my desire. That should have been a warning to me. Again, I didn't care. Life was flying by me like a .762 round. *But whose life was it?*

"I'm not passed out; I can't pee. I don't remember Lucy not letting me pee."

"Well I know a way that might help you out with that—turn on the water."

In the tiny barracks bathroom, I turned on the shower from my spot on the commode and continued to sit, unable to coax my bladder into action. I don't know how long I sat there. I heard Miller rustling around in my room. My roommate's room.

"Ah, fuck it," I said, bored with the bladder-on-acid situation, yet feeling anxious about Miller's presence and the decision before me.

I hung my towel up and walked out into the room, where Miller had turned on my lava lamp and was staring at it. He suddenly noticed me and sat up quickly, knocking my copy of *Heart of Darkness* to the floor. I should have seen that as a sign. A sign that the next years of my life would be peppered with things I should have passed on—marriage to Miller in Copenhagen not too many months later being number one on that list. But also continuing to believe that the operators of the military industrial machine gave a rat's ass about me, my fellow soldiers, or the Constitution. The sign was there. I saw it. But it whizzed right on past me. I rejected the opportunity to save my future in that moment, giving in to ignoring the pain and pushing forward numbingly as my main problem-solving tactic, just like the pain in my feet from my boots. Instead, I pulled the trigger and charged ahead.

"The queen of towel world is ready to open the capacitor. Are you ready?" I said.

He looked up and smiled.

RECORDINGS FOR LATER LISTENING
Benjamin White

SERGEANT MAJOR HILL

He did his research;

Digging in the dumpsters
To find which soda cans
Were being crimped by soldiers
To use as makeshift marijuana bongs

And then he would stand
By the soda machines
And quietly watch;
Simply observe

Until he concluded

His pot smokers
Were grape soda drinkers
Who parted their hair

Down the middle—

They don't hand out
Sergeant Major stripes
To just anybody.

LCDR JEFFRIES, USCG
FORMERLY BM3 JEFFRIES, USN

The Navy fired
The five-inch shells
At the Viet Cong

Leaving empty brass canisters
Without any useful purpose

Unless you were lucky enough
To go to shore
On the mail run
In the liberty boat

Where the shells
Could be traded
To Vietnamese women
For all the things
Vietnamese women
Could offer young sailors,

And it was a black market,
Free enterprise,
Free exchange,

So when the sailors left

The Vietnamese women
Traded the brass casings
To the Viet Cong
For food and safety.

Then the shells were repacked,

And the Viet Cong
Fired them back
At the Navy.

SPEC4 BOWES

Bowes was from Florida

Far away from the comfort
Of Fort Walton Beach,

So when he was absolutely infatuated
With Elke who worked
At the McDonalds in Ansbach,
He simply couldn't talk to her;

Only going in
For Big Macs and French fries
And to watch her—

Intimidated by language
Culture, distance,
And foreign logistics.

"If I had my truck here,
I'd talk to her."

HANK

Henrietta
May not have understood the humor

When we called her "Hank"

A Spitzname

Then again,
She may not have cared enough to understand,

For she was proud
Independent, and not really
Interested in our occupation.

When Sergeant Schaffer
Reminded her once
America had won the war,
She didn't talk to any of us
For six months.

GERMANY BY THE CASE

The end-of-day formation
Fell out at 1700 hours

And right after the evening meal
Cases of German beer
Would let themselves in
To visit the barracks room
Full of soldiers

The empty bottles would pass out
Around zero-two
Knowing the soldiers had to get up
To run PT at six

And day after day
It was the same routine
Lasting two or three years

When they returned to the States
Those soldiers would look back
And tell their friends
How much they hated Germany.

DARK DUTY
SPEC4 BLAINE

The Black Forest
Was dark and dense
And night made it impossible
To see anything a soldier
Was put on guard to see,

So Blaine took
The silent solitude
Of midnight-to-two
As a chance
To masturbate,

Happy to report back
He had ejaculated
On the FDC track
Where our sergeants

Were safely sleeping.

SERGEANT NEWMAN (DELICATESSEN)

We killed the slug.

Watching it dissolve in a coat
Of C-Ration salt
Sprinkled out onto the fender
Of the Platoon Officer's Jeep.

It wasn't our most humane act of the morning,

And Sergeant Newman knew it, so

Having sharply recognized
Unauthorized amusement,

He came over to point out
Our evil transgressions.

"You shouldn't do that," he said,
Authoritatively representing the slug,

"That's a delicatessen in some countries."

HOMETOWN HOTTIES SCIENTIFIC SURVEY
Terrell Fox

S omeone jostled me awake. I opened one eye and saw
Sergeant Max at the foot of my cot, looking disheveled
and sweaty, wearing only a dusty pair of blue boardshorts
and untied combat boots. He slapped a rolled-up magazine into the palm of his hand and said, "Sir, we have a problem."

I was trying to take a post-dinner nap, resting up in the sti-
fling heat of our operations tent, far out on the western edge of
Camp Dwyer in Helmand Province, Afghanistan. No one in our
Supporting Arms Liaison Team got enough sleep, so we crashed
out whenever and wherever we could. Max rarely interrupted
my naps unless it was a crisis, like a troops-in-contact situation
or a no-comms scenario. He looked concerned but not stressed,
so I figured it wasn't a dire emergency. He obviously felt it was
important enough to wake me up, so I opened my other eye and
asked, "What's up, dude?"

He unrolled a battered *Maxim Magazine Top 50 Hometown
Hotties* article and pointed to the numerically ranked pictures
of artfully photoshopped girls and their corresponding local
American cities. He waved it around like I hadn't read it, and
the dozens of other out-of-date magazines in the tent, countless

times before. "Sir, this list is bullshit. We've been arguing about it for a week and we need you to arbitrate for us. You can be impartial about hot chicks, right?"

"Yes," I lied. He was out of his damn mind if he thought that anyone except Olivia Munn would ever be number one, but she wasn't anywhere in that particular issue, so I felt comfortable with my lie.

Sergeant Max didn't notice my poker face. "Awesome," he said. "We're trying to rearrange this list to more accurately reflect reality because *Maxim* sucks and the editors there are idiots."

I sat up, curious. "Of course they are. Well, what's your plan? How are you going to go about figuring this thing out?" It had already been a long day, full of the mind-numbing minutiae of war: re-submitting convoy rosters that changed on an almost hourly basis due to the inscrutable whims of disconnected senior officers; listening to conflicting intelligence briefs from competing government agencies about how we were somehow simultaneously both winning and losing the hearts and minds of the local nationals; and managing improperly filed logistics requests that never seemed to get routed to the correct supply unit on the first, second, or even third try. I didn't want to do any more work than I had to, even for a bunch of airbrushed boobs.

Max scrunched his nose. "Sir, we thought we'd just jerk off to these pictures and see which one takes the least amount of time to bust a nut to. Then that one would be the hottest and we'd just kind of go from there." He grinned as if verbalizing his plan made it sound stupid, which it was, but I was wide awake now, and invested in the novelty of his idea. It wasn't the crisis I expected but it was still intriguing. It sure beat the hell out of writing the nightly SitRep.

I held out my hand for the magazine spread and Max handed it to me. I looked at the display of tanned bikini bodies and talked through the process with him. "That could work, I think, but we'd need a control group. And we'll have to control for individual efforts, personal tastes, times of day, times between jerk off sessions, and probably put a limit on the whole shebang. Maybe go top 10 instead of the full 50? How about 10 girls in 10 days? Otherwise people might get chafed and I don't need Doc on my case about why none of us can walk around without bleeding and crying."

"Sir! Yes! That's the best." Max knelt down by me. I grabbed a pen and a notebook and tossed them over to him. We sketched out our plan together.

"OK, so, who all's involved in this thing? Everyone?" I asked. Max nodded. "Doc, too."

"Good," I said. "He can keep us in hand lotion and wet wipes. Let's make a list with our names across the top, and then a list down the long axis of the page for each girl and her hometown, and we can fill in the grid with the start, stop, and total elapsed time in each of the boxes."

Max drew the grid and filled in the Marines' names, first by rank, and then by last name, alphabetically.

"We need a control group, though," I said. "A baseline reading of standard non-sexy jerk-off times."

Max grunted in affirmation and added in another row for the control group. I reached past him to my desk and picked out a *National Geographic* from a stack of porn mixed in amongst my science magazines. I thumbed quickly through it and found a picture of an alpaca. I tore it out.

"Everyone jerks off to the alpaca first," I told him. "They'll check in with me, take the alpaca to the shitter, rub one out, and bring it back, hopefully unsoiled. I'm going to be pissed if someone cums on the alpaca. I'll clock people in and out and write their times on the sheet."

"What about the time it takes to walk to the port-a-shitter and back?" Max asked. "Some people walk faster than others. Anderson walks like he has a lit firecracker up his ass, and Boaz shuffles around like he's an old man who forgets his own name."

He had a point. "Margin of error, I guess? I don't know. I'm not going to follow you all with a stopwatch and stand outside waiting while you guys whale on yourselves, if that's what you're getting at. Not even for science."

Max frowned. "That makes sense, sir, but still—too many errors. They'll start compounding and skew the fuck out of the results."

Him and his goddamn computer science degree. "We're not going to the friggin' moon, dude. We're just timing the masturbation sessions of a bunch of men in the middle of the desert. Totally normal stuff."

Max nodded and turned back to the notebook.

"So," I said. "We'll have to go in order, just down the final top 10 list, like in the magazine, so that as the days go by and people get tired, there's a consistent change in times correlated to the individual girls. We won't know for sure what the errors will be, but we can at least conclude they'll be sort of in the ballpark of each other, right? And I don't think anyone's an unstoppable Jerkinator, so there shouldn't be any crazy outliers. I guess everyone gets Portland first, yeah? Good thing, because she has awesome hair."

"After the alpaca," Max corrected.

"Yes, after the alpaca. Also, if the alpaca wins, all of you have duty forever, because seriously." I said it mostly as a joke, but then the more I thought about it, the more worried I got. Our small unit operated in relative isolation from the rest of the Marine Corps and we were only about halfway through our deployment. We existed in our own little world, working directly with the Afghan National Army, and everyone on the teams had already experienced their fair share of scary, disturbing, frustrating, and traumatic events: the Taliban hanging little girls from trees; sleeping in the dirt next to burning drums of shit and diesel fuel; requesting more pallets of water and getting boxes of hats instead; the chow hall running out of cookies—black humor kept us sane, but having someone develop a gross new perversion on top of it all was a legitimate leadership concern of mine.

One team steadfastly refused to put on pants unless they were actively taking RPG fire. Another wanted an absurd amount of hot sauce so they could "burn each other's assholes so hard" in a self-perpetuating cycle of MRE-related shit-centric pranks. I even had to stop a team from ordering t-shirts with "We Watch Crush Porn" emblazoned on them, right above a detailed cartoon of a lady's high-heeled foot stomping a baby duck to death. They wanted to take pictures of themselves wearing the t-shirts and then send the pictures back as a thank-you/fuck-you to the Baptist knitting group who had sent them a giant stack of quilts so that the team didn't catch cold out in the desert in the middle of summer. This current jerk-off adventure seemed pretty tame in comparison.

"Sir," Max said. "Ten girls, 10 days, after the initial alpaca, and you hand out the pictures in order, start the clock, we go jerk off, come back, turn in the picture, and you stop the clock?"

I confirmed the plan. "Yep. Sounds like a good use of our time."

"Beats walking around, waiting to get exploded out there, sir." Max stood up and turned to leave. "I'll go let everyone know, if you want to cut out the pictures."

"I'm on it," I said. I flipped open my pocket knife, took the pages of pictures over to my desk, and started cutting.

Max paused on his way out of the tent and turned back. "Oh, sir, are you participating? Who's going to time you?"

I focused on slicing cleanly along the edges of the pictures. I didn't want to slip, cut out some poor woman's eyes or something, and accidentally open up yet another dark, weird fetish avenue for my teams to explore during their downtime. My mental list of things that I worried over for them and about them grew longer by the day. "You know, I think I'm going to stay impartial on this one, dude," I replied. "Your mom sent me a picture of her. I'll just jerk it to that, like I always do."

"That's fucked up, sir."

"Everything's fucked up here, dude. Everything."

SURVIVAL

Dennis Williams

I lie face up in the warm tropical mud feeling light-headed from loss of blood. My attention, however, is concentrated on a slender, young North Vietnamese Army (NVA) soldier standing above me with an AK-47 rifle pointed at my chest.

STILL PATROLLING THE JUNGLE 50 YEARS LATER

I was a US Army rifleman during an almost forgotten battle in the Vietnam War during the 1968 Tet communist offensive. We fought mostly the NVA, the regular full-time soldiers. The Viet Cong guerrillas—known as VC or Charlie—also participated.

The battle, capture by the enemy, and deaths of many members of my unit formed the basis of nightmares and anxiety that I dealt with by avoiding thinking about it for years.

The first hint of a problem was about five years after discharge, when selling my 1967 Mustang to a young Vietnamese man who lived in Little Saigon, a growing immigrant community located in Westminster, California.

During long and hard bartering over the price, I sweated, my hands shook, and anger grew. I told the Vietnamese guy that negotiations were over and I would only sell the car now and for cash. He bit, but to my surprise and dread, I mistakenly left my wallet in the car and had to track him down in Little Saigon at night.

By the time I retrieved my wallet I was back on patrol in the jungle, a place I definitely did not want to revisit. I have sold cars before without a problem, and my overreaction startled me.

Besides bad dreams, I walked around lugging an irrational fear of the Vietnamese people. I didn't want to hate, and the whole experience was like carrying a 900-lb rucksack full of rocks.

Worse, I cried when trying to talk about the war. While discussing Vietnam with a male navy friend in a restaurant, I fled in tears, to my embarrassment. This must have puzzled and amused the other customers who wondered what the two grizzled vets were up to.

When medically discharged due to my wounds in 1969, the VA offered no treatment for PTSD—if that's what I had—and I never bothered to get a diagnosis.

I needed to find a way to lighten my load, rock by rock, so I developed self-therapy. My program simply involved tracking down and confronting war demons. This idea dawned on me from visiting a storage space shared with my recently-divorced first wife. Entering the room caused raw, intense feelings of loss and failure, but frequent visits to access my stuff eventually diluted my dark mood.

I began attending Vietnamese New Year Tet festivals in Little Saigon and made friends with Vietnamese people at work. I ate frequently at Vietnamese restaurants where the food was good and the people friendly. I also began researching my unit's history to learn who died, who was wounded, and what actually happened that day in battle.

Now in its 50th year, my therapy program is still ongoing. I'm still occasionally haunted by Vietnam in bad dreams and I get angry if I think too much about the war. Maybe my therapist was incompetent.

THE CURIOUS INCIDENT OF THE MAN WEARING A WHITE SHIRT

My unit was Alpha Company, 1st Battalion, 6th Infantry in the
Americal Division. I was a rifleman and an assistant machine
gunner, and my job was mostly to hump steel canisters of 7.62
mm ammunition belts and feed the M-60 machine gun during
a firefight. I was shocked the first time I saw a dead enemy body
crumpled like litter along the trail.

We fought in combat assaults to mostly cold LZs and laid
night ambushes somewhere near Chu Lai, about 60 miles south
of Da Nang. I did my best to avoid sniper fire and booby traps
set along the trail. I shot at an elusive enemy—mostly faceless VC
irregulars—who retreated into tunnels or faded into the jungle
after a brief, intense firefight.

During the 2½ months I served in Vietnam, Chu Lai was
relatively quiet. But one incident stood out.

I was on the late-night watch of a platoon-sized ambush covering a road alongside a village. While most of the platoon slept, my
job was to watch for the enemy. The night was very still. Trip flares
guarded both ends of the trail, along with two M-60s at either end:
a classic ambush setup. Filling in for the machine gunner while he
slept, I sat cross-legged with a M-16 on my lap, alert, rifle on safety.

This was a free-fire zone where residents were considered hostile and anything moving should be shot. Charlie mostly operated
during the nighttime. From a nearby hooch, obscured by dense
foliage, I heard two voices, a woman and a young person speaking
in Vietnamese. Didn't know the language, but it didn't take a PhD
in linguistics to understand the tone of an apprehensive woman.

The young, reassuring voice answered. Obviously the two did
not know about our ambush right outside their door.

Suddenly, out popped a young Vietnamese man wearing a
white shirt and loose, black trousers. He stepped onto the path,
avoiding the trip flare. He was about five feet away from us in
the dark, moonless night while he walked past.

He carried no gun, nor backpack. His hands were empty and he wore a white shirt. I thought, "If he's Viet Cong, why the hell is he wearing a white shirt at night and where's his weapon?" I was confused and angry at the ambiguity.

I flashed to grim kudos I might have gotten from the guys for wasting a VC. Some RA (regular army) types of my unit did not like or trust draftees and here was my chance to earn their respect, to prove my worth. But my goal was to come home alive, and I didn't care how many enemy I killed, or medals I earned.

The Vietnamese man walked past me, his back a clear target. Despite all the "Kill Viet Cong" we chanted in training, my morality and upbringing rebelled at killing, especially shooting somebody in the back. I saw my enemy as I saw myself: a civilian. I was in Vietnam only a month and not yet battle-hardened. My rifle remained on safety.

Unaware of instant death several feet away, he incredibly walked past sleeping soldiers towards the trip flare at the other end of the ambush. I watched with horrified curiosity.

The trip flare crackled and hissed, suddenly lighting the night like an angry, phosphorous ghost. I was surprised no shots were immediately fired. Anxious shouts came from alarmed soldiers and the machine gun finally barked into life.

I heard crashing through the jungle going back to the hooch. The woman's voice cried out in anxiety.

Our ambush position compromised, we moved on to another location. I never learned if we got a confirmed kill that night, and I kept my mouth shut. I was uncertain as to whether I did right or wrong.

TET AND THE BATTLE OF LO GIANG

Tet happened about one month after the ambush. The NVA launched a massive countrywide assault late January, 1968, against

the South Vietnamese Army, US Forces, and allies. The commu-
nists assaulted multiple South Vietnamese cities, including the
US Marine compound at Da Nang.

Over the next several nights, mortars and rockets pounded
the base, followed by a ground assault. A number of Marines
were killed and wounded defending the airbase, and aircraft were
destroyed.

On 7 February, the US Forces commander ordered two bat-
talions of Army infantry troops to strengthen defenses south of
Da Nang. You know the Marines are in trouble when they need
rescue by the Army.

My platoon and another, along with the command group, advanced on a skirmish line to Lo Giang—a small farming hamlet—
to investigate reports of enemy activity. The 1st platoon and the
mortar unit held back in the rear.

A heavy barrage of enemy mortars, rockets, heavy machine
gun and small arms fire welcomed us as we advanced across the
open field. We dropped behind a small earthen dike surrounding
rice paddies, and returned fire to a tree line where we thought
enemy soldiers were hidden.

The battlefield noise was deafening and fearsome. Mortars exploded everywhere, bullet rounds snapped overhead, and adding
to the chaos were cries of "medic!" from the wounded.

Our platoon leader was killed and the sergeant wounded. I
took over the M-60 when my buddy Ralph, the machine gunner,
received a blast of shrapnel to the face, which also sprayed me.
Ralph was a big and serious man from Wisconsin and I patched
him up as best I could. He ran to the rear looking for medical
treatment, but died in the muddy field by enemy fire.

It suddenly became eerily quiet except for moans of the
wounded. The enemy was now advancing. The machine gun
was empty, as I had shot the rest of the ammo. I was alone and
defenseless. I had traded my rifle to Ralph for the machine gun
and carried no sidearm.

No leadership. No orders. No nothing. I looked along the dike and was amazed to see no US troops. The order to retreat was given, but failed to reach us. My only choice was to low crawl to the rear and resupply.

I hoped the foot-tall rice stalks would provide some cover, and I crept on my belly where I bumped into our wounded medic. I dragged him with one arm and the machine gun with the other in the slippery rice field until my arms gave out. I placed him behind a dike and would send help once I got back. (Years later, much to my relief, I found that Doc had survived.)

I didn't get far until enemy troops spotted me and began firing. I saw five or six NVA troops in pith helmets and khaki uniforms advancing. A large breaking wave of gut-churning dread smacked into me.

Rounds cracked overhead and splashed into the mud until one tore into my lower right leg, shattering the tibia. It felt as if a baseball bat whacked me in the shin.

A NVA soldier cautiously came up and pointed his AK-47 to my chest. I was uncertain what to do and military training definitely did not cover negotiating with the enemy for your life. Maybe a dose of common sense would help.

"Hey, buddy," I said in a conversational tone and pointed to my bleeding leg. "You got me good and I could sure use a medic." I didn't think I'd get medical help, but thought talking calmly might help.

The soldier was young, probably my age. He looked uncertain, standing there for what seemed a long time. I imagined his AK-47 round slamming into my chest and wondered what it was like to die. I felt no emotion. My life did not flash before me, nor did I think of family, friends, or flag. It was like I had stuffed all thoughts and feelings into an envelope and mailed it to myself for opening at a later time.

The Vietnamese soldier lowered his rifle, lifted my machine gun, and walked away, much to my relief.

I managed a quick tourniquet around my thigh with a belt. Unarmed and badly wounded, I decided to play dead. I bit hard on my lower lip and spit the blood down my chin so it looked like I was dead. Another group of Vietnamese soldiers came, and one robbed me of my new Omega watch I'd recently bought at the base exchange. Apparently, I did look dead.

Enemy troops then got into a furious firefight with the 1st Platoon. "Friendly" rounds popped overhead and augered around me into the rice paddy. Enemy soldiers lay in the prone-firing position in front of the "dead" American and I was so close as to get a muddy Ho Chi Minh sandal in the head. One by one, enemy soldiers were killed.

I was amazed to be alive and without further wounds. I was hazy from loss of blood and giddy with joy when one of our guys carried me fireman's style off the battlefield, where I was medevaced by helicopter to a field hospital, and then on to the States.

SURVIVAL

The battle of Lo Giang was over and so was my short, intense, and bloody career with the US Army. By nightfall, the enemy had retreated and the battle was a tactical success for US Armed Forces. The butcher's bill for A company was 19 killed and 35 wounded, a large number for a unit that started with 131 men. A lieutenant from my unit told me that living through that action was a "not so minor miracle."

Why did I survive?

Maybe it's because I habitually wore plain fatigue shirts with no name, rank, unit patch, or decoration. Snipers looked for leaders and a "nobody" was less a threat if captured. After the battle, a few guys from my unit were found with hands tied behind them and shot in the head. I never saluted officers in the field because snipers sometimes didn't know the difference.

Or maybe it's because I tried to keep my head, remained flexible, kept a positive attitude, volunteered for nothing, and struggled for homecoming minus a body bag.

After years of putting the puzzle pieces together, I slowly realized that the best reason I lived is because of the dumb good luck to run into an enemy soldier who shared my reluctance to kill. Most warriors are not natural killers, but are forced to do so by war.

Through the years, my nightmare script improved from victim soldier lying on his back to a survivor who counter-attacked the enemy with kicks that occasionally landed me on the bedroom floor. My wife also helped by soothing bad dreams, and friends listened patiently to my story.

Nowadays my rucksack is lighter and I stand taller. A few light rocks remain, so I guess I'll continue to fight in Vietnam, during the nights, until the end of my days.

LESSONS LEARNED

Aramis Calderon

PFC Harrison had been unaccounted for the last ten hours. My buddy Wallace suggested his location: "Hey Watt, maybe he's jerking off in one of those abandoned bunkers."

The sound of our laughter echoed in the concrete cavern, temporarily blocking the background noise of running diesel generators. The hangar was partially buried, and from a distance resembled a burial mound. It was large enough to hold a warplane, and the Iraqis in the nineties used these types of fortifications and reinforced concrete structures to keep their shitty MiGs from getting blown up by our bombers. Now we used them as shelters to keep our Marines from getting blown up by shitty mortars.

I was fatigued. Wallace grabbed my rifle as I passed it to him. I took off my flak and dropped it on the concrete floor; the Kevlar clipped to my armor made a hollow *clonk* sound. I took my rifle back, slung it muzzle-down, and thought about Wallace's idea.

I said, "Harrison probably would."

The thought of dropping trousers and, like Wallace would say, "punching the clown," in one of the unused bunkers at Taqqadum Airbase was a joke but totally within possibility.

Wallace lit a haji cigarette. The smokes he favored lately had the name "Miami" on the package. "He's a weirdo," he said.

I wiped my eyes; sand mixed with tears and made mud. "It better have been good. I'm going to haze that shitbird."

We'd been looking for PFC Harrison for the last two hours. In a few more hours it would be sundown, and everyone in the platoon had already come back from the day's operations. No one had seen Harrison since morning formation.

I said, "Can you believe Harrison had the balls to be UA after he was late to formation at zero six thirty?"

Wallace took a deep drag and shook his head. "I heard he fell asleep on fire watch last night, too. He clearly doesn't know how to not get caught."

"Why don't you teach him how to skate like you?"

Wallace shrugged and adjusted his three-point sling. His cammies had sweat stains in the outline of a flak jacket. "Ramirez's gonna quarterdeck him first."

Staff Sergeant Ramirez had sent out Marines from the platoon to check out the usual places where we escaped Iraqi Freedom: MWR tents, chow halls, and the chapel. "Wherever he is, that fucker is gonna learn."

Wallace blew out smoke from his nostrils. "Yeah, he's going to learn a lesson." A Humvee pulled up to the entrance of the hangar. Wallace made his lips into a straight line. "Looks like Gables turned up empty handed."

Corporal Gables dismounted, full battle rattle, and marched toward us. He spit a nasty stream of tobacco juice. "I'm going to haze the shit out of him when we find his ass." He stank of acrid sweat, mixed with the smell of diesel.

Wallace scratched his balls. "Preaching to the choir, Corporal."

I knew Gables was not in a mood to be fucked with, so I kept my mouth shut.

Gables adjusted the three-point sling on his rifle, slowly took off his Kevlar, and clipped it to a D ring on his flak jacket.

Another Humvee pulled up. It was Ramirez. His stocky frame jumped out as soon as the vehicle stopped. He took off his gear and neatly stacked it on the driver's seat. Ramirez grabbed his sidearm out of the chest holster on his flak and walked towards us. I started fidgeting with my blouse; I knew we were going to get our asses chewed out again.

Wallace flicked off his cherry and field stripped his smoke. "Shit."

Ramirez's demeanor was usually somewhere between pissed off and murderous. He walked towards us slowly, weapon pointed to the deck, his finger straight and off the trigger. He never took his eyes off us. He looked full of rage and disappointment at the same time.

Ramirez tucked the pistol in the waistband of his trousers behind his back. He had the froggy voice of a Drill Instructor. "Have you found Harrison yet?"

Gables took the chew out of his mouth and threw it to the ground. As one, we assumed a modified parade rest position. Gables said, "Staff Sergeant, we are only waiting on Hicks to come back from the MWR tent. We checked every other place. We checked—"

Ramirez made a high degree knife-hand to Gable's face and yelled, "Where the fuck is Harrison?"

He lowered his hand and pointed at me.

I swallowed hard and said, "Staff Sergeant, we've been looking for hours."

The veins on Ramirez's temple were the size of carotid arteries. His eyes were red-rimmed. He said, "I don't give a rat's ass. How do you lose accountability of one Marine? In a combat zone?! For ten hours?!"

Each question felt like a slap. I looked up to Ramirez like a father. A dysfunctional father, but one that stuck around. I feared his disappointment more than IEDs and firefights. I stammered, "I...I don't know, Staff Sergeant."

Gables shifted his weight side to side and cleared his throat. "We'll find him. He's probably just sore from getting his ass chewed this morning."

Ramirez ignored Gables and looked at Wallace. He waited for something to come out of his mouth.

After an uncomfortably long silence, Wallace said, "Um, err, Staff Sergeant."

Another Humvee pulled up and interrupted our ass chewing. Hicks got out and reported,

"Harrison was not at the MWR tent, Staff Sergeant."

Ramirez shook his head and pinched the bridge of his nose. "OK killers, listen up. No one secures until we find Harrison. Gables, send some Marines to the chow hall to get box nasties. Tell everyone else to keep looking for Harrison. Look anywhere, use your fucking imagination. We have until eighteen-hundred and then this is a DUSTWUN, the Company office gets informed, and we expand our search to outside the wire. Go."

We all said "err" and the Platoon Sergeant walked to his vehicle, geared up, and drove off. I looked to Gables with my palms up and said, "I don't know where else the fucker could be."

Wallace lit another one of his Miami smokes. "This is bullshit. Harrison's a grown ass man. If he wants to be UA, fuck him."

Gables snapped, "Shut the fuck up, Wallace. All you do is bitch."

Wallace adjusted himself and shrugged. "A bitchy Marine is a happy Marine."

The NCO shook his head and got his notebook out. "Watt, go wherever you might go. Like Staff Sergeant said, use your fucking imagination. Report back here at seventeen forty-five. Hicks, get back in the Humvee, take fucking Wallace, and get chow. I'm going to find the rest of the Marines and pass the word. Go."

Wallace sighed loudly and put out his cigarette again. He put his armor on slowly and slung his rifle. He said, "Maybe he just blew his fucking brains out in one of those bunkers."

Everyone went to execute their orders faithfully, or in the case of Wallace reluctantly. Carefully, I laid my rifle down on my Kevlar and wondered why it mattered where this Marine was right now. Putting my armor on, I noticed the weight had become more difficult to bear as the deployment went on. I had always thought the more you carried something, the stronger you got.

What a strange idea Wallace had, Harrison committing suicide just out of the blue. Who would do that in a place where people were actively trying to kill you? Harrison survived the Battle of Fallujah, ambushes in Ramadi, and hundreds of miles on IED-laden roads; there was not a scratch on him. Ramirez had even started to think he was a good luck charm.

I listened to the distant engine of a Cobra Gunship flying somewhere over me, probably on the way back from a mission. I stepped out of the hangar, rifle casually slung down across my body, in time to see the flares launched from the fuselage. It's not unheard of for a Marine to suck-start a rifle. Some guys lose it when Jody gets into their girl's panties. But I didn't know if there was a Dear John letter for Harrison. I wasn't even sure he had ever had a girlfriend.

The sand under my boots was mixed with gravel to help control dustups in the equipment lot. I didn't know where else to look, but if I just kept going, someone would eventually find him. The Corps had taught me this was all just a waiting game. Get through twelve weeks of boot camp, seven-month deployments, and your four-year enlistment. No one could stop time. Unless you quit.

Quitting. Something about the word was shameful. Wallace's comment bothered me more than I admitted.

There was just sand under my boots now in this part of the lot. My feet were taking me to a bunker at the far end. It looked like a short grey pyramid with a flat top. Hicks had wanted to hang out there to drink booze he had smuggled from home, but Wallace said it was bad luck to drink in a bomb shelter.

There was no door at the entrance. Old Arabic graffiti lined the inner walls. There were only concrete stairs going down into the black. I descended. The Velcro rip of my Surefire pouch echoed in the chamber. I pressed down the rubber button of my light.

No training can prepare you to see blood on someone with the same uniform.

The bunker was cool, dark, and quiet. Everything I pointed my flashlight at was grey. Except for Harrison. He was sitting up against the wall opposite the entry stair. There was blood on the wall behind him, all over his blouse and on the floor around him. His rifle was across his left leg, the butt between his thighs. His right thumb was hanging on the trigger, and his left arm was relaxed on his side. I could not look at his face.

I stood there mute. And then I cursed everything I could think of: the sand, the heat, the Iraqis, the enemy, and this Marine. This boy. He was the youngest and most inexperienced in our platoon. This was his first deployment and I never liked him. He was immature. He fell asleep on duty chronically and was obnoxious when playful. I was callous and called him an idiot often. But I never wanted this to happen.

My knees were getting weak, and my lungs struggled to get a breath. I sat down against the wall, opposite his body, and tried to get my shit together. *We saw you at morning formation. Gables and I chewed you out for being late. You also fell asleep on post last night. So we yelled at you and sent you away. We never checked up on you. We never asked why you couldn't perform your duties well. We never cared. Not Ramirez, not Gables, not thirty Marines, and not me. I'm sorry.* I wiped the mud from my face and stood up.

There was a weight on my chest, heavier than the plates in my armor, and like my armor, I would have to learn to carry it. "We didn't look after you in life, Harrison. We're going to look after you now." The bunker echoed the promise and sealed the bargain.

FRESH AIR

Brian Simpson

t was pretty early into my first 18 years, spent shuttled eight times between five of Maryland's foster and group homes, that I understood what it meant to be seen as a number instead of a human being. It motivated the biggest decision of my life to date: if I was just going to be another number, there should at least be some purpose behind it. So I joined the Marine Corps, and for all of its testosterone, it was the least violent and most stable environment I'd known.

The Marine Corps gave me my first opportunity to be around white people who weren't in a position of authority over me; no social workers or cops, just ordinary poor kids like me, a lot of whom unintentionally helped me realize I wasn't nearly as dumb as I'd grown up thinking I was, at least by comparison.

Upon completion of boot camp, I was all in. The Corps was a place where a nobody could become a somebody; a meritocracy where the smart, fast, and strong rose to the top. No math tests that lacked obvious relevance to my life, this was going to be the beginning of my climb to the top. I loved the Marine Corps, and based on everything they told me and despite all the ass kicking they dealt out, the Marine Corps loved me.

My first time in the Middle East was March of 2003 and began somewhere in the middle of Kuwait. At the time, no one was sure if we were going to actually invade Iraq or not. No other group of people debated this topic more heavily than the Marines of MACS-1 EWC. No Marine in the EWC debated the topic more heavily than Lance Corporal Simpson—that's me—who had several hundred bucks riding on the issue.

The EWC stands for Early Warning and Control. Our job was to man an awesome state-of-the-art radar intercept system that could see some classified distance away, the first to detect planes and missiles launched by an enemy. My personal responsibility was to maintain an advanced RADAR interface. Most of the stuff never breaks, so most of my time was spent playing spades and board games.

*

Our mandate was to assume any missile that was launched contained some sort of biological weapon, and to alert the entire camp right away. Of course, none of this really mattered to me at the time because we weren't actually at war with anyone yet, and as I mentioned before, I had several hundred bucks bet on the issue.

Every single day of every single week, for the 2 months we'd been in-country, we had biological weapons drills 5–7 times a day, to prepare for the very likely scenario that we would be attacked by a biological weapon, contingent upon the very unlikely scenario that we would actually go to war.

By now I'd been in the Marine Corps long enough to find nothing strange about preparing for a threat that was either unlikely, outdated, or completely non-existent. This is the military way of life, the means by which it justifies its outrageous budget and ego. By week three, we'd had so many drills that we'd broken our military-issued NBC Nuclear/Biological/Chemical alarm, and had to use a modified 7-ton truck horn in its place through a jury-rigged process involving high voltage cabling, an industrial generator, and Satan.

The result was a noise that sounded like the opening ceremony of the apocalypse, or as I liked to imagine it, an elephant if you set its nuts on fire and rolled it down a bumpy hill.

When you heard the alarm, you had to stop what you were doing, scream *GAS, GAS, GAS!!* while you were finding and putting on your mask and hazmat suit, then run to the nearest trench or bunker and wait to be given the all-clear.

Wearing a gas mask when it's 90 degrees outside with zero percent humidity is comparable to putting a condom on your face and then manning a BBQ grill. Being made to do it countless times, for what always ended up being a drill, resulted in almost everyone becoming complacent long before we created the ol' truck horn.

We'd be sitting in the bunker playing cards, joking around, hating life, with someone mumbling obscenities through their carbon filters, and because you had to stop and run to the closest bunker to you, the people you ended up in the bunker with were often totally random.

At times, I found a bunker that contained only my friends, and on one of these occasions, I decided that it would be a good idea to cheat, loosen my straps, and put my headphones in. It turned out that my lieutenant looked a lot like my buddy Tom when he had a gas mask on.

The lieutenant was clearly not pleased with my music listening. It could have been me, or it could have been that he didn't feel that 50 Cent's *Get Rich or Die Tryin'* was a classic, but either way, my punishment was to make a 1:100 scale replica of the great wall of china out of sandbags. Sandbags that I had to fill myself while wearing my gas mask.

I hate gas masks; I won't even smoke weed out of them.

On March 17th 2003, I'd been in Kuwait for a couple of months, and I found myself fresh off my shift and right in the middle of a heated game of Trivial Pursuit. I don't remember anything else about the night except the card I drew, on what may or may not have been my winning turn.

The question on the card was, "In 1996 the US military tested all their gas masks for defects. What percentage were found to be defective?" I lost the game because I guessed ten percent. The answer was fifty.

Fifty percent. Fifty. Percent. I reflected on all those trust-building exercises that we'd done before we left, when they showed us a video of a goat being vaporized by a gas that Saddam most assuredly was in possession of.

When we were still in America, we'd all went to the gas chamber to test our equipment against tear gas. Since we were assigned specific individual masks, the exercise was supposed to help us build confidence in our equipment, but because we ended up being a few masks short at the gas chamber, a handful of Marines in my platoon—myself included—ended up not even being able to test the mask that we would ultimately end up deploying with.

I told every single Marine I passed on the way back to my tent that night. "Did you know that your gas mask might not work? It's a 50/50 shot! FIFTY. FIFTY. They made us do all those drills, and the damn thing doesn't even work FIFTY PERCENT OF THE TIME!"

I was like a manic Paul Revere running through tent city.

"I knew it!! I knew it!! We're nothing but a number to them. Agent Orange in Vietnam, LSD in WW2, Tuskegee experiments, and now this!"

I mean, If the people that made Trivial Pursuit knew this… then how the hell could the military not?

Unless they did.

I had my whole situation pegged all wrong. The military isn't a race to the top; it's a struggle to stay in the middle, a contest to see how far the system can fail before it's forced to admit it needs change.

Here I was trying so desperately to escape the fate of staying a nobody, I didn't see the alternative I'd chosen: in the Marine Corps, you're not nobody, you're anybody. You're just another cog in the machine, replaceable, expendable, a number on some colonel's spreadsheet.

No one took my rants seriously though, because not only had we grown complacent about the NBC drills, we'd also grown complacent about the possibility of going to war with Iraq. I was putting my revolutionary complex on display out of outrage, but not fear, because the truth was I still slept like a baby, confident that what I learned about my gas mask would never matter because it would never be tested.

Never bet against a Bush going to war. The very next morning, we woke up, were called into formation, and informed that the war had already started in the middle of the night. From this moment forward, there would be no more drills.

"Any alarm sounded from this moment forward is the real deal."

Almost immediately after we were dismissed, just as I was starting to think about all the money I'd lost on that stupid bet, the alarm sounded. In an instant, the complacency of the past few months was exposed as suicidal behavior.

All the Marines moved like madmen, scrambling to get the little bits and pieces of equipment we'd come to take for granted, trying desperately to remember all the procedures that might save our lives.

Sitting in a ditch in the desert, facing death with a good portion of the people I cared about all around me, and all I could think about was that goddamn Trivial Pursuit card and that goddamn goat. I couldn't stop visualizing how the goat evaporated, its skin falling to the ground like there were no bones or organs inside. I could hear the instructor's voice, so very clearly, describing the symptoms of being infected by this gas.

I'm not imagining this, it's happening to me. I'm dying. These pools of sweat building up around the rubber seals on my forehead, my cheeks, and on the back of my neck will start to burn at any moment, right before I lose control of my bowels and my soul, and evaporate into nothing like the victim of some Mortal Kombat finishing move.

I've feared for my life before, but I always believed I could at least affect the situation in some way. Now I was at the mercy of the numbers. It all came down to two coin flips: a 50/50 chance the incoming missile contains bio-weapons, and a 50/50 chance that my mask would work if it did.

I was supremely aware of every single sensation; every single nerve ending in my body was vying for my attention, while my mind dissociated. I scanned the trench line with almost smugness, thinking, "these poor bastards don't even know how close we are to death right now, so confident in their protection."

I was slowly losing my mind. Imagining how awesome it would be to not be about to die. What I would do for just one more breath of fresh air. It would feel like being born again. I wanted that breath of fresh air so bad I couldn't stand it. The feel of the cool breeze on my face, and the refreshing, non-poisonous air filling up my lungs, like being released from a hostage situation into a sauna, and afterwards running right into a walk-in freezer, made of Valyrian steel and York Peppermint Patties.

I've already made up my mind that I'd rather go out like Private Pyle than that goat. I clicked my M-16 from safe to unsafe, put the business end under my chin, put my finger on the trigger, and waited for the gas to affect my nervous system, and the resulting twitch to finally make me, literally, the no-one I'd never wanted to be.

That's when I heard the two sweetest words in the English language echo from the distance.

"ALL CLEAR!!"

All clear…

All clear.

ARCHAEOLOGY

Wendy Hill

I tell my children stories about their father, the ones I can remember. He was a Marine, an Osprey pilot, and before that a CH-46 helicopter pilot. I tell them how he almost crashed on his first deployment when the huge piece of metal that keeps the rotors attached to the helicopter cracked in mid-flight. I tell them how the pilots in the other helicopters thought they were watching thirteen people die as the aircraft plummeted toward the desert floor, but that Russell managed to land it, saving the lives of everyone onboard.

When we were first married, in our early 20s, Russell and I worked on the thoroughbred horse farm his father still manages. I tell our son and daughter how Russell once caught a lime-green garden snake outside the foaling barn and put it down his shirt. How he planned to go up to their grandfather and tell him he had a stomach ache while the snake writhed around on his belly. How the snake bit him and he just laughed and poked it back down, biting him twice more before he let it out, laughing.

When Elton John's "Tiny Dancer" comes on the radio, I tell Warren and Adrianne how their father used to sing the words wrong to aggravate me. How he would tilt his head back and croon,

"Hold me closer, Tony Danza." I tell them how he actually cared what other people had to say. How he would never sit back and watch the Marines under him do all the work but would jump in to help sweep or organize tools or turn a wrench. How they loved him for it. I don't tell them that he never read a book all the way through, or that he thought college was overrated. I don't tell them that every time he got on a motorcycle, his body became one with it, or that he was the fastest guy at the track almost every time he went, or that he could ride a motorcycle sitting backward. I don't tell them that he sometimes flirted with waitresses right in front of me. That he could be irresponsible: with money, with his own safety, with time. That he would often procrastinate.

The stories are my version of him. I am editing their father: considering which faults to share and which to bury with him. Considering how far I can err without creating a father on a pedestal they can never reach, or a version of him that doesn't live up to the original.

Warren started preschool at the age of four, six months after his father died in a motorcycle accident. That first year after Russell's death, and even the second, Russell was always in the picture, tall and imposing, despite being made of lines and circles. And the pictures seemed endless, as if Warren drew us everyday to communicate a grief he couldn't quite put into words.

Now that Warren is six and in kindergarten, the drawings are less frequent, more jarring when he extracts them from his Spiderman backpack. They are simple. I am the tallest, with long brown hair and a red rectangle for a dress. Warren has drawn himself almost as tall as I am. His sister, Adrianne, is shorter, in a pink rectangle dress and pigtails. My three-fingered hands stretch out toward my children on either side. We are all smiles. My stomach sinks, but I tell him how beautiful his drawing is. Warren proclaims proudly that this is our family.

A canopy of birch and oak sheltered our yard in California. At the back edge of the property, a small creek ran between the canyon wall and our shaded yard. In one of the few flat areas of grass was a trampoline, and a tire swing hung over the creek, about eight feet before a six-foot waterfall. Almost every afternoon Russell would take three-year-old Warren down to the creek, roll up his pant legs, and step with him into the cold mountain runoff. They would look for bugs, and if one of them found a praying mantis or a stick insect—their favorites—they would both bend to inspect it. Then Russell would lift Warren into the tire swing and push. Warren would squeal, and Russell would laugh: a paternal call and response.

The tire swung back and forth, back and forth. Floating a half-turn every other push. Warren would cling to the rope, his bent legs resting on the tire, his soft brown hair lifting in the wind.

Those moments only exist for me now. The kids were too young to remember. Russell is gone. I am trying to preserve their father's papers and photos and possessions, and my memories, so I can pass some knowledge of who he was down to them. But I forget things all the time. I forget to help Adrianne pick out something to take to school for show and tell. I forget to brush my teeth. I forget what day it is.

Six months after Russell's death, I packed up the kids and moved back home to Texas. I bought a too-big house and left the boxes where they landed. My new home office is a jumbled shrine. His things are hung, stacked, and scattered.

All of his things have become irreplaceable. He will never write another note in his own handwriting, never buy another pack of gum at a gas station, never pose for another photograph. I bought a fireproof safe to keep some of his things in. The couch is threadbare, but I don't want another one, because he sat on this one. I can't get rid of his underwear.

I do throw away his old motorcycle helmet, jacket, and gloves. I sell the spare parts for his now-totaled bike to one of his friends. After they are gone, I feel as if I have removed a half-dozen loaded guns from the house. When my children ask how Daddy died,

I tell them the truth. He was as good as anyone could be on a motorcycle without being a professional. He did everything he could to be safe. Motorcycles are just dangerous.

The contents of the room fluctuate with my grief. The mounds of Russell's possessions—model airplanes, childhood drawings, the contents of his desk—grow and shrink as I try to organize them. I begin to sort his clothes, transcribe our text messages, put photos in order, but I never finish.

I imagine Warren and Adrianne as little archaeologists, trying to unearth the bones of their father's life, holding up shoes and hats they've disinterred, old letters, a college ring inside a carved wooden box from Afghanistan.

Sometimes I forbid them to play with his belongings; I want to save what is left for the future. But other times I relent, thinking they will have a better sense of who he was for having played with his things as children. I let them dress up in his too-big shirts, clank his marbles against the kitchen countertop, drop his old phones between the couch cushions.

I can stand a week of this, maybe less, before the fear of losing these remnants overwhelms me, and I gather them up and lock them in the office.

*

Every afternoon, when he wasn't deployed, Russell would come home from work in his rumpled desert flight suit, smelling of jet fuel and Old Spice deodorant. He would sink into our overstuffed brown couch, and one-year-old Adrianne would crawl into his lap. He might rub the down of her head, or gaze into her big eyes. She liked to pull the velcro patches off his flight suit—the black rectangle with his name, rank, and a pair of gold wings; and the squadron patch, a white knight on a tan background. When she pulled them off and stuck them back on, the velcro made a ripping sound. *He's ours. He's theirs. He's ours. He's theirs.*

I would tuck myself in beside them, Warren on top of me, all of us trying to get as close as possible. I'd lean into him, my nose against his shoulder and breathe him in.

Russell would tilt his head down toward Adrianne's tiny hands, their heads almost touching, watching as she worked to free the patches. He died before she ever called him Daddy.

Russell was deployed when Adrianne was born. My C-section was planned for September 15, and the squadron's executive officer sent him out on a flight the night before, to transport ballots for the 2010 Afghan parliamentary election. When the plane had maintenance issues, he and the other pilot were stuck for three days in the Afghan desert with a cargo hold full of ballots and no way to call. I had hoped he would at least be able to Skype. I wanted him to see her for the first time when I did, but it was three days before he was able to call.

When he came home four months later, I rented a beach cabin for a week. He sat on the couch, a layer of fine desert sand still muting the green of his camis, and he held his daughter for the first time. He smiled at her while Warren clung to him. It was the first day of the best year of our marriage, and the first day of our last year together.

The house was drafty but beautiful, just steps from the ocean. It was January, so the neighborhood was deserted, and the house felt like our own insular world, comforting after having so much distance between us. The cold sea air seeped under doors and through the cracks around windows. I made roast beef and German chocolate cake, but he was too busy staring at Adrianne to eat. He gave her a bottle, played trains with Warren. I hung back a little, content to be in the same room as him and watch as his presence filled the void in our son that I hadn't been able to do anything about.

Eventually Adrianne fell asleep, and Warren started watching a *Thomas the Tank Engine* video. Russell sat next to me on the living-room floor, shielded from Warren's view by the couch, and unbuttoned my jeans. He slid his hand down and put two fingers inside me. I held my breath until he placed his other hand on the back of my neck and kissed me.

Warren started to sing. I said, "Let me put him in bed," but Warren wanted us both to tuck him in. So we helped him brush his teeth and put on his white-and-green frog pajamas, and the three of us lay down on the pullout couch outside the master bedroom. Warren snuggled in between us; Russell watched me as he rubbed Warren's back. When Warren fell asleep, we got up carefully and went downstairs to a secluded bedroom.

A sliding glass door faced the beach, and the sound of waves crashing penetrated the quiet. The hallway light was just bright enough that I could see his face, tender and boyish and how close the water was at high tide. He'd been gone so long. My body had held life and brought it forth since he'd last seen me.

"You never did eat," I said.

He put his arm around my waist and pulled me closer. "I don't want to eat," he said. "I just want you."

Most nights, Russell bathed the kids. He would put them in the tub, soap them up, and then dump water over Warren's head to rinse the shampoo away. Warren never complained, even though he would have screamed if I'd done it that way. I had to put a washcloth over his eyes, tilt his head back, and gently pour the water over his hair. After the unceremonious rinsing, Warren would play with his toys—foam letters and numbers and little frogs and fish. When they were finished, Russell would send both kids out into the hallway, naked and bundled in towels, and I would scoop them up, rub lotion onto their warm skin, and wriggle their arms and legs into cotton pajamas: polar bears for Adrianne; fire trucks for Warren. I'd read Warren a book, make Adrianne a bottle and rock her to sleep. Tiptoe out of her room, milk and drool on my shoulder, my chest still warm from holding her. Crawl into bed with Russell, put my head on his chest as he wrapped his arms around me.

*

We met in German class, a year before our college graduation. He worked construction on a nearby golf course, drove a ten-year-old Range Rover he'd paid for himself, and liked to drive off-road in places he wasn't supposed to. On Valentine's Day we went to a Korean restaurant and ate eel. He gave me a little stuffed dog with "I love you" written on it. I laughed and told him he should be more careful when picking out gifts; some girls would hold him to a message like that. On the way back from the restaurant he took a shortcut through the bumpy field near my duplex, and I banged my head on the passenger-side window just hard enough to hurt. He cradled my head, kissed it, and said, "I do, you know." And I asked, "You do what?" even though I knew what he meant. "I do love you," he said, and he kissed me again. I could feel the thud of his heart against his chest and I told him I could stay in that spot forever and always be happy. He said that was silly; at some point we would need to get up and go to school, to work, to the grocery store. All our softer moments tempered by his pragmatism.

Inertia blooms. Flowers. Sometimes I don't feed the kids lunch. I go days without bathing them. Our world shrinks, the walls lean inward. I watch my children become more and more bonded to each other, creating their own language as I forget the vernacular I shared with their father. I'm a distant buoy they can't quite swim to. When I look outside myself I see water; still, milky, blue like a stone.

I walk outside to sit in the garden, pull my skirt up around my thighs in response to the heat. I light a cigarette, blow smoke at a leaf-footed beetle. Newly sprouted weeds arc up and over the stone planters, thin slivers of photosynthesis. I don't want the children to lose their father to death and their mother to grief. They need me to be fully alive.

When I was a military wife, I imagined widowhood would be a tightening, a shrinking of the self. My hair in a sedate bun, a black blouse buttoned up to my throat, lighting candles at shrines. But widowhood is a loosening, an attempt to forget the past and to recreate the self. I pick up men in hotel bars, let my hair down, and answer to no one. Widowhood is a reckoning: I am not exempt from tragedy, but I am also not the one who died. Keeping my husband's memory alive, as purpose or duty, feels too much like martyrdom. But the kids deserve to know him, and he deserves to be known.

Three years after Russell's death I decide to organize some of his things. Among the clutter I spot a recordable book, *Twinkle, Twinkle, Little Star.* Russell sent it to Warren when he was on deployment. I open it expecting to hear Russell's deep, raspy Texas accent. Instead there is only silence. The batteries are dead.

Fearing the recording hasn't survived, I grab a screwdriver. The batteries are not only dead but corroded, and after I clean out the plastic compartment and replace them, the book offers up only a discordant warbling.

I don't have another recording of him talking to the kids. I cry for two hours, and then send a message to a widowed friend, needing to tell someone who will understand. She tells me to put foil between the battery and the connection and try again.

I rush to the kitchen for the aluminum-foil box and bend over the book, tearing tiny slivers of foil to wedge around the batteries. I open the book and hear a faint static, then his voice: "Twinkle, twinkle, little star. How I wonder what you are."

I tell my friend she is my motherfucking hero, and I immediately record a backup. My relief is transcendent, so light I could float on it.

Each year without Russell brings a gradual, almost imperceptible lessening of our grief. We grow the way small trees do when they are covered in vines; slowly.

I don't tell the kids when their dad's birthday passes. We don't bake birthday cakes for our dead. Think of the effort, the time, the flour on the floor, bits of batter dripped, the sticky sugar and milk. Meanwhile the kids need their cups filled, their asses wiped, their foreheads kissed. And there is no one but me to do it.

We don't visit the cemetery. I took them to see their father's grave once, and then never again. Time spent at the cemetery is time we could be reading a book together, or watching a movie, or playing outside.

Days after I repair the *Twinkle, Twinkle, Little Star* book, while I'm driving the kids to school, Warren asks me about the waterfall. Surprised, I ask, "What waterfall?"

He looks out the car window at fields of languid cows and says, "The one in California."

"I know that waterfall. What do you remember?"

"There was a trampoline, and the water was cold." I glance at him in the rearview mirror. He is still looking out the window, his six-year-old face serious, brow furrowed.

"Do you remember who used to take you down there?" I ask, resisting the urge to offer any hints. I don't want to alter his memories with my suggestions.

Warren breaks into a smile, "My daddy did, and he jumped on the trampoline with me, and when he would jump even a little bit I would bounce really high. My daddy was the best at that."

So many times I've wished he would have just one real memory of his father, one experience that was truly his. And he does. And it doesn't change his absence.

Russell used to hug me quickly, tightly, then release. He would do this three or four times in a row, always making a *humph* noise as if he were really exerting himself. I do it to the kids now, and they do it back. Adrianne calls it a Daddy hug.

The kids love the "Daddy games." Her favorite is to look me "eye to eye," the way Russell and I did when we were in a goofy mood. She will come near me, positioning one eye so close to mine that she becomes a blur of white and brown, and I feel her eyelashes and mine mingling. We chant, "Look me eye to eye, eye to eye," in silly voices and then roll away from each other, laughing.

Warren and I have staring contests. I always lose. Russell claimed no one could possibly be worse than I am at staring contests. I can't go longer than five seconds without blinking or giggling at one of Warren's funny faces.

I try to resurrect these little traditions that made up our family culture, to keep them alive. But a resurrected thing is always changed in some fundamental way. Our version of these traditions, this new family of three, loses some of the dimension and nuance they had when I shared them with Russell.

I imagine Warren and Adrianne as visitors in a museum. All the displays tell them something about their father, themselves. They take turns putting on his flight helmet and pretending to fly an airplane. I think of all the history that helmet holds: the memory of his flights, the near misses, the dirty jokes told in the cockpit, and the moments when he stared at the landscape below him in wonder. I struggle to keep him at just the right distance, and I watch my children thrive without him. I try not to think about the way he held them, how much he wanted to watch them grow. I see them living, and I see them press their faces to the glass.

WAR PORN
Matt Young

When we are deployed to Iraq in early 2006, no one touches us, so we touch ourselves. We spend hours in port-a-shitters, abrading our dicks with calloused, dusty hands. We trade smut from device to device and become so familiar with the content of the movies that we reference our favorite parts with time stamps to one another during patrol breaks. We hold communal viewing parties; the tinny sounds of the stars' moaning and grunting and the slapping of meat blasts from computer speakers and is absorbed by the shoddy raw pine construction of our combat-engineer-built hooches. Our elbows kiss, our jaws set—faces hard with anticipation of the money shot that will throw us from ourselves for a moment and make us believe this is all it takes to be a man back home in the world we left behind.

We just want to be touched. Maybe the movies and the masturbation are good enough. Or maybe we think we've evolved, that we've reached a higher plane of existence beyond the need for the love and touch of any but ourselves. But we haven't. Without the pressure of fingertips on the napes of our necks and the surf-crashing sound of skin caressing skin in our ears, we close up like wounds.

When we *are* touched during deployment, it is because we have been injured. Someone is applying a pressure dressing or holding us down to keep us from hurting ourselves further—pinning flailing arms and stabilizing cervical spines after IED explosions. Or there is an angry mob of people who have been without power or running water for days or weeks, and they are grabbing our utilities and guns and flesh and spitting in our faces. Or someone has died, and we are being hugged in a stinking mess of tears and desert-dried, salted skin.

We grow afraid of touch—horrified by the very meaning of the gesture. It becomes some kind of terrible omen. To be touched means to acknowledge death is imminent.

And then we don't die, and we return home not a year later, covered in a sickly rind of noncontact. We answer standardized questions about our mental health—our senior Marines tell us to lie, lest we be hauled away to some dark psych ward—and a chaplain tells us not to be abusive to our wives if we have them, and our seniors give us one final speech about how our mission is to not burden our loved ones with the events of the deployment, and we're heaved from the sweaty, rough embraces of our platoons to our real families for one month of post-deployment leave.

Our families operate like boning knives—their goal to slice away until we are raw and pink and small. Our goal is to dull the knife in any way possible.

Our families try to stand close to us. They try to tell us we did what we had to do. They try to ask us what war was like.

We try to always halve the distance between them and us—that way we never truly touch. We try to answer questions how we think we should—Yes, sir. No, sir. God, country, Corps, sir. We try to tell them it was their letters and care packages that helped the most. We do not talk about blood or explosions or masturbation or pornography.

We all try as best we can.

At night, our girlfriends and wives and partners touch us. They nuzzle the curves of our necks and breathe in our ears while they kiss along our hairlines and grind their pelvises against our hip bones. All we can think of is the stink of overloaded port-a-shitters or endless mounted patrols punctuated with IED explosions and the smell of burnt hair or roomfuls of dry-lipped men—gaunt faces dancing in the light of a computer screen, hearts beating in time with some porn star's thrusting.

What's wrong? they ask.

Nothing, we say.

Tired, we say.

Drunk, we say.

We've aroused suspicion that something might be wrong. We are failing the mission. Before more questions begin, we shut our eyes and push through the olfactory hallucinations, replace the images in our heads with the soothing lubricity of whichever skin flicks we've best memorized, and try to remember how to perform like men. Like humans. We mimic the grunting and sloppy kisses of the films playing across the backs of our corneas, and we feel the bodies beneath our own become tentative, so we ask, Yeah, baby, you like that?

Silence.

In the dark we cannot see their faces, they become faceless, no longer our lovers. We imagine the bitten lips and rolled back eyeballs of porn stars and decide they love every minute of it. With each thrust, we tell ourselves a new story, attempt to rework another memory. Silence becomes inexpressible excitement, speechless amazement of our prowess. We think we've fucked them speechless. We stop asking how they like it.

When we orgasm, we shoot our load through time and space back to Iraq, into those meltingly hot Humvees and filthy shitters and rooms full of boys pretending to be men watching other men, who are pretending to be a certain kind of man desired by pretend women, fuck those pretend women.

We find empty spaces on racks and the swollen plywood floor, squeeze our bodies between hardened biceps and chiseled thighs, and the spicy mixture of wintergreen chewing tobacco and flatulence settles in the back of our throats. We take our seats.

It is us they're watching on the computer, looking into the future, while onscreen we're only looking to the past. The camera angles and framing turn us into not much more than cock and balls and flexing hamstrings and every once in a while a stage face that could be pain or ecstasy. Good, we think. We've done it right. We feel like big men again. Now we're all just waiting for the money shot.

CONTRIBUTORS

SUSANNE ASPLEY is a retired Sergeant First Class, US Army Reserve, having served 20 years as a photojournalist with tours in Cuba, Kuwait, Bosnia, and Panama. Somewhere in there she earned her drill sergeant hat. Aspley also served in the Peace Corps, Thailand, 1989-1991 and worked in England and Israel.

She is the author of two novels, *Granola, MN* and *Ladyboy and the Volunteer*, along with three bilingual children's books. She now enjoys her kids and rescued pit bulls in Minnesota. Her website is www.aspleywrites.com.

SYLVIA BOWERSOX served one tour in Iraq as an Army broadcast journalist, and two tours in Baghdad as a State Department portfolio press officer. She has a MA in English from Chico State University, and is now a MFA student in the Creative Writing Workshop at the University of New Orleans. She lives with PTSD, and writes about her experiences in both wars. She has been honored by multiple Pushcart nominations. Her work has appeared in the journal O-Dark-Thirty, *Tethered by Letters, Solstice Literary Magazine*, Mortar Magazine, Bramble Literary Magazine,

The Washington Post, and the anthology, *It's My Country Too*. She lives in Wisconsin with her veteran husband Jon and her black Labrador service dog, Timothy.

NIKKETA BURGES, from San Antonio, Texas, is a former Army medic and a dog mom to her two rescue mutts. She is a high school dropout with an AA from San Antonio College. When she isn't academically underachieving, she can be found working on her prized 1978 El Camino, "Selena."

ARAMIS CALDERON is a Marine veteran with a pen. His current AO is Tampa, Florida, where he meets every week with fellow veteran writers in the DD-214 Writers' Workshop. He is working towards his MFA in Creative Writing at University of Tampa.

JOSHUA CALLAWAY proudly served as an airborne infantryman in the US Army until he was medically retired in 2014. He now lives in Santee with his three sons and their Miniature Pincher, Gingie. He goes to school full-time and has aspirations of becoming a novelist.

COLLEEN CAMPBELL served nearly two decades in the US Army, starting and ending her career in Iraq. She's in her first decade as a full-time writer, editor, and art explorer. In order to be close to both the ocean as well as mountains, she's currently living in the Pacific Northwest. When not writing, she's cooking up today's fresh catch or hiking with her two dogs.

JENNIFER D. CORLEY has a background in writing and media. You can find her work in such places as the website *Hobart,* and the printed anthologies *States of Terror Vol. 3* and *Black Candies: Gross and Unlikeable,* among others. She has won awards from Slamdance Film Festival and Lonely Planet, and was also an accepted participant in *Tin House Magazine's* Writers' Workshop for

Short Fiction. Most recently, she's serving as independent producer, editor, and music supervisor for the KPBS/PRX radio series *Incoming*, and as an editor for the accompanying books. She serves as Program Director for the literary arts nonprofit So Say We All.

JOHN DIFUSCO After discharge from the military, John DiFusco attended Riverside City College and California State University Long Beach as a theatre major. He has received the NY Drama Desk Award, The LADCC Award, LA Weekly, NAACP Theatre, Drama-Logue, Robby Awards, and Valley Theatre League Awards. In 1968, he was awarded the USAF Commendation Medal for Meritorious Service in Vietnam. He has appeared in numerous films and television shows. Go to www.johndifusco.com for a full biography.

SAGE FOLEY is a 28-year-old gay woman from Prosperity (SC), Boston, Guam, San Diego and New Orleans. She is a retired surgical tech, veteran of the Navy, ex-wife and ex-bartender, current yoga teacher, student, and writer, dedicated to exposing the god that is in every human body and the shit they call reality outside of it.

MICHAEL FORAN lives in Ware, Massachusetts, and teaches Saturday morning Literature classes at Holyoke Community College. His most recent writings have appeared in *The Magazine of Literature and Libations, Paradise Found: An Anthology of Poetry about Northampton, Mass, Plum Literary Journal, Proud to Be: Writing by American Warriors, volume 4, Driftwood Press* and the *Ocotillo Review.* He is a former member of the 82nd Airborne Division where he served as an infantry fire team leader with A Troop, 1/17 Cavalry.

TERRELL FOX is a graduate of the MFA creative writing program at the University of Washington Bothell. He is a former Marine who can't draw, paint, sing, dance, play music, take pictures, sculpt, or throw pottery, so he writes as his way of artistic expression. His work has been published in *Proximity Magazine, Ricky's Backyard, Holy Shit Journal,* and *Clamor.* He also has work in *Black Candies: The Eighties.* He was recently selected to be a group leader for *Planting the Oar,* a literature-based veteran/civilian discussion group sponsored by the National Endowment for the Humanities. Terrell can be reached on Twitter @FogButWithAnX.

ALLISON GILL is a Navy veteran, San Diego resident, and community organizer working for the federal government. In addition to her public service, she is a member of the Veterans of Film and Television, and is a working comedian and actor. She appeared in the Oscar-nominated documentary *The Invisible War* and travels the country speaking at universities about Military Sexual Trauma. She recently earned her doctorate in health administration and works closely with the military, veterans, and Congress on a number of issues relating to access to health care for our heroes. Allison has worked with the Geena Davis Institute on Gender in Media, and has created non-profits to raise funds and awareness for veterans' transition assistance. In 2012, her work earned her a nomination for San Diego Magazine's Woman of the Year.

COLIN D. HALLORAN served as an infantryman in the US Army, deploying to Afghanistan in 2006. He writes about this experience in his debut book, 2012's *Shortly Thereafter,* a memoir-in-verse that was named a Massachusetts Must-Read Book of 2013. His follow-up poetry collection, *Icarian Flux,* was published in 2015, and explores themes of PTSD and post-traumatic growth through metaphor, persona, and experimental form and narration. In addition to poetry, his essays have been published broadly, including in 2016's *Retire the Colors* and in translation in Japan. He also has a short story featured alongside two dozen veteran writers in the anthology *The Road Ahead: Fiction from the Forever War.* When not writing or teaching writing, Halloran leads creative writing workshops for veterans and their families in an effort to promote healing and connection through the arts. He can be found online at www.colindhalloran.com, facebook.com/colindhalloran, and on Twitter @poetinpinkshoes.

WENDY HILL graduated with an MFA in nonfiction from Sierra Nevada College. She is the nonfiction editor for *Bridge Eight Magazine* and was the co-managing editor of the *Sierra Nevada Review* from 2016 to 2018. Her work has appeared in *The Sun* and she is currently at work on a memoir about grief and identity. She lives in Houston, Texas with one husband, five kids, three dogs, and a cat. In her free time she likes to hide in her room and hope no one knocks on the door. She is reluctantly on twitter at @WJHMartin.

JUSTIN HUDNALL serves as the Executive Director of So Say We All, a San Diego-based 501c3 literary arts organization, and is an Independent Producer with KPBS for the veteran writer radio showcase, *Incoming*. His prior career was in international emergency aid with the United Nations in New York and South Sudan. He graduated from NYU's Tisch School of the Arts with a BFA in playwriting, is a San Diego Foundation Creative Catalyst Fellow, and is a PEN USA Teaching Fellow.

MICHELLE KEROUAC is a Navy Nurse Corps veteran. After serving six years in the Navy, she obtained her Masters Degree in Nursing and Post Masters as a Family Nurse Practitioner. She continues to be touched indirectly by the realities of military service through her work as a Primary Care Provider serving Veterans. She has shared her creative nonfiction in So Say We All's VAMP showcases, and through publication in *Collateral*, an online literary journal.

BROOKE KING served in the US Army, deploying to Iraq in 2006 as a wheel vehicle mechanic, machine gunner, and recovery specialist. Her work has been published in *O-Dark-Thirty*, *War, Literature, & Arts*, *Prairie Schooner*, the Hudson Whitman Excelsior Press Anthology *Retire the Colors,* as well as many other publications and literary accolades. Brooke's memoirs, *Full Battle Rattle,* was published by University of Nebraska Press, and *War Flower: My Life After Iraq*, by Potomac Books in 2019. Currently, she teaches nonfiction and war literature at Saint Leo University's MA Creative Writing Program.

DELIA KNIGHT is a writer living and working in the Neon Oasis of Las Vegas, Nevada. Her play *Disappearing Act* (produced by InnerMission Productions) made its world premiere debut in December, 2015. *Disappearing Act* is inspired by her brother's experience in combat and his homecoming. Her play deals with the complexity of reintegration into civilian life, the expectations of family, and the cost of war and veteran suicide. Besides veterans' issues, Delia is passionate about time with family, smart cocktails, and making cakes from scratch. She is currently working on turning scraps of notes into full blown stories and a one-woman cabaret about her Tinder experience in Vegas. You can find her highly edited offline exploits at her online home, www.shelovedsandwiches.com.

SINDRE LEGANGER With his background in the radio documentary department of the Norwegian National Broadcaster (NRK) and as a feature writer for *A-magasinet* (Norway's biggest feature magazine), Sindre Leganger has a broad experience in journalistic storytelling both through sound and text. In 2016 he made several projects for an international audience, among them "Wood Fighting With Steel" for the American podcast *Love + Radio*, and the radio documentary *The Man is Falling* for BBC/Falling Tree Productions. He also made the podcast *Skuddet på Toftøy* for *A-magasinet*, which in 2017 was awarded best podcast of the year at Norway's Prix Radio.

BRANDON LINGLE 's writing has appeared in various publications including *Incoming, The American Scholar, The Normal School, Guernica, The New York Times At War,* and *The North American Review.* His work has been noted in five editions of *The Best American Essays.* He's served in Iraq and Afghanistan with the Air Force. A California native, he currently lives in Texas and edits *War, Literature, and the Arts.*

DAN LOPEZ got into a car accident that was bad enough for Denver MEPS to disqualify him from going to boot camp for two years. Thank God he had the crazy-ass recruiter that he did. One day on his lunch break, while he was sitting at the tire shop he was working at, out of the blue Gunny Gray hit him up and said, "These fuckers are taking guys with pins in their legs, get the hell up here." August 11, 2003, he shipped off to MCRD in San Diego, California.

TENLEY LOZANO holds an MFA in Creative Writing from Sierra Nevada College and was a fellow at *The War Horse's* 2017 writing seminar at Columbia University. Tenley's writing has appeared in the web series *Permission to Speak Freely, The War Horse,* the anthology *Incoming: Veteran Writers on Returning Home,* and in the San Diego Museum of Man, among others. She was awarded *Crab Orchard Review's* 2017 John Guyon Literary Nonfiction Prize. Tenley is a Coast Guard veteran living in San Diego, California, where she works as a ship design engineer and technical writer.

FRANCISCO MARTÍNEZCUELLO was born in Santo Domingo, República Dominicana, and raised in Long Island, New York. He has been writing short stories and journaling since he was a teenager. His passion for literature and writing continued throughout his 20 years of Marine Corps service and helped him understand the impact of war on our nation's veterans. He's a 2017 Virginia Center for the Creative Arts Fellow and a member of So Say We All. Publications include: *Incoming, Split Lip Magazine, The War Horse, Beautiful Things—River Teeth, Collateral Journal,* and the *Dominican Writers Association.* Learn more at themotorcyclewriter.com.

STEVEN NEICHIN served with the Green Berets in Vietnam, returning in May, 1969. He now lives alone in the Norwegian woods.

MICHELLE NIELSEN is a Marine Corps veteran who served four years in the Marine Corps and was stationed at places like Camp Pendleton, Twenty-Nine Palms, and Camp Fuji Japan from 2007-2011. She immediately began college in Los Angeles after separating from the military and earned her Master's degree in Organizational Psychology. She has recently relocated to the Orlando, Florida area in order to pursue a career in human capital consulting. She is a volunteer enthusiast with the American Red Cross, and in her free time she is passionate about writing. Her hobbies include: watching movies, learning about astronomy, and going snowboarding, hiking, scuba diving, and skydiving.

JOSEPH S. PETE is an award-winning journalist, an Iraq War veteran, an Indiana University graduate, a book reviewer, a photographer, the editor-in-chief of the *Northwest Indiana Literary Journal* and a frequent guest on Lakeshore Public Radio. He is a 2017 Pushcart Prize and Best of the Net nominee who has had a play staged at the Detroit Heritage Theatre Festival, showcased his photography at the Oddtropolis Art Show in San Francisco, read his work for the Fictitious series on the iO Theater stage, and was named the poet laureate of Chicago BaconFest, a feat that Geoffrey Chaucer chump never accomplished. His literary or photographic work has appeared or is forthcoming in more than 100 journals, including *Anti-Heroin Chic, The Tipton Poetry*

Journal, Voicemail Poems, Dogzplot, Proximity Magazine, Stoneboat, The High Window, Synesthesia Literary Journal, Steep Street Journal, Beautiful Losers, and more. He once learned the ancient secret to writing a good bio, but promptly forgot it.

KURT SAVAGE is a writer who still works for the US Navy to pay the bills. He joined the US Navy after graduating from high school in 1979. Following his training as a Fire Controlman, Kurt's first two assignments were as a Close-In Weapon System technician aboard USS JOHN F KENNEDY (CV 67) and USS SAVANNAH (AOR 4). After serving as part of the commissioning crew of USS GARY (FFG 51), Kurt served as a Close-In Weapon System instructor at Service School Command, Great Lakes, Illinois. After his initiation as a Chief Petty Officer, Kurt joined the commissioning crew of USS COWPENS (CG 63), where he served as Leading Chief Petty Officer of the combined Gunnery and Cruise Missile divisions. On 17 January 1993, the 212th anniversary of the Revolutionary War battle for which his ship was named, Kurt led the crew in a Tomahawk missile strike against targets in Iraq. Following a tour as an instructor at Fleet Combat Training Center, Pacific in San Diego, Kurt returned to sea in USS ELLIOT (DD 967) as Leading Chief of Strike Warfare division. He retired from the Navy in 2002, and now lives with his family in La Mesa, California.

JAMES SEDDON retired from the Navy in 2015 after 21 years of service as a surface warfare officer and staff officer afloat and ashore in active and reserve billets. He served in the Middle East and the Far East, including deployments to Egypt, the Persian Gulf, forward deployed naval forces out of Japan, Korea, and a deployment from 2009–2010 to Afghanistan, where he served on the staff of US Forces Afghanistan. He's active with Iraq and Afghanistan Veterans of America (IAVA.org). His day job is managing the Enterprise Network Operations team for a major research university. He received his BS in computer science from the University of Southern California.

BRIAN SIMPSON is a stand-up comedian and writer based out of Los Angeles, CA. He is the host of the popular Black History podcast *BS with Brian Simpson*. His background as a foster child and Marine Corps veteran has led to a rare combination of life experiences that he manages to channel into an aggressively hilarious and refreshingly unique point of view. He is widely considered one of the best up-and-coming comedians in the nation today.

ADAM STONE is a retired Marine Corps Gunnery Sergeant with 20 years of service, including multiple combat tours in Iraq and Afghanistan, and numerous peacekeeping deployments around the world. He is raising four kids while beginning his college career in pursuit of an English literature degree.

ASHLI TAYLOR is originally from Polk County, FL, and rediscovered her love for writing while deployed to Afghanistan during her service in the US Army. After her enlistment was complete, she moved to California to pursue her dream of showcasing her poetry and her love for acting. She has had the opportunity to be in two plays, two music videos, a web series, and a national commercial. Her ultimate goal in life is to be an inspiration and to be the voice for those whom have not found theirs.

MARIAH SMITH is an Army Lieutenant Colonel currently stationed in Washington, D.C. A military police officer by trade, she now works as a legislative liaison. She's been deployed to Djibouti, Iraq, and Afghanistan (three times). When she isn't at work, she and Bunny can be found at the family farm in the Shenandoah Valley of Virginia. Mariah's goal for life after the Army is to spend half the day writing and the other half riding her horse, Avalon.

JONATHAN TRAVELSTEAD served in the Air Force National Guard for six years as a firefighter and currently works as a full-time firefighter for the city of Murphysboro, and as co-editor for *Cobalt Review*. Having finished his MFA at Southern Illinois University of Carbondale, he also turns a lathe, crafting pens under the name Scorched Ink Penturning. His first collection, *How We Bury Our Dead* by Cobalt Press, was released in March, 2015, and *Conflict Tours* (Cobalt Press) was released in 2017.

BENJAMIN WHITE As he was earning his MFA from the University of Tampa, Ben White thought he was a poet. But he has since found out he is not a poet at all. He is a witness. What he writes is testimony.

NICK WILLARD served in Afghanistan during the 2014 draw-down. The war continues, and he wonders if he'll have to go back someday. These are the author's views and not those of the US government or Department of Defense.

DENNIS WILLIAMS fought in Vietnam after being drafted into the US Army. He is a writer and photographer who lives in San Diego, CA, and worked in local government media relations and corporate communications producing news releases, articles, web content, and photographs. His most enjoyable career highlight was as a freelance writer for magazines and other publications while cruising the Sea of Cortez, Mexico, in a sailboat. Dennis holds a BA degree in journalism and an AA in photography.

DERRICK WOODFORD's current job with the federal government inspired his move to the San Diego area over ten years ago. When not working, Derrick pursues his interests in creative writing and filmmaking. He holds a MFA in Creative Writing and a Certificate of Completion from UCSD Extension in Video Production.

ELLEN WRIGHT grew up in Chula Vista, California and continues to live in San Diego. In her spare time, she enjoys collecting
postcards, tattoos, statement earrings, and ignorantly ambitious
mechanical projects. She currently works as a hairstylist but
maybe someday will listen to her mother, who has always said
she should do something with writing.

MATT YOUNG holds an MA in Creative Writing from Miami
University and is the recipient of fellowships from Words After
War and the Carey Institute for Global Good. His work can be
found in *Tin House, Word Riot, The Rumpus,* and elsewhere. He is
the author of *Eat the Apple* (Bloomsbury, 2018), a memoir about
his time as an infantry Marine. He lives in Olympia, Washington,
where he teaches writing.

54913828R00152

Made in the USA
Middletown, DE
14 July 2019